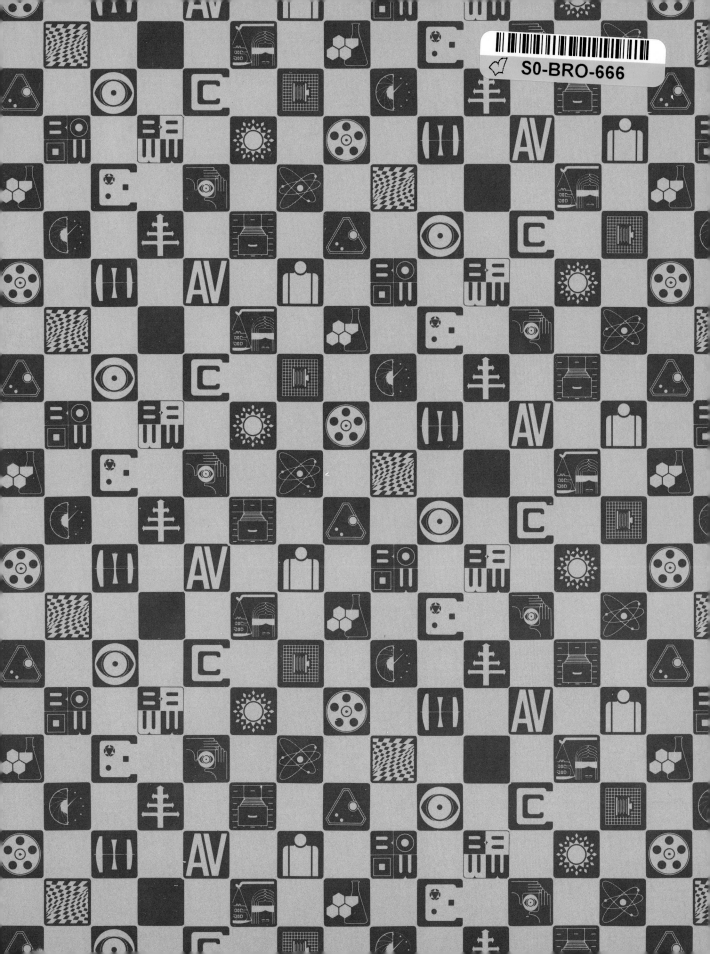

Encyclopedia
of Practical
Photography

Volume 13
Sli-Tran

Edited by and published for
EASTMAN KODAK COMPANY

AMPHOTO
American Photographic Book Publishing Company
Garden City, New York

Note on Photography

The cover photos and the photos of letters that appear elsewhere in this encyclopedia were taken by Chris Maggio.

Library of Congress Cataloging in Publication Data

Amphoto, New York.
    Encyclopedia of practical photography.

    Includes bibliographical references and index.
    1. Photography—Dictionaries. I. Eastman
Kodak Company. II. Title.
TR9.T34   770′.3   77–22562

ISBN 0–8174–3050–4 Trade Edition—Whole Set
ISBN 0–8174–3200–0 Library Edition—Whole Set
ISBN 0–8174–3063–6 Trade Edition—Volume 13
ISBN 0–8174–3213–2 Library Edition—Volume 13

Manufactured in the United States of America

Editorial Board

The *Encyclopedia of Practical Photography* was compiled and edited jointly by Eastman Kodak Company and American Photographic Book Publishing Co., Inc. (Amphoto). The comprehensive archives, vast resources, and technical staffs of both companies, as well as the published works of Kodak, were used as the basis for most of the information contained in this encyclopedia.

Symbol Identification

 Audiovisual

 Biography

 Black-and-White Materials

 Black-and-White Processing and Printing

 Business and Legal Aspects

 Chemicals

 Color Materials

 Color Processing and Printing

 Equipment and Facilities

 Exposure

 History

 Lighting

 Motion Picture

 Optics

 Picture-Making Techniques

 Scientific Photography

 Special Effects and Techniques

Special Interests

 Storage and Care

 Theory of Photography

 Vision

Guide for the Reader

Use this encyclopedia as you would any good encyclopedia or dictionary. Look for the subject desired as it first occurs to you—most often you will locate it immediately. The shorter articles begin with a dictionary-style definition, and the longer articles begin with a short paragraph that summarizes the article that follows. Either of these should tell you if the information you need is in the article. The longer articles are then broken down by series of headings and sub-headings to aid further in locating specific information.

Cross References

If you do not find the specific information you are seeking in the article first consulted, use the cross references (within the article and at the end of it) to lead you to more information. The cross references can lead you from a general article to the more detailed articles into which the subject is divided. Cross references are printed in capital letters so that you can easily recognize them.
Example: *See also:* ZONE SYSTEM.

Index

If the initial article you turn to does not supply you with the information you seek, and the cross references do not lead you to it, use the index in the last volume. The index contains thousands of entries to help you identify and locate any subject you seek.

Symbols

To further aid you in locating information, the articles throughout have been organized into major photographic categories. Each category is represented by a symbol displayed on the opposite page. By using only the symbols, you can scan each volume and locate all the information under any of the general categories. Thus, if you wish to read all about lighting, simply locate the lighting symbols and read the articles under them.

Reading Lists

Most of the longer articles are followed by reading lists citing useful sources for further information. Should you require additional sources, check the cross-referenced articles for additional reading lists.

Metric Measurement

Both the U.S. Customary System of measurement and the International System (SI) are used throughout this encyclopedia. In most cases, the metric measurement is given first with the U.S. customary equivalent following in parenthesis. When equivalent measurements are given, they will be rounded off to the nearest whole unit or a tenth of a unit, unless precise measurement is important. When a measurement is considered a "standard," equivalents will not be given. For example: 35 mm film, 200 mm lens, 4″ × 5″ negative, and 8″ × 10″ prints will not be given with their customary or metric equivalents.

How Articles are Alphabetized

Article titles are alphabetized by letter sequence, with word breaks and hyphens not considered. Example:

> Archer, Frederick Scott
> Architectural Photography
> Archival Processing
> Arc Lamps

Abbreviations are alphabetized according to the letters of the abbreviations, not by the words the letters stand for. Example:

> Artificial Light
> ASA Speed

Contents
Volume 13

Slides and Transparencies, Mounting

There are three widely used ways of mounting slides and transparencies for projection. The first is in plain cardboard mounts, similar to those in which photofinishers usually return processed transparency films. The second involves a variety of plastic and metal mounts, with and without glass, into which the transparency is placed and the parts of which are snapped together. The third method involves binding the transparency with a mask of some kind, between two pieces of glass, and sealing it around the edges with tape. A fourth, less-usual technique of cementing transparencies to glass is also described in this article.

Mounts

Cardboard. Cardboard mounts are available from many manufacturers in a variety of sizes. The common 50 × 50 mm (2″ × 2″) size is usually available with several mask openings. For casual use, mounts are supplied already sealed on three sides; the film is slipped into the mount, and the fourth side is sealed by touching it with a heated iron. For mass production, mounts are supplied flat. The mount consists of a single piece of cardboard, which is folded in half; the film is inserted, and then three sides sealed. Several auto-matic heat-sealing presses are available to perform this operation; some are inexpensive enough for amateur use.

A great many different mask openings are available from different manufacturers; several of the usual sizes are shown in the accompanying illustration. There is less standardization in mounts for larger transparencies, and in many cases these are made by the user to suit the equipment. The biggest problem seems to be with transparencies made on 120 roll film with an image area of 57 × 57 mm (2¼″ × 2¼″). The standard mount for this size image is 70 × 70 mm (2¾″ × 2¾″). This has never attained any great popularity, however. Transparencies in this format are used mainly for reproduction, not for projection, and they are not often mounted. A similar slide mount is made for the 6 × 4.5 cm (2²/₅″ × 1⁴/₅″) format, but it is not widely used.

If your slides will not be subjected to rough handling or if they will be kept continually in slide trays or magazines, cardboard mounts will be highly satisfactory for long-term slide usage.

Plastic and Metal. A variety of plastic and metal mounts are offered in several formats. Some of these are merely metal binders intended to reinforce the edges of the ordinary cardboard mount, which is inserted in the metal frame without modification. Others are made to hold two small pieces of very thin glass; the unmounted transparency is inserted between the two glasses and inserted into a metal frame for use. Similar mounts are made of plastic.

Another type of plastic mount is merely a two-piece plastic frame. The film is inserted between the two pieces, which are snapped together without other sealing or fastening devices. Such a plastic mount is made for 110-size camera slides; it has the correct picture area opening, plus a small window to show the frame number. The outside dimensions of this slide are 30 × 30 mm (1¹/₅″ × 1¹/₅″), and the mask opening is 12 × 16 mm (½″ × ⅔″).

This is a typical cardboard slide mount. Mounts are supplied sealed on three sides by the manufacturer. The transparency is simply inserted into the open side of the mount, and the mount is sealed with the touch of a heated iron.

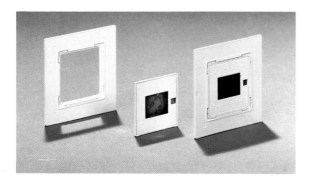

A sampling of plastic slide mounts. (Left) A mount for 50 × 50 mm (2″ × 2″) slides. (Center) A mount intended for 110 slides for a 110 projector. (Right) A composite mount that permits screening 110 slides in a conventional 35 mm slide projector.

Several makes of plastic mount are supplied for 57 × 57 mm (2¼″ × 2¼″) transparencies, including a new size, having outside dimensions of 85 × 85 mm (3½″ × 3½″). This may conceivably fit some English projectors intended for 83 × 83 mm (3¼″ × 3¼″) slides, but is slightly over-size (the English slide is approximately 82.5 × 82.5 mm). There may be some European projectors made for 85 × 85 mm (3½″ × 3½″) slides, but they are not usual in the United States.

For 83 × 102 mm (3¼″ × 4″) slides, plastic mounts are provided by Polaroid Corporation for black-and-white slides made on their 46-L and 146-L transparency films. These have a mask opening 65 × 83 mm (2½″ × 3¼″).

Glass. The oldest method of mounting projection slides is to use a glass cover over the image. Originally, lantern slides were made on glass plates, 83 × 102 mm (3¼″ × 4″) in size; for use, a paper mask was placed on the emulsion side of the plate, a cover glass placed over this, and the whole bound with gummed paper tape.

When the first slides on color transparency films were made, a similar method with two glasses was used. The film was placed in a cutout paper mask, sandwiched between the two glasses, and bound with narrow plastic tape. Many people liked this method because it seemed to promise maximum protection for the color image, but in fact, it often did not.

Binding slides in sandwich fashion between two cover glasses did achieve flatness of the transparency, but glass-bound slides often caused problems with moisture condensation, cooling, ferrotyping, and the formation of Newton's rings—particularly with extra-bright projectors. Slides will last longer if they are not mounted in glass. On the other hand, if you expect the slides to be mishandled, it might be wise to mount them in glass. Thin sheets of cover glass plus a metal binder provide good protection against dirt, scratches, abrasion, and other physical damage. Generally, the cost of repair and replacement is much less for cardboard or plastic open-frame mounts than for glass mounts.

Slide Masks

Unusual slide masks are commercially available, or you can make your own. Besides enabling you to project in new ways, odd-shaped slide mounts can help you to "save," by cropping, slides you might otherwise discard. There are several ways of putting custom-shaped images on the screen.

You can apply ultra-thin reflective metallic plastic film tape directly to the film. This works as long as the slide is projected no more than 20 to 30 seconds; otherwise the adhesive may melt and run. One industrial tape sometimes used for this purpose is 3M silver metallic polyester film tape No. 850; it is available in several widths.

Or you can use die-cut paper masks with glass mounts, as they come, or by cutting them and using them as L-shaped croppers to create non-standard rectangular openings.

Those who want to use plastic pin-register mounts can buy them with various-size openings, with or without glass. Plastic pin-register mounts, while probably among the more expensive options available to you, are supplied with locating pins for frame-to-frame registration for the easiest possible routine mounting of perforated film. And they are sometimes offered with associated film cutter/punchers for trimming and routine mounting of odd-size pieces of film.

To create custom-shaped masks photographically, you can make them by photographing black-on-white artwork with high-contrast litho film and sandwiching the resulting film masks with image-

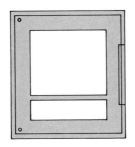
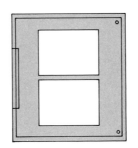
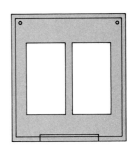

(Right) These are a few of the many styles of plastic pin-register mounts.

By multi-imaging in special slide masks, it is possible to create a single slide that tells a story—in this case the steps in the traditional making of Italian bread. Photos by Ettore Trauzzi.

carrying films in glass or glassless mounts. In order to minimize focus problems, place image-carrying films uniformly on the side of the mounts facing the projection lens.

The simplest way of achieving a wide-screen effect is through the use of conventional 35 mm slides that have been specially composed and mounted so that they are cropped down from the top and up from the bottom to yield the desired wide-screen proportions. A slight modification of this system involves the super-slide type of transparency, using the same cropping techniques at top and bottom. These slides can then be projected with conventional 50 × 50 mm (2″ × 2″) slide projectors on a screen having the same proportions as the transparency.

For presentation in large auditoriums where arc-type lantern slide projectors are used, the same technique can be applied to the 83 × 102 mm (3¼″ × 4″) slides.

Using Cardboard or Plastic Mounts

Typically, cardboard or plastic mounts are simple to assemble and use. Follow the instructions accompanying the slide mount you are using. Some mounts require special care in cutting the individual frames apart and may even require trimming the edges of the film to fit the mount. When this is necessary, a guide is usually provided with the mounts. Handle the film carefully by the edges only. Orient the transparency according to instructions with the mount. Mounts that are sealed on

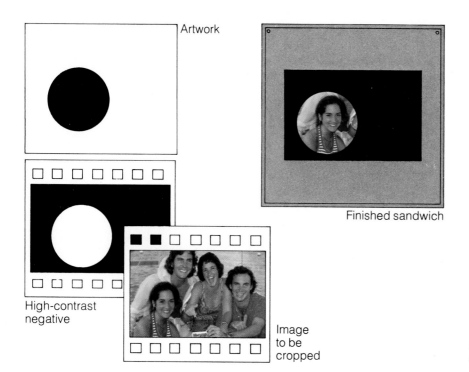

Artwork

Finished sandwich

High-contrast negative

Image to be cropped

The steps in using a high-contrast negative to custom-make a mask are shown here.

three sides require extra care in inserting the transparency. Cardboard mounts usually have a thermosetting adhesive. Use a commercial mounting press or a moderately warm (synthetic-fabric setting) household iron to seal the mount.

Plastic mounts and some types of metal mounts are supplied with or without glass. Use the same care in handling and trimming slide frames as noted above. Orient the film according to instructions with the mount. Normally, mounts with glass are clean and require no attention; but if the glass becomes dirty or fingermarked, clean it as described in the following section. Snap-together plastic or metal mounts are especially useful for assembling multiple-image slides or those with special mounts. They can be used, disassembled, and reused easily.

Mounting Slides in Glass

If other people handle your slides, or if you yourself handle them a lot, you can mount the slides in glass to protect them from dirt and scratches. Some dirt can be removed with film cleaner, but there is no way to remove a scratch. A scratched slide is a ruined slide. So do not take chances with valuable slides—protect them with glass.

Although mounting slides in glass will protect them, it will not prolong their life. For the longest useful life of slides, proper storage is most important. All dyes may change in time, but you can keep such changes to a minimum by keeping slides in a cool, dry place and in the dark if possible. Slides that are properly cared for will have a useful life of many years.

Cleaning the Glass. To glass-mount your slides, you will need a special thin cover glass. Some slide cover glass is precleaned and ready to use when you open the box. If you accidentally get fingerprints on the glass during the mounting procedure, remove them with a soft, lintless cloth.

If the manufacturer of a particular cover glass provides no assurance that the glass has been cleaned, rinse each glass in a solution of ammonia water. To make the solution, add one-quarter cup of household ammonia (the kind *without* soap) to a pint of water. Wipe each glass with a lintless cloth, and make sure that the glass is completely dry before placing it next to the film.

Making a Single-Glass Mount. If you handle slides carefully and store them in trays, you can use cardboard mounts without concern about the slides being damaged. However, after projecting the slides many times, or perhaps when changing the slides from one tray to another, the cardboard mounts may become bent at the corners. If this happens, the slides may not drop properly into the projector.

It is easy to fix a bent cardboard mount without having to remove the slide from the cardboard and remount it. A single slide cover glass and a metal binder can be used.

First be sure to remove any dust from the glass and the slide with a camel's-hair brush before mounting them together, because dust inside a glass mount will be very obvious when the slide is projected. Then place one piece of glass over the emulsion side of the slide that is in the cardboard mount. (The emulsion side of the slide is the dull side. If your slides were processed by Kodak, the emulsion side has "Processed by Kodak" printed on the cardboard mount.) Slip the glass and cardboard mount into the metal binder with the glass facing the side of the binder that has the printing on it and the top of the slide at the closed end of the binder.

The metal binder will straighten out the bent corners of the cardboard mount so that the slide will fall into the projector easily, and the glass will protect the emulsion side of the slide.

Making a Double-Glass Mount. Mounting a slide between two pieces of glass will protect both sides of the slide. This type of mounting also provides the opportunity to crop any unwanted areas out of the slide. Sometimes cropping can transform a good slide into a great one. For each slide, you will need a mask, two pieces of slide cover glass, and a metal binder or some binding tape.

Although it is not necessary to wear white gloves when mounting the slide in the mask and in the cover glass, you may wish to take this added precaution to avoid the possibility of getting fingerprints on either the film or the glass.

To mount the slide in the mask:

1. Remove the film from the cardboard mount by cutting off a wide edge of the mount with scissors. Make the cut halfway between the edge of the mount and the edge of the film. Insert your fingernail into the opening in the cardboard and pry the mount open. Lift out the piece of film, holding it by the edges to avoid fingerprints.
2. Open the mask and position it so that the half with the tabs is on the bottom if you are mounting a horizontal slide, and at the right if you are mounting a vertical slide. Slip the film under the tabs in the same orientation that you want to see on the screen. The emulsion side should face away from you.
3. Close the mask and look at the slide closely to determine if it should be cropped. To crop a slide, cut a piece from another mask and use it to cover the unwanted area. Secure the piece of mask in place over the original mask with a small piece of tape. Masks of special shapes and sizes are available from your photo dealer.
4. Place a piece of clean cover glass on each side of the slide mounted in the mask. Open the glass and carefully remove any dust from the glass and the slide by using a camel's-hair brush.

Binding Glass-Mounted Slides with Tape. To bind the glass-and-mask sandwich with tape, follow the steps given here. Make sure you roll the glass firmly and evenly along the center of the tape in order to make a strong binding.

After the slide has been projected many times, the adhesive may begin to ooze out along the edges of the tape and can cause the slide to jam in the projector. This stickiness can be removed with a solvent; or you may prefer to remove the tape, clean the cover glass, and then cover the edges with new tape.

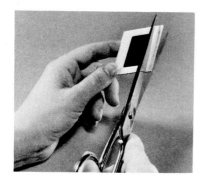
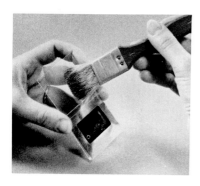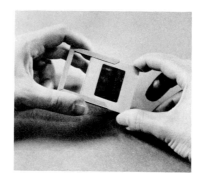

These are the key steps in making a double-glass mount. (Top left) Use a scissors to free the transparency from the cardboard mount. (Top right) Masking, if desired, is done with a piece of opaque high-contrast film held in place with tape. (Bottom left) Clean any dust from both the glass and the slide itself. (Bottom right) Add the metal binder supplied with the mount.

1. Remove the film from its mount. Open the mask and slip the film under the tabs, emulsion (dull) side down; fold the mask shut. The aluminized side faces the lamp during projection. Dust the slide and the glass with a soft camel's-hair brush.
2. Unroll 10 inches of tape. Hold the glasses tightly together against the adhesive side of the tape, ½ inch from the end of the tape. Roll the slide along the center of tape until three edges of the slide are covered.
3. Cut off squarely the extra ½ inch of tape on the first edge. Miter the end for a corner. Fold down the tape along the first edge, except at the corner.
4. Tape the fourth edge firmly, cut the tape flush, and miter the end for the corner.
5. Miter all remaining corners. Cut from the corners toward the center of the slide, holding the scissors at a slight angle.

6. Fold the tape down on the remaining edges to complete the binding. Spot label the lower left corner, aluminized side, with a pressure-sensitive label.

Newton's Rings. Newton's rings are irregularly shaped, rainbow-colored patterns caused by partial contact between the extremely smooth surfaces of the film base and the adjacent cover glass. Newton's rings ordinarily are not bothersome when slides have been properly bound with masks.

You can avoid Newton's rings only by preventing contact between the two smooth surfaces. Glass-mount valuable slides soon after processing before severe drying or repeated high-wattage projection has permanently set a curl toward the emulsion. Use the mask in the intended manner, with both the tabs and the aluminized half of the mask between the smooth film base and the cover glass. Do not anchor two opposite edges of the film with tape. If extremely accurate positioning is required, anchor the film only along one edge, and be sure that the opposite edge of the film has some

Slides and Transparencies, Mounting

freedom to expand when it is first heated by the projector.

If Newton's rings appear in spite of the above precautions, spray anti-offset powder* (grade 3 or fine) from a squeeze bottle onto the film and the side of the cover glass that will be next to the film. All you need is a mist of powder; if you can see the anti-offset powder on the film or glass, you have used too much. Remove any excess powder with a camel's-hair brush.

If anti-offset powder is unavailable, rub the glass surface with a wad of damp cotton that has been dipped in a fine abrasive, such as Grade 00 pumice (available at paint stores). The minute scratches caused by the abrasive will usually break the contact between the film base and glass enough to prevent Newton's rings. Following this treatment, and before you bind the transparencies, clean the cover glasses *thoroughly*, since any abrasive bound inside the slide can scratch the film.

A special "no ring" glass can be used to prevent Newton's rings. This glass has a coating or an etched pattern on one side, and this side of the glass should go next to the smooth (base) side of the film. Use a regular cover glass next to the emulsion side of the film.

Newton's rings will not harm your slides and will usually disappear as the temperature of the entire slide rises. However, if the film emulsion has continued contact with the glass, and if the slides are stored at high humidity, ferrotyping marks may eventually show on the film. Unlike Newton's rings, these marks are practically impossible to remove.

Condensation. When glass-bound slides are projected with high-wattage or arc projectors under conditions of high humidity, moisture will evaporate from the film's emulsion. This moisture may condense on the inner surface of the cover glass and also, very slightly, on the film. This condensation will be visible on the screen until the slide warms up enough to evaporate the moisture. Avoid storing slides in damp places, such as basements, especially during the summer months. You

Some photographers prefer a glass-mounted slide bound with tape, as shown here. Repeated projection or prolonged exposure of taped slides to lamp heat may cause the tape's adhesive to ooze. The stickiness can be removed with a solvent or the tape can be replaced.

may want to store the slides with a desiccant, such as silica gel. Moderately dry storage will usually keep properly bound slides free of condensation.

Glass-bound slides that have been projected frequently can cloud up because of repeated moisture evaporation. This is particularly true if they have been projected at high temperatures. If you notice such an effect in your own slides, take them apart, clean them, and rebind them.

Cementing Transparencies to Glass

Binding slides in sandwich fashion between two cover glasses will achieve flatness of the transparency, but glass-bound slides often lead to problems with moisture condensation, cooling, ferrotyping, and the formation of Newton's rings— particularly with extra-bright projectors.

One technique that has proved to be satisfactory is to cement the transparency to a single sheet of cover glass. Such action should enable you to retain the desirable attributes of both open-frame and glass-sandwich slide mounts.

---

*Anti-offset powder is used in the printing industry. It is sold by graphic-arts suppliers, listed under "Printing Equipment and Supplies" in the Yellow Pages of your telephone book.

The method of cementing described here provides a bond that is permanent under most conditions of use and storage and, when properly done, will result in a picture area that is free from air bubbles, dust, and dirt. It is possible to position the transparency accurately on the slide, and the film will be removable in case of an error in mounting. Finally, the method requires only simple apparatus and materials, most of which can be made at home or obtained easily.

Transparencies that have been processed recently cement best. Old transparencies—especially those that have been projected frequently—and any that are severely curled, bent, or cracked may not adhere well to the glass.

To a great extent, operator skill in handling the procedure will determine how satisfactory the results will be. Therefore, you should begin with expendable, freshly processed slides and practice until the technique is mastered.

Constructing a Mounting Box. Although the cementing technique could be carried out on a conventional light table, construction of a special-purpose mounting box can speed the operation.

Materials Required. The following materials are needed to build a mounting box.

1. Box—approximately 250 × 300 × 200 mm (10″ × 12″ × 8″).
2. Lamp (40-watt), socket, and cord.
3. Rigid plastic panel, the same length as the box and approximately 50 mm (2 inches) narrower. This can be made of plastic, such as Bakelite or Synthane, or, if plastic is not available, of tempered hardboard or plywood.
4. A sheet of diffusing glass, such as opal glass, about half the size of the plastic panel.
5. Semirigid matte Vinylite sheet or a similar material 50 × 300 × 0.2 mm (6″ × 12″ × 0.008″).
6. Double-coated masking tape.
7. Standard slide mount or mask.
8. Small beaker (50 ml).

Construction. Cut an opening 75 to 100 mm (3 to 4 inches) square through the top and near one

Illustrated here are the dimensions and construction details for making a mounting box.

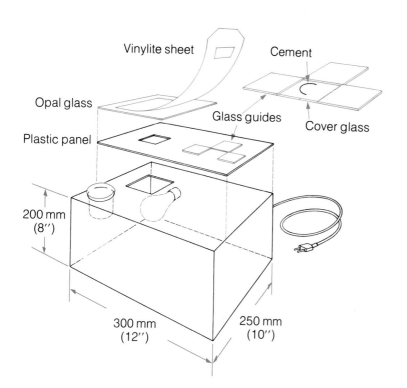

Vinylite sheet

Cement

Opal glass

Glass guides

Cover glass

Plastic panel

200 mm (8″)

300 mm (12″)

250 mm (10″)

end of the box. Mount the lamp inside the box, with the lamp surface about 50 mm (2 inches) below the opening.

Next, cut a square 65-mm (2½-inch) aperture in the panel of rigid plastic so that it will come directly over the hole in the box. Fasten the panel to the box with double-coated masking tape.

Now cut a hole large enough for the beaker on the top of the lamp end of the box, in an area of the top that is not covered by the panel. This location of the beaker will enable the heat from the lamp to keep the cement fluid.

Then with double-coated tape, affix the diffusing glass to the plastic panel, over the aperture.

Finally, stick one end of the Vinylite sheet, matte side down, to the diffusing glass with double-coated tape, leaving the opposite end (tab) free and extending slightly past the end of the box. The two corners at the free end of the Vinylite sheet can be cut off, leaving a tongue about 75 mm (3 inches) wide.

Lift the tab and roll it back over the illuminator. With two small pieces of double-coated tape, attach the slide mount to the matte side of the Vinylite sheet, 50 to 75 mm (2 or 3 inches) from the free end. Position the mount so that it is over the illuminator and, with a sharp, hard-lead pencil, draw an outline of the mount aperture on the matte surface of the sheet.

Now attach two larger pieces of double-coated tape to the mount. Next, roll back the Vinylite sheet onto the plastic panel, making sure that there is good adhesion where the slide mount comes in contact with the plastic panel. Then peel back the Vinylite sheet very carefully by loosening the small pieces of tape so that the slide mount will remain on the plastic panel.

With double-coated tape, fasten three pieces of slide cover glass to the panel (to serve as guides), in close contact with three sides of the mount. Remove the mount. In order to produce precisely mounted slides, the space formed should be an exact fit for the 50 × 50 mm (2″ × 2″) cover glasses to which the transparencies are to be cemented.

Finally, apply four small pieces (13 mm [½-inch] square) of the double-coated tape to the matte surface of the Vinylite sheet, just outside the corners of the penciled outline of the aperture.

Cementing Procedure. To use the mounting box for cementing transparencies to glass, assemble the additional materials and equipment listed below, prepare the cement according to the instructions, and follow the detailed procedure.

Materials and Equipment.

1. Roller—rubber or composition 50 to 75 mm (2 to 3 inches) long. This should not be of the glue/glycerine type. A printer's brayer (inking roller) is suitable and can be obtained from a printing supply house.
2. Medicine dropper.
3. Viscose sponge.
4. Plain unflavored gelatin.
5. Ammonium hydroxide (or strong household ammonia).
6. Diluted wetting solution such as prepared from Kodak Photo-Flo 200 solution.
7. Slotted rack for holding cemented slides on edge.
8. Slide cover glass 50 × 50 mm (2″ × 2″). Thickness: 0.8 mm (.030 inch).
9. Cotton gloves (small, medium).

Cement. The cement is made with plain unflavored gelatin, such as Knox Sparkling, Grayslake, or other edible grades not containing sugar or artificial coloring. Pour approximately 15 ml (1 tablespoonful) or the contents of one envelope into 60 ml (¼ cup) of water and warm until it dissolves. Cool to room temperature and then add about 1 ml (¼ teaspoonful) of ammonium hydroxide (or strong household ammonia) and 1 ml (¼ teaspoonful) of diluted wetting solution. Filter the mixture through a finely woven cloth or, preferably, a cotton pad. This solution will set to a stiff gel at room temperature and therefore must be kept slightly warm while being used. The solution spoils quickly and will not keep more than a day or two unless it is refrigerated.

Procedure. Lift up the Vinylite sheet tab and roll it back over the illuminator.

Place the transparency (emulsion side up) so that the desired part of the image is aligned within the pencil-line aperture. Now press all four corners of the transparency against the pieces of tape.

Holding the tab in a raised position with one hand, place a clean cover glass on the panel in the space formed by the three fixed cover glasses. Then use an eyedropper to apply about 1 ml of gelatin solution in a U-shaped bead to the cover glass.

Next, take the roller and as you lower the Vinylite sheet to which the transparency is attached, roll the transparency into contact with the cover glass so that the roller advances the bead of cement across the slide as it travels. It should take only one or two seconds to traverse the film. If the motion of the roller is too slow, the film will not adhere to the glass. If the rolling operation is too fast, there is an increasing risk of entrapping air bubbles. The pressure should be neither too heavy nor too light; the natural weight of your arm is about right.

After a few seconds, lift the Vinylite sheet tab to which the glass cemented to the transparency is now attached. Wipe excess gelatin solution from the mounting position with a moist viscose sponge. The cemented unit should now be removed from the Vinylite sheet by a twisting, sliding motion rather than by a direct pull. For about 30 seconds after mounting, the bond is somewhat delicate and a direct pull may loosen the film and cause air to be entrapped. Wipe the Vinylite sheet and the four adhesive patches carefully with the sponge to remove the gelatin solution, and then wipe the slide. By the time the slide is removed from the Vinylite sheet, it can be wiped quite freely and can even be rinsed under lukewarm water to remove any excess gelatin.

In practice, it seems to be more efficient to laminate 10 or 12 slides in a group and then to suspend operations for a few minutes while the sponge is thoroughly rinsed with warm water. Additional wiping of the slides with a thoroughly clean sponge will remove all the gelatin from both the film base and the glass surfaces.

Several hours are required for the moisture in the cement to diffuse through the film base; therefore, the slides should not be projected until they have had time to dry completely. It is usually most convenient to place the slide on edge in a slotted rack for drying.

Remounting. Should it be necessary to remount a transparency, soak it in water at room temperature for a few hours or possibly overnight.

The transparency can then be peeled from the glass readily. The layer of gelatin can be washed off under warm water by gently rubbing the emulsion with the fingers. After rinsing the film in distilled water, allow it to dry. The transparency will then be ready for remounting.

Identifying and Orienting Slides

It is possible to write directly on the mount of most cardboard or plastic mounts. Label slides with title, date, and other pertinent information including your name if you intend to submit slides to contests or club competitions. When glass-mounting slides, you can write the necessary data on the white side of the mask before putting the mask between the pieces of glass. Gummed labels should be used with care, since they may cause slides to stick together or to catch in the projector gate.

Mark slide mounts for correct orientation in the projector. When a slide is held so that it reads correctly, a "thumb spot" should be applied in the lower left-hand corner of the mount. You can mark the mount directly, apply a gummed-paper or pressure-sensitive label, or add a dab of bright nail polish for the spot. When the slides are turned upside down for projection, the labels appear in the upper right-hand corner, facing the lamp. You can add numbers to these labels. Cardboard slide mounts can be notched with a punch to mark the orientation.

 ## Slow-Motion Photography

In motion-picture production, film *exposed at a greater than normal rate* and projected at a normal rate will appear to slow the tempo of motion or action in a scene. Slow motion is defined for convenience as any camera speed faster than normal up to 64 frames per second (fps). Rates beyond 64 fps are considered high-speed photography. (*See:* HIGH-SPEED PHOTOGRAPHY.)

Slow-motion photography requires a camera that can be set at frames-per-second rates faster than 18 fps for 8 mm and super 8, and faster than the 24 fps standard for both 16 mm and larger motion-picture formats.

Higher camera speeds can also be used to minimize vibration or camera movement; when film shot at faster-than-normal speeds is projected at normal speeds, there is a greater apparent space between irregular movement and the images appear to be steadier.

In technical photography, slow motion can be used to examine movement that is normally just too fast to analyze visually or in normal-speed motion pictures. In Hollywood-type movies, slow motion is used for special effects such as dream sequences. When moving models or miniatures are photographed in slow motion, a closer sense of reality is achieved. This is the standard technique for movie sequences with model ships, model bridges collapsing, or in explosions and similar effects.

• *See also:* HIGH-SPEED PHOTOGRAPHY; MODEL AND MINIATURE PHOTOGRAPHY;MOTION-PICTURE PRODUCTION; MOTION STUDY; PROJECTORS; TIME-LAPSE PHOTOGRAPHY.

Snowflake Photography

Snowflakes are fascinating objects. They are, in one sense, all of a pattern; yet, no two are alike. Because of the arrangement of hydrogen and oxygen atoms in the water molecule, an ice crystal always has six sides, but the molecules join randomly to form larger crystals with numerous branches.

Photographing snowflakes presents some interesting problems. The flakes are very fragile and will not stand rough handling. More important, they contain only a very small amount of water, and a snowflake on a dry, cold surface will evaporate in minutes.

Equipment

Snowflakes vary in size from a few millimetres to an inch across. Photographing them is a project in photomacrography. A long-bellows view camera with a short-focus lens or a 35 mm single-lens reflex camera with extension tubes will serve. Some workers prefer to use a microscope with a mechanical stage and a low-power objective. The eyepiece can usually be omitted. Coupling devices are used to attach a single-lens reflex camera to the microscope.

For photomacrography, the lighting equipment is simple. An electronic flash ring-light unit surrounding the lens is excellent. An auxiliary incandescent light source may be needed for focusing. It should be of low wattage and placed as far as possible from the outfit to avoid heating the specimen.

With a microscope, the usual microscope illuminator can be used. However, it will require the addition of a heat absorber or water cell to cool the light beam.

Working Area

Snowflakes can not be photographed indoors. By the time a good specimen has been caught and brought indoors, it will have already started to deteriorate. In a warm room, it will evaporate in seconds. A photographer must therefore work outside or in an unheated shed or garage. Heavy clothing and gloves will have to be worn while working. It is useless to attempt to do any snowflake photography if the temperature is above freezing.

Snow Conditions

The temperature at which snowflake photography is possible depends somewhat on the thickness, size, and texture of the snow and whether the temperature is rising from a very cold period or falling from a point above freezing. If the temperature is rising after a cold period, photography can continue until actual thawing commences.

Studying the weather map is helpful. The western quadrants of large storms or blizzards produce beautiful flakes. Such a condition may be identifiable even without a weather map. Usually the wind is from west to north, and the barometer is at 750 to 760 mm (29.6 to 29.9 inches) and slowly rising. Perfect crystals are more likely to be found when the snowfall is not too heavy and the flakes are small. Quality and quantity of good specimens change sharply as a storm progresses.

Collection and Photography

For collection and photography, you will need a sharp-pointed wooden splint (toothpicks will do), a feather duster, some individual feathers, and a blackboard about 30.5 cm (1 foot) square. The blackboard should have stiff wire or metal handles at the ends, so that the hands will not warm it.

Catch the snowflakes on the blackboard as they fall, and examine them with a hand lens. Sweep the board as necessary with the feather duster. Continue this until two or more promising specimens are seen.

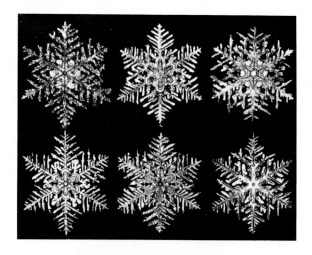

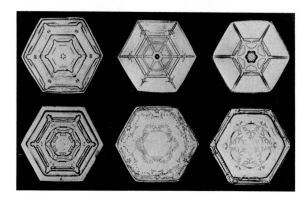

Wilson A. Bentley, a Vermont farm boy, was given a micro-scope for his fifteenth birthday. He combined this with a studio camera and began photographing snowflakes. In 1931 a volume of 3,000 Bentley snowflake photographs was published. The photos above are from Bentley glass-plate negatives in the collection of the National Archives.

From here on you must work fast. Transfer a likely specimen to a glass slide. Surrounding the specimen with two or three additional snowflakes retards evaporation. The slides must be kept cold.

Transfer the slide at once to the camera stand or microscope stage, center it quickly, and focus. If a microscope is used, you will discover that the center of most snow crystals is made up of tiny air tubes. Focus sharply on one of these. Immediately expose.

You cannot, of course, take the time to measure the exposure with a meter. If electronic flash is used, make some preliminary tests using salt crystals or some such material as subject matter. Establish a few standard exposures for different magnifications. Use the same approach with a microscope.

Because the snowflake lasts only a few minutes, it is important to work as fast as possible. Even when in doubt, take the picture. Be prepared to use a good deal of film. Photograph every promising crystal and make selections later. If you hesitate in deciding among several good specimens, you may find that they all have disappeared.

With a macro setup, place the snowflake on a black background and photograph it by frontlight. This defines the form and outline of the flake well. You may find, however, that you do not get the inner structure of the crystal with this lighting.

Using a microscope and glass slides, try making pictures by transmitted light. This brings out the inner parts of the crystal very well, but because there is little contrast between the flake and its background, the outline will not be very distinct. Modified dark-field illumination can be used to good advantage in this situation.

Handling Snowflakes

It may be possible to photograph the desired flakes directly on the blackboard with the macro setup. Also, some photographers use a set of small boards or paddles, covered with black velvet or plush, on which to catch and photograph promising specimens.

If a microscope is used, transfer the flakes from the board to a glass slide without damaging or breaking them. This can be accomplished with a sharp-pointed splint, pressed gently on the flake until it adheres. Pick up the flake and drop it on the cold glass slide. The microscope should already be roughly in focus, either from focusing a test slide or from photographing previous flakes.

Once the selected flake is placed on the glass slide, press it flat against the glass with the edge of a feather. Quickly place the slide on the microscope stage, center it, and make final focusing adjustments. Immediately make an exposure. Recheck the flake to see if it is still in good condition. If it is, make another exposure, possibly with a different exposure setting. Speed is important. Whatever setup is used, you must be able to focus and photograph the specimen without having to remove any part of the equipment. If you do not have a single-lens reflex camera, your microscope must have a beam-splitting eyepiece, so that the slide can be viewed with the camera in place and ready for exposure.

Plastic Replicas

To experiment, you might try making plastic replicas of snow crystals for later photography. To form the replica, mix a dilute solution of polyvinyl formal in ethylene dichloride, chill the solution, and drop small amounts of the chilled solution onto selected crystals. Set the treated crystal aside for the plastic to harden and the ice to evaporate. Since the dilution, the temperature, and the type of crystal are interrelated, experimenting will be necessary to find a successful combination. Once the plastic has hardened, the replica can be handled at room temperature. Cementing the replica to a glass microscope slide is a good way to preserve it permanently. Carefully made plastic replicas can preserve much of the detail of the original snow crystal.

Films and Processing

Since snow crystals are white, there is normally no benefit to be gained by using color film. For frontlighted photography, any medium or fast black-and-white negative film is suitable. When using a microscope setup with transmitted light, somewhat higher contrast may be desirable. Special-purpose films for photomicrography are available. Depending upon the film-developer combination used, a moderate increase in contrast can be gained by developing negatives about 20 percent longer than recommended for pictorial material.

Negatives can be printed normally, either by contact or enlargement. If the picture was made against a black background, the snowflake will stand out dramatically.

Flakes photographed by transmitted light will have exquisite detail, but may lack contrast and be without a clearly defined outline. Various techniques of photographic and hand masking can be used to overcome this.

Color

Do not neglect color films entirely. Even the white crystals show a hint of color from clear prismatic branches. There are methods of introducing color into the highlights or backgrounds when using transmitted light and dark-field illumination. Employ colored filters rather than an opaque stop for dark-field illumination in the microscope. With any lighting arrangement of more than one light source, try colored filters over one or more of the sources. Even portions of a ring-light flash can be covered with filter segments of one or more colors to add color to highlights.

• *See also:* COPYING; DARK-FIELD ILLUMINATION; PHOTOMACROGRAPHY; PHOTOMICROGRAPHY; WINTERIZING EQUIPMENT; WINTER PHOTOGRAPHY.

Sodium Bisulfite

Sodium acid sulfite, sodium hydrogen sulfite

Acid preservative used in nonhardening fixing baths as a preservative for pyro and as clearing bath in reversal processes.

Formula: $NaHSO_3$
Molecular Weight: 104.06

White, crystalline powder, soluble in water, insoluble in alcohol. It has a faint odor of sulfur dioxide.

Sodium Bromide

Restrainer in developers, less used than potassium bromide, but works in exactly the same way.

Formula: $NaBr$
Molecular Weight: 102.91

White or colorless granules or powder. Sodium bromide absorbs water from the air but is not deliquescent. It is freely soluble in water and somewhat soluble in alcohol.

Sodium Carbonate

Carbonate of soda, sal soda, soda ash, washing soda

Principal accelerator used in developers of moderately high activity.

Formula: Na_2CO_3 (anhydrous—"soda ash")
           $Na_2CO_3 \cdot H_2O$ (monohydrated)
           $Na_2CO_3 \cdot 10H_2O$ (crystals—"washing soda")

Molecular Weight (respectively): 106.00
                              124.02
                              286.16

White powder (anhydrous), white crystalline granules (monohydrated), or colorless crystals (crystals). It is soluble in water, insoluble in alcohol. The three forms are not equivalent in strength, but may be substituted for each other in the following proportions:

> For 100 grams of anhydrous, use 117 grams of monohydrated, or 270 grams of crystals.
>
> For 100 grams of monohydrated, use 85 grams of anhydrous, or 230 grams of crystals.
>
> For 100 grams of crystals, use 37 grams of anhydrous, or 43 grams of monohydrated.

Sodium Chloride

Table salt, sea salt, rock salt, muriate of soda

Used in sensitizing printing-out papers, and in certain ferricyanide bleach formulas and reducers.

Formula: $NaCl$

Molecular Weight: 58.45

Colorless, transparent crystals or crystalline powder. For photographic use, avoid common table salt sold in groceries because it contains certain other ingredients, such as iodine and various anti-caking agents. Occasionally, grocers carry special salt for canning and preserving, and this is essentially pure sodium chloride. For sensitizing, however, it is probably better to order USP or reagent grade sodium chloride.

Sodium Cyanide

Used in reducers, in intensifiers, and in restoring daguerreotypes, because it dissolves silver salts but not metallic silver.

Formula: $NaCN$

Molecular Weight: 49.02

White deliquescent granules or lumps, freely soluble in water.

DANGER: Cyanides are intensely poisonous and should be handled only in a well-ventilated place, with rubber gloves. Never pour used cyanide solution down a sink drain; any trace of acid in the drain will cause the evolution of deadly hydrogen cyanide gas.

Sodium Dithionite

Sodium hydrosulfite

Used as a dye bleaching agent, also as a fogging agent in reversal processing.

Formula: $Na_2S_2O_4$

Molecular Weight: 174.10

White powder with typical sulfide odor (like rotten eggs). It is very soluble in water, oxidizes in moist air, and may, in fact, ignite spontaneously if left in an open container in a damp area. Sodium dithionite is an extremely powerful fogging agent, and traces of the material on workbenches or suspended in the air can cause serious damage to photographic materials. Therefore, solutions of sodium dithionite should always be prepared away from the darkroom, and all utensils must be thoroughly washed after solutions are prepared.

Sodium Ferricyanide

Red prussiate of soda

Used in reducers, toners, and similar solutions, in place of potassium ferricyanide when the latter is not available; the potassium salt is preferred.

Formula: $Na_3Fe(CN)_6 \cdot H_2O$

Molecular Weight: 298.97

Deep ruby-red crystals, soluble in water. The crystals are very deliquescent and are difficult to store; for this reason, the sodium salt is seldom used. Potassium ferricyanide is not deliquescent.

Sodium Hexametaphosphate

A water-softening agent and a mild detergent commercially sold under various trade names such as Calgon. Sometimes sold combined with detergents; for example, Calgonite.
Formula: $(NaPO_3)_n$
Molecular Weight: Some multiple of 101.98

White, flaky crystals or granules, soluble in water, with an alkaline reaction. It has the property of keeping calcium and magnesium salts from precipitating, even in boiling solutions. In photographic applications, it is known as a sequestering agent.

Sodium Hydrosulfite

Another name for sodium dithionite. (*See:* SODIUM DITHIONITE.) This chemical is also sometimes referred to as sodium hyposulfite. This usage should be avoided because of possible confusion with sodium thiosulfate, which is also called sodium hyposulfite in older books.

The name sodium hydrosulfite is also applied, on occasion, to another chemical with the formula $NaHSO_2$, molecular weight 88.06. This chemical is not used in photography.

Sodium Hydroxide

Caustic soda, soda, lye

Strong alkali, used as an accelerator in high-contrast hydroquinone developers.
Formula: $NaOH$
Molecular Weight: 40.00

Available in small pellets or sticks; very soluble in water, alcohol, and glycerin. When dissolved in water, sodium hydroxide causes the evolution of a great deal of heat; therefore, it must always be dissolved in cold water, and the solution allowed to cool before use. If sodium hydroxide is dissolved in hot water, the added heat will cause the solution to boil violently, possibly spattering.

DANGER: Sodium hydroxide is a caustic poison; it can cause very painful burns on the skin if allowed to remain in contact with it.

Sodium Metabisulfite

Sodium pyrosulfite

An acidic salt of sulfurous acid, used as a preservative in developers, also as an acidifier in nonhardening hypo baths.
Formula: $Na_2S_2O_5$
Molecular Weight: 190.12

Colorless crystals or white powder, soluble in water. While it is analogous to potassium metabisulfite, sodium metabisulfite is rarely found; when specified, it may be substituted for by sodium bisulfite, which is commonly available.

Sodium Metaborate

An alkali salt, used as an accelerator in developers of medium activity; the akalinity of this salt is about midway between that of borax and that of sodium carbonate. It has two advantages over sodium carbonate: (1) It allows control over the activity of the developer by varying the amount of alkali, and (2) it does not produce a gas when neutralized with an acid, hence there is no danger of blistering a negative if an acid stop bath is used.
Formula: $NaBO_2 \cdot 4H_2O$
Molecular Weight: 132.88

Colorless crystals or white powder, freely soluble in water.

NOTE: Kodalk, a proprietary alkali marketed by Eastman Kodak Company, is chemically similar and can be used in the same way, quantity for quantity.

Sodium Sulfide

Used in toning of prints, also as a substitute second developer in reversal processes where a brown image is acceptable. Used in some silver-recovery procedures.

Formula: $Na_2S \cdot 9H_2O$
Molecular Weight: 240.19

Colorless or yellowish crystals, very deliquescent, freely soluble in water. Sodium sulfide is also available in anhydrous form (Na_2S), which contains no water. If using the anhydrous variety, use only one third as much.

CAUTION: Sodium sulfide solutions should be mixed outside the darkroom; traces of sulfide can fog sensitized materials very badly. If used solutions are discarded down a sink drain, follow with a good amount of running water, so that no residue is left. Such residue would react with acids to produce poisonous hydrogen sulfide gas, which also has a strong fogging action on films and papers.

Sodium Sulfite

Preservative in developers; also used in acid fixing baths to protect the hypo from acid. It is mildly alkaline, and in some developers, notably Metol-only and Amidol formulas, no accelerator is needed.

Formula: Na_2SO_3
Molecular Weight: 126.05

White crystals or powder. The crystal version contains 50 percent water, and so twice as much is needed as of the anhydrous (desiccated) variety. Freely soluble in water, insoluble in alcohol.

Sodium Thiocyanate

Sodium sulfocyanide, sodium rhodanide

Used in developers for reversal processes, and formerly used in fine-grain developers as a substitute for potassium thiocyanate. It is also used in gold toners.

Formula: NaSCN
Molecular Weight: 81.08

Colorless or white crystals, very deliquescent; sometimes dissolves in the water it absorbs from the air. Store in well-closed bottles away from light, and protect from traces of iron, which cause reddish stains.

• *See also:* AMMONIUM THIOCYANATE; POTASSIUM THIOCYANATE.

Sodium Thiosulfate

Sodium hyposulfite, hypo, antichlor

Main constituent of fixing baths and a principal ingredient of Farmer's reducer.

Formula: $Na_2S_2O_3 \cdot 5H_2O$
Molecular Weight: 248.19

White, transparent crystals, varying in size depending upon grade. Ordinary commercial hypo comes in large crystals that are difficult to dissolve; the photo grade is usually in small prismatic crystals known as "rice crystals." There is also an anhydrous grade, in the form of white powder, but this is rarely used. It is soluble in water, causing a large absorption of heat. Thus, if hypo is dissolved in cold water, the solution is chilled a good deal, and the chemical is difficult to dissolve. For this reason, start with warm water when making hypo solutions.

• *See also:* AMMONIUM THIOSULFATE.

Soft-Focus Effects

The deliberate use of soft focus is an important expressive technique in many kinds of pictorial photography and a common practice in much professional studio portraiture. In pictorial work, soft focus is used to de-emphasize details and blend tones in a way that enhances the sense of a romantic mood or an atmospheric effect. It is especially effective in spreading highlights to create an overall soft glow, or accents of gently dazzling brilliance.

In portraiture, the question of whether or not to use soft focus may be a matter of personal

Soft focus can be achieved by diffusion or, as in the photograph above, by using a lens deliberately designed to retain a moderate amount of spherical aberration, which can be controlled to produce the desired degree of softness. Photo by Bob Clemens.

The effect of such aberration is to image a point, not sharply as with an ordinary lens, but with a halo of decreasing intensity around it. The effect is to diffuse and reduce the contrast of the fine detail in the image. With most soft-focus lenses, the amount of spherical aberration, and therefore the degree of softness, can be controlled either by stopping down the lens or by altering the separation between the component elements. Some older portrait lenses, however, relied on a measure of chromatic aberration to achieve softness. This type of aberration is not affected by reducing the lens aperture. A lens made especially for soft-focus effects is often designated a "portrait lens." It is different from a "portrait attachment," which is a positive supplementary lens used in combination with a camera lens to achieve focusing—and thus larger images—at closer-than-normal distances.

Some soft-focus lenses have special diaphragms that permit stopping down without minimizing the softening effect. These may have multiple holes to permit light from all areas of the lens to form the image. Another type has blades similar to shutter blades that come into the lens area from the edges, making the effective part of the lens star-shaped.

Soft Focus by Diffusion

Any device that moderately diffuses light will produce a soft-focus effect when used in front of the camera lens. Diffusion disks are made in standard sizes for mounting just like filters; some have clear centers so that the softness occurs only in the outer areas of the picture. Diffusers are often improvised from screen or net material, or from a sheet of glass smeared with petroleum jelly or a similar substance; this approach makes it easy to leave a clear area wherever desired in the picture.

Diffusion in front of the camera lens spreads the highlights into the shadow areas for a dazzling or glowing effect. When a negative is being printed, diffusion under an enlarger lens spreads shadows into the lighter areas of the print, which tends to dull the highlights. Camera-lens diffusion is usually preferred—enlarging diffusion is used when an existing sharp negative requires softening.

When making reversal prints from slides or transparencies, diffusion at the enlarger provides

preference, but most photographers find that the customer would choose a softer, more flattering image when given a choice. Consequently, few studio portraits are made with the kind of sharpness that records every wrinkle, line, and blemish. Such a portrait may appear somewhat crude unless the sitter has practically flawless skin. Otherwise, an inordinate amount of skillful retouching may be needed.

Soft focus is not out-of-focus blur; it cannot be achieved by putting the lens out of focus. It requires either a soft-focus lens, or a means of diffusing the image-forming light as it enters the camera lens, or leaves the enlarging lens.

Soft-Focus Lenses

Soft-focus lenses are specially designed to leave a moderate residue of spherical aberration.

the same effect as diffusion at the camera lens. The same devices may be used for enlarger diffusing as for camera diffusing, whether printing from negatives or positives.
• *See also:* DIFFUSION; PICTORIAL PHOTOGRAPHY; PORTRAITURE; SHARPNESS; SPECIAL EFFECTS.

Solarization

Exposure begins the job of reducing silver halide crystals to grains of metallic silver; development completes the job. For a given development, the amount of silver produced is related to the amount of exposure each area has received. Depending upon the emulsion, a certain exposure is sufficient to cause all the halides in an area to be reduced by development, producing maximum density; if even more exposure is given, no more density can be produced. However, with gross overexposure—perhaps about 1000 times normal, or more (it varies with the type of material)—there will actually be a decrease in the density of that area upon development. This phenomenon is represented on a characteristic curve by a downward turn of the shoulder, after it has reached the peak of maximum density. In a print, areas that lie on this downward slope will have reversed tonality.

The overexposure reversal effect was observed by daguerreotypists in the earliest days of photography and was named *solarization,* for only direct sunlight had sufficient intensity to cause it. Solarized areas in a daguerreotype commonly had a blue-gray color. A photographer who was not skilled enough in judging exposure to prevent a white shirtfront or similar area in a portrait from solarizing was looked down upon by professionals as a "blue bosom boy."

Changes in emulsion design over the last 75 years have produced films in which it is very difficult to create intentional solarization. In long time exposures outdoors at night, a street light overexposes during an exposure that is sufficient to record detail on a dimly lit subject. The negative image of the light bulb itself may have less density than the surrounding halo and may print black. This is true solarization. A related phenomenon sometimes occurs accidentally when an area of

This daguerreotype shows solarization in the blue-gray cuffs and collar of the subject. It was caused by an error in exposure, common in early photography. With modern emulsions, solarization is actually a difficult effect to create. Photo courtesy International Museum of Photography, Rochester, N.Y.

film is exposed to a sudden intense light, such as a streak of lightning, during the course of a longer exposure to much weaker light. The affected area will print with reversed tonality, which has given it the description "black lightning" effect. (*See:* CLAYDEN EFFECT.)

Reversed tonalities are frequently used in pictorial photography for expressive effect. They are not the result of true solarization, but are created in the darkroom by exposing an emulsion to white light after development is partially complete; the techniques are described in the article SABATTIER EFFECT.

Some direct-positive materials are pre-exposed by the manufacturer just to the solarization point. A further normal exposure in a camera causes the material to produce a direct-positive image with regular development.
• *See also:* CLAYDEN EFFECT; EXPOSURE; SABATTIER EFFECT.

Soundstripe

For sound recording, a magnetic oxide coating can be placed on the photographic film base in the form of a narrow soundstripe. Typically, the soundstripe is coated on the base side of the film and, where possible, on the edge away from perforations. A narrow stripe may also be placed on the opposite edge of the film, to provide uniform winding of the film on the roll. Camera films in super 8 and 16 mm formats can be supplied with soundstripe for live recording during filming. Soundstriping can be applied to silent films after processing, or even after editing of the film, for later addition of sound.

• *See also:* MAGNETIC SOUND FOR MOTION PICTURES.

Special Effects

While the motion-picture producer might consider special effects in a more restrictive sense, for the purpose of this article any set of nonroutine photographic techniques might be considered to produce a special effect. Special effects are as varied as the needs and desires of the photographer. In a sense, each special effects effort is an experiment because special effects are nonroutine, and frequently unpredictable, operations.

There are few rules that can be followed in creating special effects. The work is often experimental, and mistakes are common. Only considerable experience in creating special effects will give the photographer uniform results.

Special effects are achieved in many ways, and there are no specific classifications. However, the work is generally accomplished in three basic ways: (1) in the camera, (2) in the darkroom or motion-picture laboratory, and (3) by a combination of these techniques.

Special effects done in the camera simply means that all the elements of the completed image are created on the original camera transparency or negative. This can be done by imaginative use of what is *in* the camera (the film), what is *on* the camera

(Top) Unusual effects can result from choice of film stock, as in this landscape on infrared (false-color) film. Photo by John Stone. (Bottom) The use of double exposure outdoors created this interesting silhouette effect. Photo by Dennis Hallinan.

Multiple-image lenses used in front of the camera lens are surfaced in such a way as to divide a single subject into several identical images. This multi-imaged photograph of a Mexican cathedral viewed through a field of poppies has the dreamlike quality of a mirage floating in air.

This photograph was created by covering the top half of the camera lens with a No. 25 red gelatin filter; a No. 47 blue filter was placed at the bottom of the lens. Photo by Keith Boas.

Special Effects

(Right) A high-contrast original was used to produce this image making use of the Sabattier effect. The Mackie Line around the image is very evident. Photo by Barbara Jean. (Below) Reticulation was used to add interest to this photograph, which has strong design quality and large plain areas. This is a print from a black-and-white negative. Photo by Keith Boas.

(lenses, filters, accessories), or what is *in front* of the camera (colored lights, projected images, stroboscopic illumination).

Many more special effects are created in the darkroom with nonroutine photographic processing and printing techniques. These include relatively common control techniques such as masking, dodging, intensification, and reduction; making shadow pictures without a camera; and the more exotic techniques of posterization, reticulation, solarization, and similar effects.

The third general category of special effects is the unusual work accomplished by a combination of camera and darkroom techniques. Much of this involves creating new photographs from existing pictures, such as combining several images to make one print. High-contrast pictures, titles, and tone-line negatives also fall into this category.

• *See also:* BAS-RELIEF; BLACK-AND-WHITE PRINTS FROM COLOR FILMS; COMBINATION PRINTING; DIFFUSION; DIRECT POSITIVE PAPER PHOTOGRAPHY; DYE TONING; FALSE-COLOR FILM; FISHEYE LENS; FRONT PROJECTION; GUM-

(Top) Montages can be created with high-contrast film and a color slide. Foreground subjects on high-contrast film can add a center of interest to sunsets and other scenes. (Bottom) High-contrast films make effective slides as a montage. The skyline of New York is a high-contrast positive contact-printed from a black-and-white negative. The moon is from one color slide, and the trees are from another which was taken with a multiple-image lens. Three films and a combination of darkroom and in-camera techniques create a photograph never seen in a viewfinder. Photo by Paul Kuzniar.

Further Reading: Duckworth, P. *Creative Photographic Effects Simplified.* Englewood Cliffs, NJ: Prentice-Hall, 1975; Litzel, Otto. *Darkroom Magic.* Garden City, NY: Amphoto, 1975; Ruggles, Joanne and Philip. *Darkroom Graphics.* Garden City, NY: Amphoto, 1975; Smith, Edwin. *All the Photo Tricks.* Garden City, NY: Amphoto, 1974.

Specific Gravity

Specific gravity is the ratio between the mass of a given volume of a substance, and the mass of an equal volume of pure water, usually measured at 4 C. It is a ratio and thus has no dimensions. In the case of liquids, specific gravity may be measured with a hydrometer, which is a calibrated float immersed in the liquid in question. American hydrometers are calibrated in specific-gravity units; many European countries, however, use the Baumé system, which has two separate scales — one for liquids heavier than water, the other for liquids lighter than water.

On the heavier-than-water scale, 0 Baumé corresponds to the specific gravity of pure water, hence it is equal to specific gravity 1.00, and 66 Baumé corresponds to a specific gravity of 1.842. On the lighter-than-water scale, 10 Baumé corresponds to specific gravity 1.00, and 60 Baumé corresponds to a specific gravity of 0.745. Thus, there is some overlap between the two scales.

While the specific gravity of a solution can give some indication of its concentration, there is no correlation between this and photographic activity. Specific-gravity measurement using a hydrometer is a quick way of checking the mixing procedure when packaged mixes are used. A specific gravity noticeably lower than normal (about 0.005

unit) indicates that too much water was used, or that some chemical was omitted, in preparing the solution. A specific gravity 0.005 unit or more higher than normal indicates that too little water was used or that a chemical which lowers the specific gravity was omitted.

Spectrography

Spectrographic Analysis
In spectrographic analyses, photographs of spectra (bright-colored lines) are used to detect the presence of elements, and to determine the concentration levels at which they are present. The analyses are based upon measurements of the positions (wavelengths) and the relative intensities of spectral lines. There are two principal aspects of the subject. One of these is the production of the spectrum, which involves choosing the source of the spectrum and operating the spectrograph. The other is the recording of the spectrum, which involves selecting the most suitable photographic plate or film emulsion, processing the film or plate properly, and converting the recorded photographic densities to element concentrations.

Optical-Emission Spectroscopy
Optical-emission spectroscopy is an analytical technique in many industrial, research, and medical laboratories. Spectrographic analysis is used extensively for the determination of trace elements present in concentration ranges below 1 part per million, as well as for the determination of primary constituents, such as those encountered in alloys. Analysis time is often less than that required for comparable chemical analysis.

The Spectrograph
This instrument is one of the most comprehensive analytical instruments available. One exposure can often serve to determine positively the presence or absence of over 50 elements. This comprehensiveness, in combination with the development of techniques permitting semiquantitative analyses of "random-type" samples, has extended the application of the spectrograph to laboratories whose analytical problems change from day to day.

Industrial and medical emphasis on trace analysis has revived interest in the spectrograph. Extremely small quantities of metallic elements are successfully monitored by the spectrographic technique in the manufacture of many products, such as transistors, optical goods, and semiconductors, and in the study of biological tissues and fluids. This type of analysis is difficult and time-consuming, if not impossible, by classical wet chemical procedures.

Photographic Materials
The spectral sensitivity of a plate or film, or its response to radiation of various wavelengths, is an important factor in determining its suitability for spectrum analysis. Most silver halide photographic materials exhibit a variation in contrast at different wavelengths of radiation. This gradient variation is usually greater in the region of optical sensitization; in the green-sensitive region of an orthochromatic emulsion, or in the green- and red-sensitive regions of a panchromatic emulsion.

In order to obtain maximum sensitivity in spectrographic analysis, the intensity of available radiation and spectral background adjacent to the spectrum lines of interest must be considered. When low-intensity radiation is being recorded, or when no background is present, an emulsion with high initial speed is desirable. However, when there is sufficient intensity to record an appreciable background, the best detectability will be obtained with an emulsion of higher contrast and finer grain. High-contrast emulsions produce a relatively large density change for a small change in light intensity, compared with low-contrast materials. It follows that a small intensity difference between line and background, such as is frequently encountered in trace analysis, will be magnified by a high-contrast emulsion.

In general, due to the relatively large change in density per unit change in exposure, high-contrast emulsions are usually preferred for semiquantitative analyses employing visual concentration estimations of unknowns from standard plates. However, for highest accuracy, the variation of gradient with wavelength requires more frequent calibration at closely spaced wavelengths.

Emulsions having wide exposure latitude (low contrast), and thus a single exposure, will often cover a 50- to 100-fold concentration range. This is an advantage when completely unknown samples are being analyzed. With high-contrast materials, on the other hand, it is often necessary to provide different exposure levels when covering wide concentration ranges.

• *See also:* SPECTRUM; WEDGE SPECTOGRAM.

Spectrum

The range of colors from red to blue that is seen when white light is dispersed into a rainbow by the atmosphere, or by a prism, is the visible spectrum. The colors seen are the response of the human sensor—the eye—to distinct kinds of electromagnetic energy. Sir Isaac Newton was the first man to use a prism to spread white light out into a visible spectrum. He described the colors as violet, blue, green, yellow, orange, and red.

The visible spectrum is but a very small portion of the total range of electromagnetic energy. Humans are unable to directly detect by their senses any other portion of the energy spectrum, but the body is affected by energy from other portions, such as ultraviolet, x-rays, gamma rays, and other radiations.

Photographic materials have a greater range of sensitivity than the human eye. Their sensitivity extends partly into the infrared region, beyond visible red, but primarily into the ultraviolet and adjacent regions beyond the deepest visible blue. Thus, photography makes it possible to obtain visible records of invisible energy. When coupled to other sensors and display devices—radio telescopes, fluorescent screens, and oscilloscopes are only three of thousands—photography makes it possible to "see" some aspects of virtually the entire electromagnetic energy spectrum.

The spectrum is actually a visual display that shows the ranks or orders of electromagnetic radiant energy according to two of its measurable properties: frequency and wavelength.

Electromagnetic radiant energy originates at a source and radiates, traveling in straight lines. As it

The Electromagnetic Spectrum

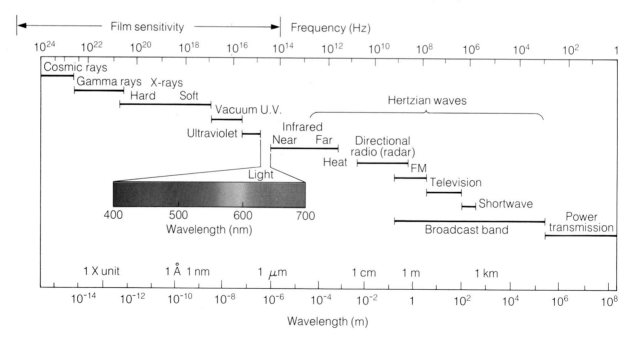

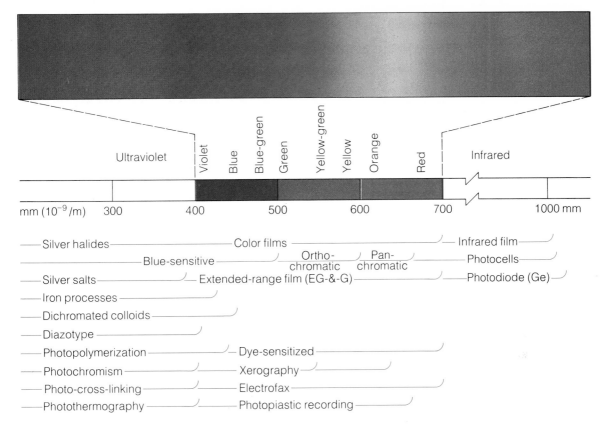

Spectral Sensitivity of Some Photographic Materials

travels, it exhibits the characteristics of both particle motion and wave motion. The distance from the peak of one wave to the peak of the next wave is called the wavelength, or a cycle. The number of waves (cycles) that go past a point in a given length of time is called the frequency. These are related by the equation

$$\text{Speed} = \text{Frequency} \times \text{Time}$$

A frequency unit is called a Hertz. Standard electrical current in the United States is alternating current and has a frequency of 60 Hz—that is, 60 cycles per second. The frequency of light is much greater than this. It ranges from about $10^{14.5}$ Hz (deepest red) to 10^{15} Hz (deepest blue).

Electromagnetic energy travels through space at approximately 300,000 kilometres (186,300 miles)

per second. Some energy at radio frequencies has wavelengths several metres long. The wavelength of energy at the frequencies of light is so short that it is measured in a unit only one-billionth (10^{-9}) of a metre long, the nanometre (nm). A wavelength of green light is about 1/50,000 of an inch in length. The deepest visible red has a wavelength of approximately 700 nm; the deepest blue has a wavelength of approximately 400 nm.

The accompanying diagrams show where various kinds of energy are located within the electromagnetic spectrum and indicate the sensitivity range of several kinds of detectors, including film.

• *See also:* COLOR THEORY; INFRARED; INFRARED PHOTOGRAPHY; LIGHT; RADIOGRAPHY; SPECTROGRAPHY; ULTRAVIOLET AND FLUORESCENCE PHOTOGRAPHY; WAVELENGTH.

Specular

The term "specular" is used in photography to describe reflection, as well as a kind of illumination and a kind of density; the opposite term is "diffuse." Semispecular or semidiffuse light is a mixture of diffuse and specular light.

Specular light is light in which the rays follow orderly paths. They may be parallel, or may diverge or converge in a three-dimensional pattern. A point source of light emits light that radiates; that is, the rays diverge in an orderly fashion from the source. Hence, such light is specular. Light from the sun is specular—by the time the light rays reach the earth, they are essentially parallel.

A specular reflection is a mirror-like reflection from glass, metal, or any surface that is smoothly polished. Such reflections conform to the law that the angle of reflection is equal to the angle of incidence, and thus reflect an image of the energy source. A significant amount of a specular reflection from a nonmetallic surface can be screened out by a properly aligned polarizer.

Light reflected from mirror-like surfaces is specular if the light itself is specular as it falls on the surface. Light in most condenser enlargers is semispecular—the light bulb is too large to emit purely specular light.

Specular density is measured from the light that passes straight through a material with essentially

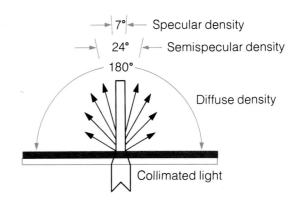

Diffuse density is a measurement taken with a solid angle of collection of 180 degrees. Specular density is measured with a solid angle of 5 to 10 degrees.

no deviation from its original path. In practice, spectral densitometers read the light within a solid angle of from 5 to 10 degrees. Readings taken over wider angles measure either semispecular or diffuse density, as illustrated in the accompanying diagram.

• *See also:* CALLIER EFFECT; DENSITOMETRY; MIRRORS; POLARIZED-LIGHT PHOTOGRAPHY.

Speed Systems

The first system for rating the sensitivity of black-and-white negative emulsions on a scale of "speed" numbers was developed by Hurter and Driffield in the course of their pioneering work in photographic sensitometry in the 1870's and 1880's. In succeeding decades, a number of variant systems evolved, each attempting to provide ratings that would permit a more accurate determination of the exposure required to achieve optimum results under various conditions. Today, a single system of arithmetic numbers is used throughout most of the world. These speeds are the same, but bear different prefixes according to the reference standard used for their determination:

    ASA—American National Standards Institute;
    BSI—British Standards Institute;

As shown in the diagram, specular reflections from a polished surface obey the law that the angle of incidence equals the angle of reflection. They therefore reflect an image of the energy source.

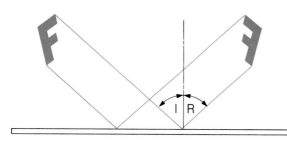

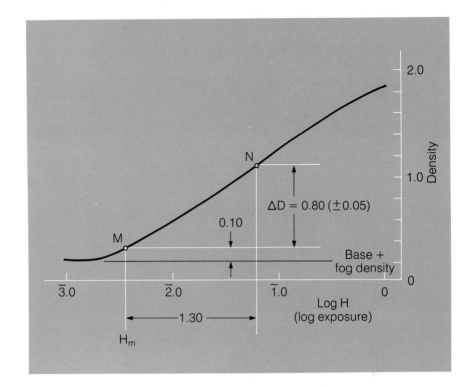

The method for determining ASA speed of pictorial black-and-white negative materials is specified in ANSI PH2.5—1972. The speed point M is located on the characteristic curve 0.10 above base-plus-fog density when a second point on curve N (which received 1.3 log units greater exposure) has an additional 0.8 density. The standard specifies developer formula.

JSA—Japan Standards Association;
ISO—International Organization for Standardization.*

A related series of logarithmic numbers, designated DIN (Deutsch Industrie Norm—German Industrial Standard), is also used with many materials of European manufacture. In the USSR, an arithmetic series of GOST (Gosudarstvenny Standart) numbers is used. Although determined by slightly different methods, they may be used interchangeably with the nearest corresponding ASA/BSI/JSA/ISO numbers.

Speed Criteria

Speeds for negative materials are derived from the exposure required to produce a certain minimum density when the emulsion is given a standard development. In the case of color negative materials, speed is determined from the average exposure required to produce a minimum density in the three (red-, green-, and blue-sensitive) emulsion layers.

The speed of color reversal films is mathematically derived from the exposures that produce certain maximum and minimum densities. Standard processing for both negative and reversal color films is that specified by the manufacturer.

Printing-paper speeds are determined from the exposure required to produce a specified middletone density. Paper speeds are less necessary than film speeds as a practical matter, but they serve a purpose in establishing printing exposures when changing from one paper to another.

Basic Method for Black-and-White Negative Films

The ANSI, BSI, JSA, and DIN standards all use the same method to locate a minimum density "speed point" in an emulsion's response. As the accompanying diagram shows, it is a point on the characteristic curve 0.1 above film base-plus-fog density, when the emulsion is developed so that a second point which received 1.3 log units more exposure has a density 0.8 ($\pm$0.05) greater than that of the speed point, M.

In practice, several samples of film are identically exposed in a sensitometer to a transmission

*Speeds for some products are now appearing with the designation ASA/ISO in anticipation of an eventual worldwide speed system.

step tablet. The exact exposure in metre-candle-seconds given each step is known. The samples are developed for various times in a specified standard developer. These are examined to identify the one that meets the necessary density criteria.

The exposure (H_M) that produced the speed-point density can be determined from the log exposure (log H) axis of the characteristic curve. The actual exposure value that produced the speed-point density (in lux seconds or metre-candle-seconds) is used to calculate the speed as follows:

$$\text{ASA/BSI/JSA Speed} = \frac{0.8}{H_M}$$

$$\text{DIN Speed} = 10 \log_{10} \frac{1}{H_M}$$

The result is rounded off to the nearest arithmetic or logarithmic scale number in a specified series (see the accompanying table).

Arithmetic and Logarithmic Speed Scales

The scale of arithmetic numbers used for ASA/BSI/JSA speeds progresses by the equivalent of one-third-stop exposure intervals. The scale numbers double (or halve) at every third step, indicating twice (or half) as much sensitivity. In practical terms, a film with twice the speed of another requires one stop less exposure to produce equal densities.

On a logarithmic scale, a change of ± 0.3 represents a doubling or halving of speed. Most modern exposure meters are marked for both ASA and DIN speed settings.

COMPARISON OF FILM SPEED RATINGS

ASA/BSI/JSA (Arithmetic)	DIN (Logarithmic)	GOST† (Arithmetic)	Weston (Arithmetic)	BSI Log; Scheiner (Logarithmic)
3	6	2.8	2.5	16°
4	7	3.6	3	17°
5	8	4.5	4	18°
6	9	5.8	5	19°
8	10	7.2	6	20°
10	11	9	8	21°
12	12	11	10	22°
16	13	14	12	23°
20	14	18	16	24°
25	15	23	20	25°
32	16	29	24	26°
40	17	36	32	27°
50	18	45	40	28°
64*	19	58	50	29°
80	20	72	64	30°
100	21	90	80	31°
125	22	112	100	32°
160	23	144	125	33°
200	24	180	160	34°
250	25	225	200	35°.
320	26	288	250	36°
400	27	360	320	37°
500	28	450	400	38°
650*	29	576	500	39°
800	30	720	640	40°
1000	31	900	800	41°
1250	32	1125	1000	42°
1600	33	1440	1250	43°
2000	34	1800	1600	44°
2500	35	2250	2000	45°
3200	36	2880	2500	46°

*The actual ANSI values are 63 and 630; manufacturing practice is to use the numbers shown in the table.
†These numbers may not correspond with those on some meters calibrated in GOST speeds; they have been chosen to be in the proper 9/10 relationship to ASA speeds.

Speed Systems

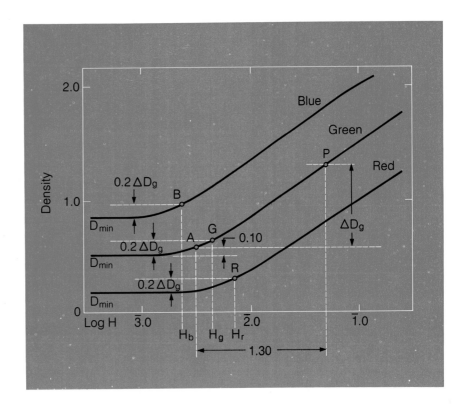

$Log\ H_m =$

$$\frac{(log\ H_b\ +\ log\ H_g\ +\ log\ H_r)}{3}$$

$ASA\ Speed = \frac{1}{H_m}$

(ANSI PH2.27—1965)

This is the method used for determining speed of pictorial color negative films.

The accompanying table compares these two major scales along with the GOST scale. The additional scales are not currently used, but are included for reference because their numbers may be encountered in older literature or equipment. The American Weston arithmetic scale was used with Weston exposure meters before the ASA system became well established. (Later Weston meters were converted to the standard scale and are clearly marked "ASA.") The BSI Log and earlier Scheiner logarithmic speeds are obsolete; they are distinguished by the ° symbol following the scale number.

Converting Film Speed Ratings

Because the systems currently in use—ASA, BSI, DIN, and GOST—are all based on fundamentally the same principles, speeds can be freely converted from one to the other.

Notice that there is a definite relationship between the numbers used in the arithmetic series. The Weston scale is the ASA/BSI scale multiplied by 0.8, and the GOST scale is the ASA/BSI scale multiplied by 0.9, and thus the latter falls midway between the Weston and ASA values.

The derivation of the BSI Logarithmic and the DIN numbers is less clear, but simple enough. It is based on the following relationship:

BSI Logarithmic speed = $10\ log_{10}ASA + 11$

Thus, for example, an ASA speed of 20 would be converted to BSI Log as follows: $log_{10}20 = 1.3$. Then

$10 \times 1.3 = 13 + 11 = 24$ BSI Log

A similar system is used to derive DIN from ASA except that the constant factor is 1 instead of 11. That is:

DIN speed = $10\ log_{10}ASA + 1$

And therefore a speed of ASA 20 would be:

$10 \times 1.3 = 13 + 1 = 14$ DIN

It should be obvious that BSI Log speeds can be converted to DIN by simply subtracting 10 from the

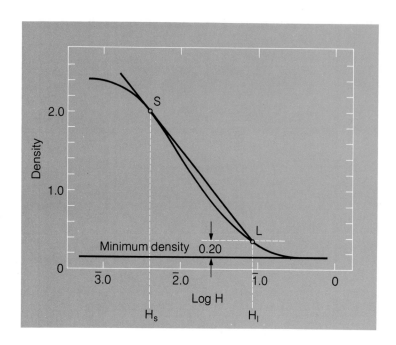

$$H_m = \sqrt{H_l H_s}$$

$$ASA\ Speed = \frac{8}{H_m}$$

(ANSI PH2.21—1972)

(Left) The speed for pictorial reversal films is determined by this set of curves.

(Right) The diagram illustrates the method for determining the speed of photographic papers.

$$ASAP\ Speed = \frac{1000}{E_{0.6}}$$

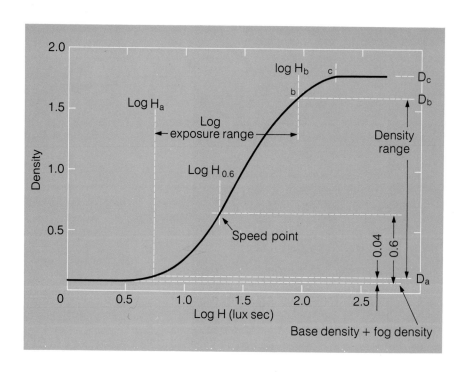

BSI number, and conversely, DIN speeds can be translated to BSI Log by adding 10 to the DIN number.

Although the old Weston system theoretically could not be converted to ASA and vice versa, what actually happened when the Weston system was abandoned was simply that the makers of the Weston meter made just one small change in the meter itself. They replaced the meter calculator dial with a new one marked in ASA numbers, which was simply the old dial with the numbers changed in a 5:4 ratio. Thus, in essence, it is legitimate to multiply an ASA speed by 0.8 to secure a setting for an old Weston meter having the original calculator dial. This is in no sense converting one film speed system to another; it is merely shifting the light measurement scale of the meter to bring it into accord with the American Standard. To be precise about it, the Weston *speed* is not being converted to an ASA *speed;* a Weston *meter setting* that will give satisfactory exposures is merely being devised.

• *See also:* ANSI; ASA, ASAP SPEEDS; BSI SPEEDS; CHARACTERISTIC CURVE; CONTRAST; DENSITOMETRY; DIN SPEEDS; EXPOSURE; GOST SPEEDS; LIGHT; LIGHT: UNITS OF MEASUREMENT; PAPERS, PHOTOGRAPHIC; SENSITOMETRY.

Splicing Film

Motion-picture splicing is the procedure of joining the ends of two pieces of film together to form a single, continuous length. Splicing is the mechanical part of editing. Editing consists of deciding the length and order of the scenes in a movie; splicing entails assembling them permanently into that order, and cutting the pieces of film to proper length.

There are two methods of splicing:

1. The film ends are joined by transparent tape.
2. The film ends are fused together, most commonly by a cement that partially dissolves the film base and welds it together. In professional work, fused splices are also made by thermal or ultrasonic energy.

Splicing Materials

Film Cement. Some cements (such as Kodak film cement) are formulated primarily for splicing films on an acetate-propionate base (Kodachrome films and Eastman Ektachrome print film 7390). They are generally available in small quantities. Professional film cements (such as Kodak professional film cement) are suitable for all films on a cellulose-triacetate base, as well as those on an acetate-propionate base. They are available in both small- and large-quantity containers.

Splicing Tape. Transparent tape for splicing is made of polyester and is self-adhesive on one side. It is available in standard film sizes with sprocket holes, in both rolls and precut tabs of the length required for a single splice. Unsprocketed tape is also available for special purposes. Ordinary household transparent cellulose tape should not be used; it lacks the necessary strength, and its cement will ooze, affecting adjacent layers on the reel and potentially causing damage to the film and to projection equipment.

Splicers. A splicer holds the two film ends in proper alignment for cutting and splicing. Registration pins engage the sprocket holes of the film; some splicers have more than one set of pins for use with various film sizes. Most models have built-in cutters that allow the film ends to be trimmed at precisely the right length for an overlap or a butt splice.

Some cement splicers have built-in scrapers (necessary for preparation of the film to be spliced), often with adjustable guides to control the depth and width of the scrape. One type of splicer, the hot splicer, has a heating element under that portion of the splicer where the film cement is applied. This element reaches approximately 38 C (100 F) and the heat, by increasing the evaporation rate of the solvents in the film cement, decreases the drying time of the splice from 15 or 20 seconds (conventional splicer, film cement but no heat) to 8 or 10 seconds.

The splicer determines the width of the splice and its location at the frame line; these factors vary according to the intended use of the film. A number of standard splices and their purposes are shown in the accompanying diagrams.

Choosing a Splicing Method

The size and location of a splice will be determined by the film's intended use (processing, print-

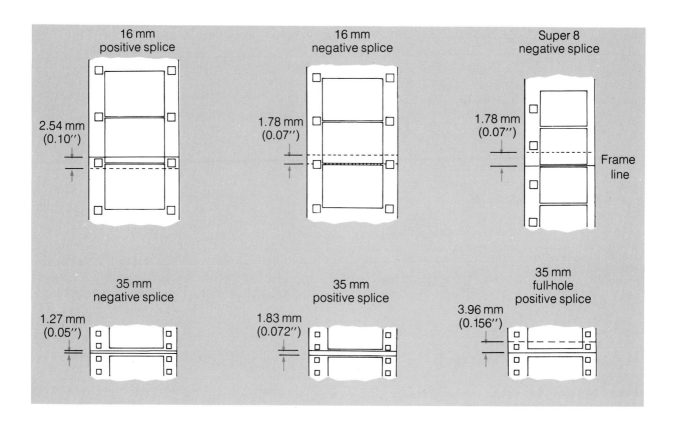

Shown are the standard splices and their dimensions in commonly used motion-picture film formats.

ing, projection). The *kind* of splice is determined by the base materials of the films to be joined.

Acetate to Acetate. Either tape or cement splicing, properly done, produces a satisfactory splice. For occasional nonproduction splicing, tape splicing is convenient, virtually trouble-free, and economical. However, cement splicing is required for some professional applications, and may be preferred by those individuals who have frequent occasion to make splices and who have become familiar with that technique.

Polyester to Polyester. Ultrasonic splicing is perhaps the most used technique for splicing polyester films. It is not necessary to scrape off the emulsion, although the splice will be neater if the emulsion is removed. With careful splicer adjustment and use, the splice can be made with nearly single-film thickness. Ultrasonic splicing can be used to splice films for projection, for processing, and in some cases, for camera exposure.

A satisfactory tape for splicing films for *processing* is 3M No. 852 Metalized Polyester Tape, or the equivalent.

To splice films for *projection only,* other tapes, such as Kodak Presstapes, can be used.

Polyester to Acetate. Only tape—including Kodak Presstapes and 3M No. 852 Metalized Polyester Tape—can be used satisfactorily. Ultrasonic and film-cement splicing will not work well.

Making Splices with Film Cement

It is a good idea to practice making splices with scrap film to learn the "feel" of the splicer and to recognize the pressure needed for proper scraping of the emulsion.

WARNING: Film cements and their fumes are mildly irritating, and they should be kept away from the eyes. The solvents used in film cements are volatile and can burn rapidly. While modern film bases are not fire hazards, the film cements can be. Film cements can damage enamel and other finishes, and the man-made fibers in clothing.

Structure of Motion-Picture Film. Motion-picture film is constructed of three layers:

1. An *emulsion* coating, consisting chiefly of gelatin. In this layer is suspended the silver or dye that forms the photographic image.
2. The *binder,* a microscopically thin layer between the base and the emulsion coating, binding these two layers tightly together.
3. A flexible film *base* that provides a strong, durable support.

Width of Splice. The two splice widths most common in film editing and repair are the *positive* splice (2.5 mm [0.10-inch] overlap) and the *negative* splice (1.7 mm [0.07-inch] overlap). These names do not refer to positive or negative film, nor do the names imply a degree of splice reliability—both splices are highly reliable when made properly. The positive splice was developed first; unfortunately, it is quite visible when the film is projected. Therefore, positive splices are suitable for film that will not be used for printing (workprints, for example). The negative splice is narrower and overlaps a different portion of the projected picture; it is less visible but just as reliable. The professional must make a negative splice if he or she is conforming (matching) original film for A and B roll printing. Many splicers can be ordered to provide scraping widths of 2.5 mm or 1.5 mm as desired.

Removing the Emulsion. For a good splice, the two top layers—emulsion and binder—must be removed completely from the section of film that will be overlapped in the splicer. The base of the bottom film must be bare and ready for fusing into the base of the overlapping film. (See the accompanying diagrams.)

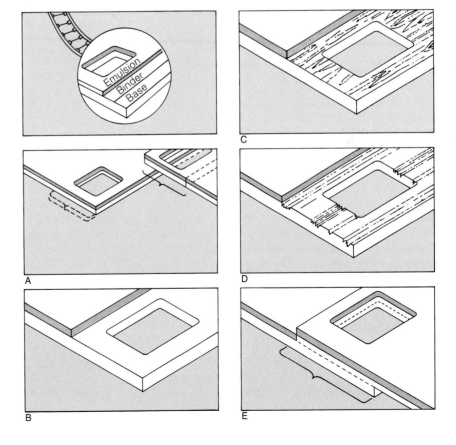

Motion-picture films are composed of multiple layers; their relative thicknesses are exaggerated here. Also shown are the steps in preparing the emulsion side of film for making a cement splice. C and D show the errors of too little and too much scraping of emulsion and binder.

Normally the emulsion and binder coatings should be moistened with water and allowed to soak for a few seconds to soften the coatings before they are scraped off. However, too much water can damage the emulsion adjacent to the splice, so use care. Be sure to take off all the binder layer, which is hard but shinier than the base. After scraping, wipe the prepared area with a clean, dry cloth or brush to remove all moisture and emulsion residue before applying cement.

Some splicers with a built-in scraper are designed for waterless scraping. Do not attempt dry scraping unless you have one of these splicers; you may tear the film at the perforations or near the edge, and the torn section will have to be cut off before preparation for a new splice can be made. If the splicer has no scraper, a razor blade, emery board, or piece of fine sandpaper can be used—*with care.*

The scraper on some splicers is equipped with guides that control the depth and width of the cut —on other splicers, however, the amount of pressure and the number of scrapes determine the depth. In any case, it is best to scrape the film with light strokes at first, then gradually increase the pressure until emulsion and binder are completely removed. If the pressure is too great, or uneven, the base may be torn, gouged, or just scraped too deeply. This produces a weak spot in the base, and a weak splice.

Preparing the Base Side. The base side, or undersurface, of the film that will be overlapping in the splicer may have oil on it, picked up in projection; also, some films are made with a thin coating on the back. If a good splice is to be obtained, any oil or base coating must be removed.

To remove oil and other coatings, wipe the back of the film with a dry cloth. Further rubbing with a cloth moistened with alcohol is often helpful, although many film editors prefer to apply a moderate amount of film cement to the base and then quickly wipe it completely off with a soft cloth. If these simple measures fail, lightly scrape the splice area of the base side. Be careful not to leave abrasive particles on the back of the film, since there is a possibility that they will spread through the roll and scratch the film.

If the film is old, it may be necessary to treat the back surface of the film base with film cement before splicing. As film ages, it becomes dry and sometimes brittle. An application of film cement acts as a conditioning agent to help prepare a good splice.

Applying Film Cement. In addition to a solvent, film cement contains chemicals that stabilize its action. If film cement is exposed to the air, the solvent will evaporate, the cement will become thick and gummy, and usually it will not make a satisfactory splice. For these reasons, and for convenience, if you are using a bulk supply, it should be kept in the original container, and a quantity sufficient for immediate use should be transferred to a well-stoppered working bottle.

Cement should be applied by brush to the prepared surface—enough to wet the complete splice area, but not so much that cement will run outside the splice when the two films are pressed together. Time counts: It is important that you close the splicer and bring the two films into contact as soon as possible after cement has been applied and keep the film under pressure for 15 to 20 seconds (8 to 10 seconds for a hot splicer).

The body and viscosity of most available film cements are such that little or no cement will be squeezed out of the overlap when splices are made properly; but if any is, the excess must be wiped off immediately with a soft cloth. Otherwise, it may adhere to and leave a smear on the preceding or following layer of film in the reel, causing damage, distortion, or wrinkle.

Films that have become very dry or that have been rolled on small-diameter-reel hubs can develop so much curl that splicing becomes difficult. Such films should be held under pressure in the splicer 30 seconds or longer (15 seconds with a hot splicer) after the cement has been applied, to allow the splice to develop adequate strength.

Checking the Cement Splice. A good splice has sufficient strength after 20 seconds to allow the film to be removed from the splicing block and wound onto the reel at normal tension.

Examine each splice for quality. A good splice is fully transparent; bubbles and hazy areas indicate a poor splice. No freshly made splice should be tested by scraping or pulling at the weld; instead, test the splice by flexing it. The splice should be slightly stiffer than the single thickness of film.

Cement-Splicing Films with a Sound Track. Cement splices on film that has a recorded magnetic sound track may cause a momentary loss in signal

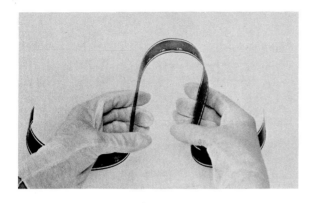

level at the splice; if the magnetic head of the projector bounces at the splice, the head loses contact with the film for an instant. To minimize this effect, make sure the butt of the splice is toward the tail end of the film so the head will drop off the splice, not run into it. The correct method of lapping the film ends is illustrated in the accompanying diagrams.

Using film cement to remove 35 mm and 70 mm magnetic sound stripes is not recommended because too much stripe may be affected. Carefully scrape the base side to remove magnetic coatings.

If the metal in the splicer becomes magnetized, a noticeable click may be heard in films that have a magnetic sound track. If this proves to be a problem, the splicer must be demagnetized.

Film that has an optical sound track can be spliced without any special attention to the direction of the splice butt, because the optical sound track is essentially a part of the film emulsion. Use blooping (opaquing) ink on optical sound film splices to eliminate pops and clicks caused by abrupt changes in the sound-track modulation at the splice.

Suggestions for Using Film Cement. For effective use of film cement for splicing, these suggestions should be followed:

1. Keep the splice clamped for 15 to 20 seconds (8 to 10 seconds in a hot splicer) after the film ends have been joined together. Insufficient drying time is probably the greatest single cause of splice failure.

(Right) When cement splices are made in films for spooling in Kodak and similar projection cartridges, the spliced film must be oriented correctly with the direction of film travel as shown. (Below) Splicing film with a magnetic sound track. Film ends should be lapped so that the butt of the splice is away from the magnetic head.

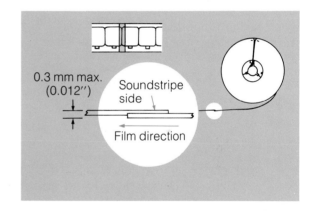

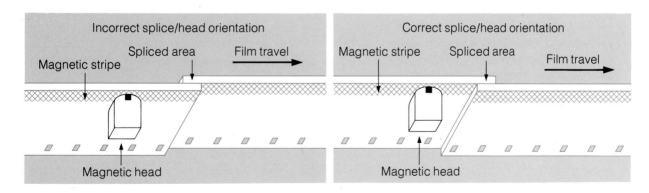

2. Never add new cement to old in a work bottle. Carefully clean out all the old and start with fresh cement daily.
3. Keep the work bottle of cement tightly covered. The solvent in film cement evaporates rapidly.
4. Keep the cement fresh and unadulterated.
5. Check the age and condition of the film. It will be necessary to remove any base coating by scraping or by applying and wiping off film cement in the splice area.
6. When scraping, do not remove more than the emulsion and binder. Remember that gouging the film base will weaken the splice.
7. Keep the splicer scrupulously clean. A buildup of film cement on the knife edge, upper pressure clamp, or pin support block can cause a poor splice. To clean off dried cement, saturate it with wet cement and wipe off with a clean cloth. Never scratch the splicer.
8. Avoid fingerprinting the film; wear lint-free gloves.

Common Causes of Unsatisfactory Cement Splices. The following are some of the common causes of unsatisfactory cement splices:
1. Old film cement from which the essential solvents have evaporated. For everyday use, film cement should be stored in small bottles that will provide the least possible air space so as to retard evaporation.
2. Insufficient drying time.
3. Emulsion or binder not completely removed from the scraped area, causing an incomplete or faulty weld.
4. Excessive scraping, scratching, or gouging of the film base, weakening the base and causing the film to collapse or break at the splice.
5. Too much delay in bringing the film ends into contact after cement has been applied.
6. Applying too much cement. Excess solvent action will cause the splice to buckle. During projection, the splice may cause difficulty in the film gate or at a sprocket pad roller.
7. Applying too little cement, resulting in an incomplete weld. Such splices should be remade, or they may come apart during projection.
8. Poor mechanical alignment of the splicer. This can cause a misaligned splice, which can catch in the projector film path and tear apart.

Tape Splices

A properly made tape splice may be considered quite permanent, but it can be disassembled at any time, if necessary, and usually without damage to the film. Tape splices can be made either with an overlap or with the two film ends butted together. The width of the overlap with tape splicing is not as important as it is in cement splicing, but it should be sufficient to prevent hinging (or collapse) when the splice is flexed. An overlap tape splice made on a bench-top splicer can be compared with a similar cement splice—with one exception. Instead of cement being used to bond the two film ends at the overlap, a piece of perforated polyester tape is placed over the overlap on both sides of the film. With special splicers, unperforated tape is used and perforated during the splicing operation. There is no need to remove the emulsion and binder from the film, although it may be desirable if the splice is to be less noticeable on the screen.

Splicing tape is available in 35 mm, 16 mm, and super 8 sizes, in perforated and unperforated rolls, and as precut tabs. There are advantages and disadvantages with each type of tape, but all types will make satisfactory splices. The main advantage of the perforated rolls is the ability to cut tapes of any length for film repair, as well as short pieces for splicing. Another advantage is the lower cost per splice. The only disadvantage is a possible time loss because the thin tape is difficult to handle with unprotected adhesive. Very thin polyester splicing tape tends to move unpredictably due to static attraction, and efforts to place it over the splice in register with the film perforations and splicer pins can prove very frustrating at times. The unperforated 35 mm tape can be used only with special splicers that are designed to punch out the perforations in the tape area.

Perforated tape tabs, on the other hand, are simple to use but tend to be somewhat more expensive. Those currently available are only four perforations (one frame) in length. When making a proper splice, the picture area in the frames divided by the splice will each contain two tape ends that can be distracting on the screen.

For esthetic reasons, and for added strength, it is desirable to make an overlap tape splice with tape sections two frames long (eight perforations). This procedure places the tape ends at a frame line for invisibility and provides for a greater adhesive area.

Making Tape Splices. When making tape splices with a bench-top or block-type splicer, the following directions are important:

1. Cut the two ends of the film to be spliced in the normal manner as you would do when making a regular cement splice.

2. It is not necessary to scrape the left-hand section unless esthetic considerations are requested. Simply bring down the right-hand section so that the two film ends are in contact on the splicing block.

3. If you are using perforated tape on a roll, it is advisable to have a few two-frame (eight-perforation) sections precut and placed on a nearby surface that will allow for easy grasp and release.

4. Lift both sections of the splicer and hold the film in position if it tends to pop up. Using your free hand, pick up a precut tape section and carefully place it over the splice, aligning it with the splicer pins and centering it so that either tape end falls on a frame line. Press the tape down carefully to hold the two film sections together. Remove the film from the splicer and thoroughly rub the tape section with a soft, lint-free cloth to eliminate bubbles and wrinkles.

5. Turn the film over and replace it in the splicer. Place a second tape section on the splice corresponding to the position of the first tape on the other side.

6. If you are using one-frame precut tape tabs, follow steps 4 and 5. In this case, however, the four-perforation tab

(Top) A one-frame perforated tape tab and a one-frame tape splice showing full-hole overlap. (Bottom) A two-frame perforated tape tab which is no longer available. The use of two frames of splicing tape—cut from a roll—can replace the tab and offer greater adhesive areas and a less visible splice.

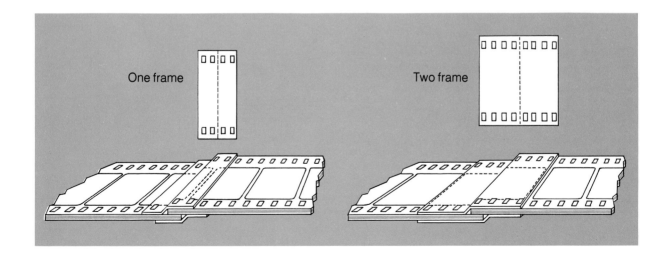

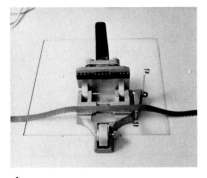

A

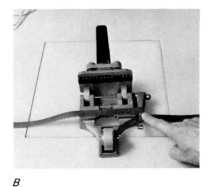

B

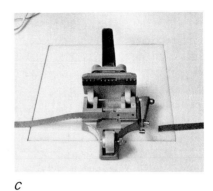

C

D

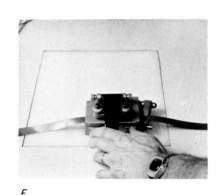

E

F

G

These are the steps in splicing 16 mm fullcoat film on a guillotine splicer. (A) Position the film on the splicer with sprocket holes over the registration pins. (B) Lower the diagonal cutting bar. (C) The diagonal cut is completed. (D) Move the film into splicing position. (E) Draw the unperforated splicing tape across the film. (F) Lowering the lever trims the splicing tape to size and punches sprocket holes at the same time. (G) This is the finished splice.

should be applied with two perforations on either side of the cut film end to provide maximum strength. To facilitate centering the tab over the splice, shift the film sections one perforation either way so that the splicer pins may be used for proper registration of the tab. When considering the standard 3.96 mm (0.156-inch) overlap width, centering the second tab on the other side of the film in a similar manner will displace the tab by the same amount. The result will be two tape ends visible in the picture area in each of the two frames adjacent to the splice.

7. When tape splices are made on film that has a magnetic sound stripe, the tape should be trimmed along one edge with scissors, so that when it is applied to the film it will not cover the sound track.

Butt Splices with Tape. A butt tape splice may be considered somewhat superior to an overlap tape splice only because it is less noticeable on the screen. A properly made butt splice depends on a precise cut on both film sections. The two cut edges must mate perfectly and be held in rigid contact, while the splicing tape is applied to both sides. If either of these requirements is not met, the splice will be prone to hinging or collapse during projection. Butt splices cannot be readily made on the splicers most commonly found in theaters and film exchanges. The precise cutting and rigid holding of the film sections that are necessary while the splicing tape is applied cannot be accomplished with such splicers. By manipulation, it is possible to cut the film so that the sections will butt in frame, but the quality of the cut will generally preclude a successful splice. Also, the lack of a means to hold the film tightly together at the butt while the tape is being applied further lessens the chances for a successful splice. If butt splicing is desirable, it is strongly recommended that you acquire a splicer specifically designed for that purpose.

Regardless of the instructions that may accompany a butt splicer, it is recommended that a two-frame (eight-perforation) tape section be used to make the splice. If one-frame precut tabs are being used, it is obvious that they need not be displaced when applied because no overlap is present.

IMPORTANT: *Do not apply tape in the picture area only.* The protruding corners of the film edge could catch at a sprocket pad roller and cause damage.

No matter which type of tape splice you employ, it is important that the film surfaces in the area of the splice be clean and free of oily deposits. Dirt will cause bubbles and blemishes, while oily film will prevent proper adhesion. If a tape splice is not aligned properly or produces wrinkles, carefully lift a corner with a razor blade or knife and peel the tab off; then replace it with a new tab. If you are splicing film with magnetic sound tracks, it might be desirable to use a one-frame tab on the track side to minimize sound interruption.

• *See also:* A AND B ROLL EDITING; EDITING MOVIES; MAGNETIC SOUND FOR MOTION PICTURES; MOTION-PICTURE PRODUCTION; MOVIE FILMS, STORAGE AND CARE OF.

Sports Photography

Anticipating action is the key to good sports photographs. Unlike other forms of photography, the sports cameraperson has little or no control over the events before him or her. The photographer must try to predict the moment of action that will produce spectacular pictures. This requires a hair-trigger state of readiness, finger poised on shutter release, gauging the exact instant to get the picture.

Experienced sports photographers follow a few basic rules that may be applied to just about any action situation:

1. Know something about the fundamentals of the sport you will be covering.
2. Know the mechanical functions of your camera equipment so you can concentrate on the sport.
3. Try to plan your shooting location and your equipment requirements *before* the event as much as possible.
4. Stay out of the way of the athletes and officials. Avoid blocking the vision of spectators. Keep off the playing field at all times.
5. Stay alert. Watch for the unexpected burst of action that tells the story; the shortstop may drop an easy pop fly, the quarterback may fumble the ball, the runner may fall at the finish line, and so on. Sports events are unpredictable, but the photographer who *anticipates* the exact instant to shoot will be rewarded with some exciting pictures. (*See:* ACTION PHOTOGRAPHY.)

Cameras and Lenses

Single-Lens Reflex Camera. Good action pictures can be made with almost any type of camera. There is a tremendous variety of equipment available to the photographer. Most professionals covering sports events favor the 35 mm single-lens reflex camera because of the vast array of interchangeable lenses available for this equipment. Modern SLR cameras offer many other conveniences: instant-return mirrors, built-in automated exposure systems, power winders and motor drives for rapid-fire sequence shooting. SLR cameras that use 120/220 film are also available for photographers who require a larger negative or transparency.

Lenses. SLR automatic lenses are exceptionally useful. The image is focused with the lens wide open. When the shutter is released, the automatic diaphragm is activated and closes the lens to the correct aperture just before the film is exposed.

The choice of lenses depends on the sport to be photographed. In some sports like basketball and track, the photographer is usually fairly close to the action, and a normal or wide-angle lens will be adequate for most pictures. Other sports like football and baseball require the use of telephoto lenses because of the camera-to-subject distances normally encountered. A medium-long telephoto lens in the 100 mm to 200 mm range is ideal for most sports. It will "pull in" action at a considerable distance. Zoom lenses in this category are also very popular. You have the convenience of a single long lens that combines the most-used focal lengths in one convenient package. (*See:* Zoom Lens.)

Extra-Long Telephoto Lenses. In selecting additional lenses for your camera, an extra-long telephoto lens like a 300 mm or 400 mm should be considered. Such lenses allow a greater choice of

Interesting effects can be obtained by use of a fish-eye lens and unusual camera angles. Opportunities for taking photographs such as this must be arranged outside of regular game times, possibly during a practice session. Photo by Don Maggio.

pictures, since it is possible to cover action at long range and still produce an image that will withstand considerable enlargement.

Unfortunately, these long focal lengths have drawbacks that create difficulties for the unwary photographer. The longer the lens, the less depth of field (zone of sharpness between near and distant points in the focused image) at any given aperture. Accurate focusing is critical, especially when the light is poor and you have to shoot at maximum aperture for correct exposure. Many of the longer telephoto lenses are heavy and difficult to hand-hold. Excessive camera movement will cause unsharp pictures. Use of a sturdy tripod is recommended, but it can also slow you down when following action from the sidelines of a playing field or stadium. A unipod is much better. This single-leg support provides most of the tripod's steadiness and far greater mobility. It is often preferred by professionals covering fast-moving events.

For special situations where it is impossible to get close to the action, experienced sports camera operators resort to extra-long (and expensive) 500 mm to 600 mm lenses. They are useful for such pictures as a baseball outfielder chasing a long fly, or a fumble in the far end zone at a football game; however, focusing and depth-of-field problems are also magnified.

Soccer games range all over the playing field, and action can be at a considerable distance from the camera or quite close to it. A medium-range telephoto lens of 100–200 mm focal length may be an ideal choice. Photo by Pete Culross.

Telephoto lenses, if used properly, can produce very dramatic pictures. They pull things together in a way the human eye cannot see by compressing space and exaggerating perspective. Near and distant objects will appear much closer together than they really are, creating graphic visual impact. (*See:* TELEPHOTOGRAPHY.)

Wide-Angle Lenses. Wide-angle lenses are an important part of the sports photographer's working tools. They make it possible to relate subjects to their environment or show the broad sweep of an event more effectively than a normal lens. The wider the angle of the lens, the greater its depth of field at any given aperture or lens-to-subject distance. Focusing is less critical because of the extended zone of sharpness between foreground and background. This asset may prove troublesome in focusing a single-lens reflex camera in bright light. The lens shows so much depth of field that it is impossible to tell where the exact point of critical focus is located. However, the wide zone of sharpness will usually compensate for minor focusing errors.

Many wide-angle lenses are likely to produce some distortion of the image at the edges of the picture, especially if the camera is not held level. The super-wide lenses (15 to 28 mm in the 35 mm format) can generate extreme distortion in subjects close to the camera. This distortion is not always desirable in photographing people, but it can be turned to your advantage by adding impact and

---

The Sports Photographer's Checklist

Before Leaving for the Game

Cameras.
Camera motors (if used).
Battery-driven cameras: sufficient spare batteries, auxiliary battery pack.
Lenses.
Tripods or high hats.
Film: spare magazines or film chambers (if used).
Exposure meter.
Several empty film cans.
Extra take-up reel.
Film-changing bag.
Miscellaneous items: tape, screwdriver, small wrenches, lens cleaner.

At the Field

Cameras loaded with film.
All lenses mounted or readily available.
Correct focus set.
Camera speed control set at desired speed.
Aperture settings determined for every part of the playing area.
Any spare magazines or chambers loaded with film and readily available.
Footage counter properly set.

Viewfinder objectives or mats set to corresponding lenses, if necessary for your camera.
Any parallax setting on viewfinder adjusted.
Filters (if needed) placed on lenses.
Spring motor fully wound and wind handle in position, if camera is spring-driven. If camera is driven by an electric motor, it should be attached, plugged in, and test-run.
Load battery-driven cameras with fresh batteries and check operation; attach auxiliary battery pack if needed.
Tripod leveled and anchored.

After the Game

Equipment dismantled and packed away properly.
Cameras or magazines unloaded.
Film cans and boxes marked and ready for shipment to processing laboratory.
Any special instructions to the laboratory that should accompany exposed film—such as how and when to return film, special processing, damaged film.

drama to an ordinary subject. For example, a super-wide-angle lens can make a midget race car appear longer and more exciting than it actually is. (*See:* WIDE-ANGLE PHOTOGRAPHY.)

Black-and-White Films

A fast, general-purpose black-and-white film is recommended for sports photography. It has enough speed (usually ASA 400) and exposure latitude to cope with a wide variety of lighting conditions. When properly exposed and developed, modern high-speed films will produce negatives with an excellent fine-grain structure and tonal range. Such films are especially useful for photographing action under low available-light levels. With special processing, they may be pushed to speeds of ASA 1000 to ASA 1600 without objectionable loss of quality. (*See:* PUSH PROCESSING.)

Color Films

Selecting a color film is a matter of personal preference. Many professionals on a sports assignment carry at least two types: a slow- or medium-speed reversal color film plus a high-speed emulsion with an ASA rating of 400. This combination is necessary because reversal color films do not have the exposure latitude of black-and-white, and the professional sports photographer must produce acceptable pictures regardless of lighting conditions.

Color negative films are handy when color prints are needed quickly. They have moderately good exposure latitude and are used by many newspapers for ROP (run of press) color reproduction of major sports events. They will also produce acceptable black-and-white prints, but the quality is not quite up to the standard of prints made from black-and-white films.

Filters

Most black-and-white sports work is accomplished without correction filters, but many photographers keep a UV (ultraviolet) filter on each lens to protect it from dust and scratches. This versatile filter can be used with any black-and-white or color emulsion without requiring increased exposure. The UV filter blocks excessive ultraviolet light in mountain and marine scenes. It knifes through distant haze, reducing the bluish tinge of color transparencies shot on a cloudy day. The skylight filter is very similar. It has considerably more ultraviolet screening action and produces slightly warmer colors.

Zone Focus and Follow-Focus

In fast-moving sports events, it is rather difficult to establish a definite spot on which to focus because the participants are constantly in motion. You will probably achieve the best results by prefocusing the camera at a specific distance where action is likely to occur—such as the finish line in a track meet, or at home plate in a baseball game—and letting the depth of field of your lens work for you. The exact distance focused on will depend on your camera position and the focal-length lens you are using.

It is important to know how your lenses perform at different apertures and focusing distances. You can estimate the depth of field and gauge when your subject is within the zone of sharpness at the point you are focused on. Most lens manufacturers provide accurate depth-of-field charts for their equipment. This information is also engraved on the lens mount, showing depth of field when the lens is set for a specific distance. For example: A typical 200 mm telephoto lens (popular with many sports photographers) focused at 15 m (50 feet) with the diaphragm set at $f/11$ might show a depth of field ranging from 14 to 21 m (45 to 70 feet), a very broad zone of sharpness. Any action photographed within this area will be in acceptably sharp focus.

Remember, depth of field is diminished as the lens aperture, or f-stop, is increased. A lens set at maximum aperture (wide open) usually requires critical focusing to create sharp images.

Follow-focusing a camera on a rapidly moving subject demands the utmost in hand-eye coordination. This skill can be perfected by taking your camera to a busy street corner or highway and practicing focusing on automobiles in motion. Try to keep them centered in your viewfinder as they speed past. As a general rule, the zone-focusing method is favored by many sports photographers because it provides them with a very high percentage of sharp pictures under difficult shooting conditions.

Basketball

A good location to shoot basketball action is from a corner of the court in line with the basket, from 5 to 8 m (15 to 25 feet) away. Another excellent location is a seat in the lower rows of the stands,

By focusing on a point just under the basket, a photographer can capture both the struggle to score and the valiant actions of the defensive players. A minimum shutter speed of 1/250 sec. is recommended for the faster action. Photo by Pete Culross.

opposite the foul line; you have a slightly higher camera angle that can be very effective. Try to pick a seat on an aisle or in the first row of a balcony. This reduces the possibility of excited fans jumping in front of the lens at a crucial moment.

An 85 to 135 mm lens on a 35 mm camera will be ideal for most overhead shots. Normal and wide-angle lenses are most effective from close-up camera positions at the sidelines of the court. Focus on a point under the basket and catch the frantic action as the team with the ball attempts to score. You are also in position to capture defensive efforts by the opposing teams as they try to keep the ball away from the basket.

A minimum shutter speed of at least 1/250 sec. is recommended, but you can shoot at 1/125 sec. to catch the action at that peak when motion is halted. An example of this is when a player is driving in for a basket, or outleaping the opposition to grab a rebound. It is possible to get the picture at 1/125 sec. if you aim for the exact instant when the players are nearly motionless in mid-air at the top of their leaps.

Fast black-and-white film will make it possible to obtain excellent action pictures even under low existing-light conditions. However, a dependable electronic flash unit is a handy accessory because the existing light is not always adequate, especially if

you are working with color. Correct exposure depends on the power and light output of the model being used. It is advisable to follow the manufacturer's instructions for best results. Use of strobe lights may be forbidden at some major college and professional games in order to avoid distracting the players. Check with school or league officials in advance to determine if there are any restrictions. Virtually all college and pro arenas require credentials.

Baseball

Except for the major leagues, photographers can usually work on the sidelines of the field as long as they do not interfere with the progress of the game. This means staying clear of the base paths at all times.

Keep one eye on the batter, even if you are expecting action at another position. There may be a hard-hit foul ball heading your way when you least expect it. Always be prepared to duck.

A batter waiting his or her turn at the plate is often a good human-interest subject—flexing muscles with several bats, carefully watching the opposing pitcher. As he or she steps into the batter's box, the picture possibilities are multiplied—the pitcher winding up to throw; the batter poised to swing; the catcher bent low, waiting for the pitch. The ball streaks in and the batter swings, face contorted with tension.

Fast shutter speeds are necessary to show the bat at the exact instant of contact with the ball—at least 1/500 sec. This motion is almost too fast for the eye to follow, and you will have to anticipate correctly. Shoot as the batter swings. If your timing is good, you will stop the ball in flight somewhere inside the batter's box—a tricky shot, but one that is worth aiming for.

Remain between home plate and first base until a player gets on base; you have both areas covered if there is action. When a runner reaches first, take a position slightly to the right of the base. If the runner gets careless and takes too long a leadoff, the pitcher may attempt a trap with a sudden throw to the person on first base. This often produces a frantic scene as the runner dives headlong at the base to evade the tag. Whether the player is safe or out, you have got a picture.

Anticipate action at second or third base when a runner is on first. These positions are best covered from a spot about halfway between third base and home plate. You can catch the runner attempting to steal second. If the batter hits a long ball to the outfield and the runner goes to third, you are well-positioned in case the runner slides into the base.

Lenses from 135 mm to 200 mm (on 35 mm equipment) are adequate for most sidelines work, allowing you to pull in the action from a safe dis-tance. To cover second base from the sidelines on a regulation-size field you will need a 300 mm or longer lens; otherwise, negative or transparency images may be too small for quality enlargements. At junior- or little-league games, you can get by with shorter-focal-length lenses because the baseball diamond is smaller and shooting distances are considerably reduced.

Photographing outfielders in action takes lots of patience and super-long lenses (400 to 600 mm). There are usually long periods of time when nothing much is happening, then a sudden flurry of motion as an outfielder chases a long fly ball. Sometimes, two fielders will go after the same ball, an especially interesting picture situation if they both leap for it. Chances are that one or both of them will take a tumble.

In day games, faces are often hard to see because of the peaked caps ball players wear. Shadows can be troublesome, and there is not too much you can do except to concentrate on pictures showing motion and form rather than facial expressions. A very low camera angle is helpful in minimizing shadows. You may have to open up a stop to register detail in the faces. Sometimes, pictures will be better later in the day when the sun angle is lower and faces are illuminated.

Night games are difficult to photograph because light levels are usually very low, especially for color. Experienced baseball photographers try for pictures

By staying between bases, you can cover two areas. An attempted steal can create a frantic action scene, which a photographer can capture on film by anticipating the probable plays. Photo by Paul Bereswill.

Sports Photography

when the action is suddenly arrested. The players appear to be in motion, but are actually poised to move. An example would be a pitcher at the peak of the windup, just before releasing the ball. Other possibilities are a batter ready to swing or a runner taking a lead off a base. By watching for moments when action is suggested, you can create excellent photographs that capture the spirit and emotion of baseball.

Football

Football can be photographed from both the sidelines and the stands (with long telephoto lenses). Covering a game from the sidelines is strenuous work. You are always in motion, following the teams up and down the field. Standard ground rules for photographers at most college and pro games allow you to work from the end zone to the 35-yard line, on either side of the field. You are not allowed between the 35-yard markers, an area reserved for players and coaches, without special permission.

At many stadiums, photographers must also stay behind a second boundary line, 3 to 8 feet from the sidelines, so officials have a clear view of the out-of-bounds area. High-school games are normally less restrictive, although many schools will

(Above) Peaked baseball caps keep the sun out of the players' eyes; unfortunately for the photographer, they also put the players' faces in shadow. Concentrate on pictures showing motion and form. (Right) The photographer who second-guesses the quarterback will be correct often enough to get images like this. Photos by Paul Bereswill.

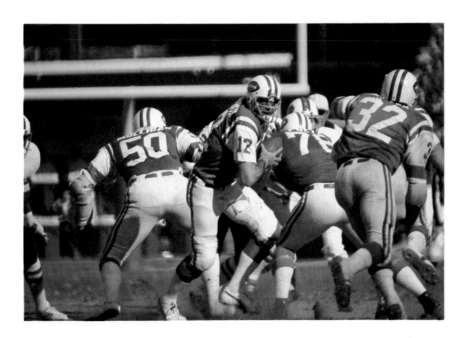

Sports Photography

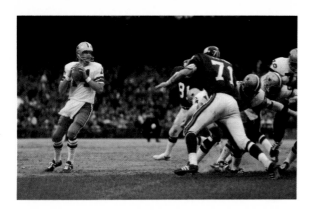

By staying ahead of the line of scrimmage, a photographer can capture the action head-on or at a 45-degree angle to the camera. Lens focal lengths between 100 and 300 mm are the best choice. Photo by Paul Bereswill.

follow the same ground rules for photographers as the colleges and pros.

Try to second-guess the quarterback, anticipating the direction of each play. You will probably be wrong most of the time, but if you understand the fundamentals of the sport, your chances of capturing an instant of peak action are substantially increased.

Stay about 10 yards ahead of the line of scrimmage. The action will be coming head-on, or at approximately a 45-degree angle. This gives you more chances to shoot than if the ball carrier and defending tacklers run parallel to the camera position. Lens focal lengths should be from 100 mm to 300 mm.

In scoring situations, when the team with the ball is deep inside its opponent's territory, get behind the goal line—in the middle, if possible—so you are ready to cover a play breaking in either direction. If there is an end run or a pass to a receiver in the corner of the end zone, you will have to react quickly to get the picture. For goal-line situations, 85 mm to 200 mm lenses are good choices, and a zoom is ideal. Longer lenses may be too restricted in field of view and depth of field to be of much value.

Keep alert for good human-interest shots when you are on the sidelines. Players on the bench cheering their teammates in the game, excited fans, the bands at halftime, and other fine details of the sport can enhance your action coverage.

Soccer

Soccer is a game of continuous movement and constantly changing ball possession. There are no "downs" as in football, where the action is halted as the teams line up to face each other.

At most nonprofessional soccer events, you are free to move around the perimeter of the field as long as you remain behind the sideline boundary stripe. Never go out on the field while a game is in progress. It is advisable to keep down when at the sidelines so you do not block the spectators' view of the game, or interfere with coaches and reserve players if you are shooting around the team areas. Also, soccer pictures generally appear more dramatic if they are shot from a low angle.

Soccer is an exciting game to cover, with some unusual picture possibilities. A player must advance the ball by kicking or butting it with the head and shoulders. Only the goalie is allowed to use hands to move the ball. This rule is rigidly adhered to. If any player except the goalie touches the ball with his or her hands, a penalty is called against the player, and the opposing team is awarded a free kick, like a free throw in basketball.

Because soccer is such a fast-moving sport, it is rather difficult to establish a definite spot on which to focus. You will probably find it easier to prefocus the camera at a specific distance, say 15 m (50 feet) from the sidelines, and wait until the players are within range. The exact distance focused on will

Because soccer is such a wide-ranging game, it is often best to prefocus your lens and wait for choice bits of action within your range. Photo by Paul Bereswill.

Sports Photography

In track events, a position midway between start and finish is a good place to use slow shutter speeds and a panning movement to create the sensation of motion. Photo by Peter Gales.

depend on the focal-length lens you are using. As in football photography, lenses from 85 mm to 200 mm are ideal for most pictures. You will need extra-long telephoto lenses (300 mm to 500 mm) to pick off shots past the mid-field point. Soccer is played on a slightly larger field than football, and shooting distances may be increased. Watch for choice bits of action in the goal area when the team with the ball is in scoring position—a player jumping to "head" the ball, or a goalie making a diving catch to prevent a score. These are among the many split-second occurrences that challenge your ability to capture highlights of the game.

Rugby

Rugby is a brutal endurance contest that combines elements of both soccer and football. While soccer permits a player to move the ball only by kicking or butting with head and shoulders, rugby rules allow a player to carry the ball football-style. Tackling is permitted, as well as passing the ball laterally or to the rear, but a forward pass to another player is forbidden. Blocking in advance of the ball carrier is also not allowed.

Rugby is even more violent than football. Players wear no helmets or additional padding, and there are no time-outs. If a player appears to be injured, the referee may choose to stop the game.

While the popularity of rugby in the United States has not been high, it is growing steadily. Many colleges now include rugby in their sports programs. In the British Commonwealth, where the sport originated in the early 1800's, rugby has a tremendous following. Attendance at important matches often rivals the gigantic crowds at the annual football bowl games held on New Year's Day in the United States.

The same principles used to cover soccer and football may also be applied to rugby. This sport is much easier to photograph, because there are many moments of arrested action—two opposing teams locked together in a "scrum," or scrimmage, to advance the ball. The goliaths of the line strain against

each other, head to head, like battling rams. There is not much movement, but the fierce facial expressions of the athletes will make for a very effective picture.

Track

There are usually very few restrictions placed on photographers at a track meet. The principal requirement is that you keep off the track while a race is in progress. The start and finish of running events can be photographed from the side of the track. Photographers may also take a position anywhere between the start and finish lines, providing the vision of judges and timers is not obstructed.

Because it is possible to work close to the track, normal or even wide-angle lenses are usually all you will need. However, the medium-long telephoto lenses (100 mm to 200 mm) are useful for concentrating on individual competitors during a race. They are also good for shooting interesting warm-up and post-event reactions by athletes.

For running events, the finish line is a good place to shoot because everyone is putting out maximum effort at that point. Select a camera angle about 5 to 6 m (15 to 20 feet) away. You will have a good view as the runners burst through the tape. Do not ignore the beginning of a race. Focus on the runners as they break from the starting blocks, or at

The first or second row of "fences" is the best camera position for hurdle events. The runners here are bunched and vaulting the hurdles in near unison. Photo by Peter Gales.

about the half-way point on the track. This is a good place to use slow shutter speeds and pan with the action to blur backgrounds. (*See:* ACTION PHOTOGRAPHY.) Working from the inside of a turn may also provide good camera angles as the runners struggle to negotiate the curve.

Hurdle Events. The first or second row of hurdles is best, because the runners are usually bunched up and jump the hurdle together. Later on they spread out too much as the faster runners take the lead.

Field Events. High jump, pole vault, shot put, and other field events are excellent subjects if you time the exposures for the peak of action—the shot as it is released, the athlete grimacing with effort, the graceful arc of a high jumper etched against the sky. Pictures of this type are fleeting, and you will need to work fast.

Tennis

At most amateur or interscholastic matches, you are free to move around the perimeter of the court. However, it is best to limit your movements while a game is underway to avoid distracting the players. Pick a location and stay there until there is a break in the action or a change of sides at the end of a game, and then move.

Although the game is played at a furious pace, there are many instances of arrested movement that are easy to photograph—a player preparing to serve as he or she throws the ball in the air, or with racket poised to return the opponent's shot. To show a player serving, focus when he or she takes position at the rear of the court. You will have plenty of time to make the picture.

To stop the player's racket at the moment of impact with the ball, a shutter speed of at least 1/500 sec. is recommended. However, it may not always be possible to shoot that fast due to low light levels. It is still possible to get the picture simply by timing the exposure for the instant when the racket is poised to strike, just as the player commences the swing. It sounds difficult, but you will be surprised how quickly you learn to anticipate when to trip the shutter.

A normal lens or medium telephoto lens is adequate for most pictures. For courtside action, the 85 mm to 135 mm focal lengths are excellent. Zoom lenses are especially useful for following the players, who are constantly changing position. For best results, prefocus the camera on a point around the center of the court and let the depth of field of your lens work for you.

Try shooting from the stands for a high viewpoint. By shooting down at your subjects, you simplify the background by eliminating distracting elements such as fencing, spectators, and officials. This frequently creates a much stronger picture.

For tight close-ups of action as seen from the stands, you will need at least a 200 mm or 300 mm lens, depending on your location. It may be possible to find a camera angle that will show both players at once, or all four players in a doubles match. This picture usually requires a camera position facing the back of the court, looking toward the net.

Golf

A professional golf tournament is one of the toughest events to cover because of many built-in restrictions on photographers. The most important

Despite the furious pace of most tennis matches, you can watch for the beginning and end of actions to get tennis pictures like these. Photos by Paul Bereswill.

rule is to stay out of the golfer's line of sight. This sport demands the utmost concentration, and even the slightest distraction is unnerving. Never shoot while a golfer is lining up a drive off a tee, a putt, or an approach to the green. The click of the shutter may spoil his or her timing and cause a miss. Motorized cameras, with their machine-gun staccato, are especially troublesome to a golfer.

Telephoto lenses from 400 mm to 600 mm are often used by press and magazine photographers covering golf tournaments. The longer the lens, the less conspicuous a photographer is. He or she can work at long range, ahead of the golfers, but out of their line of sight. A unipod, rather than a tripod, is normally used to steady the camera because it allows a greater degree of mobility.

Amateur photographers will find a more relaxed atmosphere at most public golf courses, charity, celebrity, and Pro-Am tournaments. You can work much closer to the players with shorter-focal-length lenses.

Like baseball players, golfers' faces may be heavily shaded by their caps. Watch for situations that reveal the golfer's face. The player will always look up after hitting the ball to follow its flight. That is a moment to shoot. The combination of a classic golfing position, club on the follow-through, and a suspenseful expression usually makes for a good picture.

Sand traps are great locations to show the plight of an unwary golfer who strays from the fairway. There is usually a vivid explosion of sand as the golfer attempts to knock the ball loose. The sand will act as a natural reflector to fill in shadows on the golfer's face.

For close-ups of individual golfers, try to get them on the practice tee before a match. You have more freedom of movement and may find a better variety of camera angles than is possible out on the course. Most golf courses will allow you to shoot on the practice tee as long as you do not get in the way of players warming up.

Hockey

In this fast-moving sport, a seat close to the ice is preferred for following the back-and-forth playing patterns of the teams. Focus about 8 m (25 feet) out from the sidelines, depending on your location, and as the players come within range, begin shooting.

Action around the goal area is best photographed from the side of the ice opposite the net or slightly to one side. You have a wide choice of camera angles to show the goalie trying to deflect the puck and stop a score. Watch for violent body contact as the players slam into each other. You will need a shutter speed of at least 1/250 sec. The 85 to 135 mm lenses are especially suited for most hockey pictures.

Bright interior lighting in many professional hockey arenas permits exposures of 1/250 or 1/500 sec. at f/2 or f/2.8 on fast pan film rated at ASA 800

or higher. There is a great deal of light reflected from the surface of the ice, which helps to fill in shadow areas from below. This may also result in grossly inflated meter readings that will cause trouble. Blindly following the meter may result in badly underexposed film. You may have to open up a full stop over the indicated exposure to show adequate detail in the faces of the hockey players.

Some amateur and semipro teams play in small arenas with very dim lighting. Electronic flash is needed to insure usable pictures.

Auto Racing

Motor speedways are usually designed to give the fans a good view of the action, at least for the start and finish. Many outstanding pictures have been made by amateur photographers from a grandstand seat.

Long telephoto lenses (200 to 400 mm) are required for working at the distances normally encountered. Each track is different, and in some cases shorter-focal-length lenses—such as 135 mm—are satisfactory.

A camera position near a turn is preferred, since spin-outs and crashes are most likely to occur there. Stay at least 100 to 150 feet away. This is advisable not only for safety, but also because the human eye records a wider field of view at that distance, and it is easier to follow action.

The hockey photographer should try for a seat near the ice and close to one of the goals. Beware of reflected light from the ice; it can cause an inflated meter reading, resulting in badly underexposed film. Photo by Paul Bereswill.

Panned shots of sports cars made at deliberately slow shutter speeds are often more dramatic than photographs that totally "stop" the speeding car.

The panning technique may be effectively utilized in photographing motor sports events. A moderately fast shutter speed of 1/125 or 1/250 sec. is capable of stopping fast, broadside motion and creating graphic visual effects. The subject will appear in sharp contrast to a blurred background, suggesting a feeling of great speed.

A slower shutter speed like 1/30 or 1/60 sec. will accentuate the blur and make the cars appear to be moving even faster. Zoom lenses are excellent. For some really startling images, try panning the camera and zooming the lens at the same time. You cannot predict what the finished pictures will look like, but that is half the fun. Panned shots at slow shutter speeds often capture a feeling of realism that is lacking when the action is frozen.

You may also find it necessary to use panning for frozen-action shots. Even 1/1000 sec. may not stop a race car traveling at 300 kilometres (190 miles) per hour. With correct panning technique, 1/500 or even 1/250 sec. will be sufficient. Prefocus the lens at the point you wish to shoot. Move the camera smoothly to keep the car centered in the viewfinder. As the car passes in front, squeeze the shutter but follow through by keeping the camera moving as the car speeds past. Mastering this technique takes practice, but the results more than justify the extra effort.

On race day, get to the track early and scout the best locations for photography. You may find a position around the infield fence that is closer to the track than you expected. When the race begins, shoot the cars on the first lap to show them all together. You may not get another chance. Afterwards, they are usually spread out as the faster drivers move in front.

If you are close to the track at ground level, a cardinal rule is *never turn your back on the cars.* Accidents can happen at any time. A racer spinning out of control may crash through the perimeter barrier near your position. Stay alert, and always be prepared to run. It could save your life.

Night races must be photographed by available light. Nearly all tracks forbid the use of flash because they could temporarily blind a driver, causing an accident. Pick a spot where the light level is brightest. You will probably have to push high-speed film to the outer limits—from ASA 1600 to 2000—to get pictures. Some of the smaller speedways have extremely poor lighting. In this situation, try a special-purpose film such as Kodak 2475 recording film. The recording film can be exposed at very high ratings of ASA 4000 or more. The film is quite grainy, but you can get pictures in low-light conditions that would be impossible otherwise.

Motorcycle Racing

The same camera techniques used in auto racing are suitable for covering motorcycle events. There are two basic types of competition—high-speed races, like those sanctioned by the American Motorcycle Association at different tracks throughout the United States, and "motocross." Motocross is a violent endurance contest combining high speeds over a treacherous course designed to test a driver's skill to the utmost. A motocross race may include ski-type jumps off a steep hill, mud holes, water holes, and other hazards.

Besides these formal professional events, there are numerous amateur and semipro motorcycle races catering to the special interests of hill climbers, oval, flat-track, and desert racing enthusiasts. The picture possibilities are outstanding in all of these categories.

Sailing

Sailing may be photographed from shore or from a boat. Just about any lake, harbor, or river offers a variety of recreational boating activity. To

A small power boat is needed to photograph a sailing race. Having another person at the controls of the vessel will give the photographer the freedom to concentrate on the boats. Photo by Frank Zagamno.

photograph sailing races, use a power boat whenever possible. It is more maneuverable and will allow a good selection of camera angles. It is wise to bring another person along to run the boat while you concentrate on pictures. Small powerboats are available for rental at most harbors or marinas, and there are almost always experienced boat handlers there who can take you out.

Follow the racing fleet around the course. Watch for action around a turning mark (buoy) as the boats converge. Deck activity of crews trimming sails and the boats maneuvering for position are always good. Medium to long telephoto lenses (85 to 200 mm) are essential to cover this action from a safe distance.

For informal shots of sailing activity, just about any lens will do. You do not even need a boat. There may be a variety of good dry-land camera positions, like a beach or pier, that offer a good view of the water.

Backlighting or sidelighting is most effective in boating shots. Light-yellow or red filters will darken the sky and add drama if you are shooting in black-and-white. For color, a UV or skylight filter is required to hold down the blue cast typical of marine scenes.

Water Skiing

The best camera angles are from the stern of the boat towing the skier, or from another boat running alongside the skier, from 15 to 30 m (50 to 100 feet) away. This requires the cooperation of an expert boat driver working with the photographer. Medium-long lenses (100 to 200 mm) and fast shutter speeds, 1/500 to 1/1000 sec., are recommended. Do not rest the camera on any part of the boat. Brace it against your cheek and press your elbows firmly against your body for maximum steadiness. Kneeling on a seat cushion will help pad the bumps in rough water.

Water-ski speed competition is best covered from a position near a turn. A skier is most likely to fall at this point, which can produce a spectacular photo.

Swimming and Diving

Swimming competition is difficult to photograph because the contestants' faces are underwater or hidden by flailing arms most of the time. You must watch carefully and trip the shutter only when their faces are visible. Be prepared to use lots of film. Unless you are very fortunate, you will have to shoot many pictures to get a few usable ones.

Diving is a joy to photograph. The lithe bodies of athletes plunging through space into brilliant blue water are dynamic subjects. Competitive diving events are staged from a low board, 1 m (3 to 4 feet) above the water; a high board, at 3 m (10 feet); and

Photographs from the stern of the boat towing a water skiier are best made with medium-long lenses (100–200 mm). Support the camera so your body absorbs vibration as much as possible; avoid resting the camera on any part of the boat. Photo by Jeffrey H. Hinman.

the high platform, placed from 5 to 10 m (15 to 30 feet) over the water. Contestants are judged on the accuracy of form in the execution of their dives.

Aim for the peak of action, and catch the diver in mid-air before he or she hits the water. Suggested shutter speeds are from 1/250 to 1/1000 sec. A normal lens or medium telephoto lens is sufficient for most pictures.

Besides competitive watersports, do not ignore the opportunity for good pictures at almost any local beach or swimming pool, whether public or private. People having fun in the water can be interesting subjects.

Surfing

Super-long telephoto lenses (400 mm and up) are mandatory for surfing because the best action is usually far out on the water. Sometimes a convenient pier or breakwater will put you closer to the surfers, and you can get by with a 200 mm lens, but this is extremely rare.

A few adventurous photographers who cover the sport on a regular basis use a waterproof camera like the Nikonos, or place a conventional camera in an underwater housing. (*See:* UNDERWATER PHOTOGRAPHY.) They wear swim trunks or wet suits and work in shallow water to shoot the surfers as they approach.

This close-up method will produce exciting pictures, but it can be dangerous. A surfer may be knocked off the board by a rough wave, and the board hurtled across the water out of control. The surfing photographer must always be ready to duck.

Skiing

There are few subjects more exciting than a skier speeding down a sun-drenched mountainside on a carpet of powdery snow. Early morning or late afternoon is the best time to shoot. The sun angle is lower, creating longer shadows and bringing out the texture of snow. Pictures taken at midday seem lifeless in comparison. The lighting tends to be very dull and flat.

Select a location where a skier is turning, like a downhill slalom course. Photograph it from the outside to capture the spray of snow. Another good location is at a jump to show the skier in mid-air, or sailing across a ridge against the skyline. Working from behind a jump is also good. It may be possible to include the ski resort or other scenic area in the background, thus giving an added dimension to the picture.

Good ski photography also requires anticipating the action. Work behind a jump or a mogul (man-made mounds in the piste) and expect action like this.

For stopped-action shots, 1/500 sec. will be fast enough for just about any situation you are likely to encounter. And do not forget the panning technique. It is also helpful in shooting skiing. Almost any focal-length lens can be used, according to your location. Zoom lenses are ideal—you can cover more action from one camera position.

Bright sun on snow can cause serious overexposure due to the intensity of the light. You can count on one or two stops more light under most conditions. For black-and-white film, a light-yellow or orange filter will darken the sky and produce better tonal separation between the snow and sky. Color films require a skylight filter for best results. There is a tremendous amount of ultraviolet light present in snow areas, especially in the mountains at high altitudes. A skylight filter will help control the excessive blue cast and warm up shadow areas.

Bracket exposures whenever you can. This will insure good results in difficult lighting conditions.

A small belt- or backpack will protect your equipment from moisture. Keep your camera wrapped in a lint-free towel when you are not shooting. Remember, never take your camera indoors if you plan to use it again outside within a short time. Condensation will form on the lens and all metal parts. This can put you out of business for hours.

Remember also that shutters may lose some of their accuracy in extreme cold, causing exposure problems. Again, it is a good idea to bracket exposures as much as possible.

Protecting Equipment

A sports photographer must frequently work under miserable weather conditions. For extra protection on rainy days, tape a plastic bag over the camera, leaving small openings for the lens, viewfinder, shutter release, and film wind. This method is clumsy and will certainly slow you down, but it can prevent a huge repair bill in case your equipment gets drenched. (*See:* BAD-WEATHER PHOTOGRAPHY.)

Cameras and lenses that have been exposed to rain or snow should be dried as soon as possible. Equipment that has been soaked for extended periods, or exposed to sand, will probably need a trip to the local camera repair shop for a thorough cleaning. Sand filtering through the inside of a camera will eventually ruin complex mechanisms.

A final word: Do not be discouraged if your first efforts at sports photography do not turn out too well. It may take a while to become accustomed to shooting fast action. Keep trying. Remember to anticipate, know your equipment, and learn something about the sport you are covering. Once you have mastered these basics, success will follow.

• *See also:* ACTION PHOTOGRAPHY; BAD-WEATHER PHOTOGRAPHY; COLOR FILMS; FILTERS; PUSH PROCESSING; WIDE-ANGLE PHOTOGRAPHY; ZOOM LENS.

Further Reading: Eastman Kodak Co. *How to Make Sports-Analysis Films,* pub. No. S-62. Rochester, NY: Eastman Kodak Co., 1975; Latham, Sid. *Camera Afield.* Harrisburg, PA: Stackpole Books, 1976; Olney, Ross R. *Photographing Action Sports.* New York, NY: Franklin Watts, 1976; Pfeiffer, C. Boyd. *Field Guide to Outdoor Photography.* Harrisburg, PA: Stackpole Books, 1977; Turner, Richard. *Focus on Sports: Photographing Action.* Garden City, NY: Amphoto, 1975; Zimmerman, John and Mark Kauffman. *Photographing Sports.* New York, NY: Thomas Y. Crowell, 1975.

 **Spotting Prints**

No matter how carefully dust, scratches, fingerprints, and the like have been avoided, a few unsightly spots will often appear on prints. Before a photographer can consider a print finished, the spots must be removed. Two kinds of spots most often appear on prints—black ones and white ones. Methods for avoiding spots and general techniques for dealing with those that are minor are discussed here. Information on extensive retouching of black-and-white and color prints can be found in the article RETOUCHING.

Black Spots

A black spot, which is caused by a "pinhole" in the negative, usually results from dust on the film at the time of exposure. The speck of dust, which may have settled on the film from the camera interior, prevents the light of the image from affecting the sensitive emulsion in that particular small area. Thus, when the film is developed, this tiny spot will be transparent. Prints from this negative will record the tiny, transparent spot as a small, black spot. If the spot happens to occur in a deep shadow area of the subject, it may pass unnoticed in the final picture; if it should fall in any middletone or highlight, you will want to remedy it.

Keep in mind it is much easier to correct a light spot than a dark spot. Accordingly, you should carefully inspect each negative *before* you print it—using a magnifying glass if necessary—for any transparent spots. Touch each one with opaque, using a very fine-pointed brush. Then treat the resulting white spot in the print with a brush and a bit of spotting color.

White Spots

White spots on prints are perhaps the most common type of problem. They are caused by dust or small dirt particles on the negative or negative carrier during the print exposure, or, less likely, by foreign matter that may have settled on the paper emulsion just before the print exposure was made.

As with black spots, the white variety is best prevented by keeping the darkroom and all items of equipment scrupulously clean. Especially important is brushing off the negative before printing. Once the white spots have appeared on a print, however, they can be removed with a small brush and a bit of spotting color.

Spotting Materials

Spotting media may be divided into three different types: pigments, pencils, and dyes. The choice is largely a matter of individual preference, but to some extent it is governed by the type of work to be accomplished.

Pigments for spotting prints are available either in the form of a stick of black India ink or as a pad of spotting colors containing daubs of black, brown, and white water-soluble pigment. Either can be used satisfactorily, and both are recommended for all-round spotting work.

Spotting prints with pencils is the easiest method to learn; it merely consists of lightly touching the objectionable white spot with a sharply pointed pencil until the spot has disappeared. This method also has the advantage of speed; a brush requires occasional dampening and recharging with pigment.

Glossy paper is the most difficult of all surfaces to spot. A ferrotyped, glossy surface presents no "tooth" to which minute particles of pencil lead can adhere. The best answer to this problem is to use spotting dyes. The advantage of using dyes is that they sink into the emulsion, increasing the density in the areas treated, without appreciably altering the appearance of the print surface.

For the techniques of applying spotting media, see the article RETOUCHING.
• *See also:* AFTERTREATMENT; AIRBRUSH; BLEACHING.

Spraying Prints

Spraying prints may involve applying a substance in aerosol form. The technique is usually done for any number of reasons depending on the end use of the print.

Prints may be sprayed with a relatively inert chemical product in order to protect the print itself from surface abrasion and fading. Aerosols sold in art-supply stores are often used. They are available in both matte and gloss finishes under brand names such as Krylon.

A second reason for spraying prints is that spraying is part of a step-by-step process, such as sizing prints with ordinary household starch as a part of the gum-bichromate process. (*See:* GUM-BICHROMATE PRINTING.) Prints may also be sprayed to make them more or less impervious to pigments or chemicals.

Spraying finished photographs also gives them a textured look. Spray aerosols in kit form are available through art-supply stores and commercial studio suppliers. Another use of sprays that is unrelated to the foregoing is spraying the face of a print as a part of a laminating process, and the back of a print as a step in mounting the print with adhesive.
• *See also:* AFTERTREATMENT; FABRIC SENSITIZER; GUM-BICHROMATE PRINTING; LACQUERS; LAMINATING; MURALS; PRINTS, MOUNTING.

Stabilization Process

Stabilization is a method of processing black-and-white prints much more quickly than usual by the customary develop-stop-fix-wash method. Stabilized prints are not permanent because the chemical reactions within the emulsion have been stopped only temporarily. However, such prints last long enough to serve a number of practical purposes. In fact, stabilized prints often remain unchanged for many months if they are not exposed to strong light, high temperature, or excessive humidity.

Stabilization vs. Conventional Processing

The main differences between stabilization processing and ordinary print processing are in the speed of activation or development, and in the method of treating the unexposed light-sensitive silver halide left in the emulsion after development. Stabilization processing is a machine operation. The prints are processed in about 15 seconds, and they are slightly damp on leaving the machine. However, they dry completely in a few minutes and are then ready for use. In conventional processing, the unused silver halide is dissolved by the fixer (hypo), and any traces of dissolved silver salts left after fixing are removed by subsequent washing. Thus, conventionally processed prints are stable for long periods. In stabilization processing, however, the silver halide is converted to only temporarily stable compounds; therefore, the prints have a limited keeping time. Stabilized prints can be made permanent by fixing and washing after their initial use.

The stabilization process is different from the activation process, in which the prints are developed by activation and finished by a conventional stop-fix-wash-dry sequence. Activation processors (such as the Kodak Royalprint processor) process prints in less than a minute. These prints have all the permanence of conventionally processed prints made on similar, water-resistant papers.

Common stabilization processes can be divided into two groups, according to the number of chemical solutions involved:

1. Two or more solutions: an activator and one or more stabilizers. The two-solution process is most often used for good-quality continuous-tone prints.
2. The monobath, or one-solution, process. This is generally more suitable for drawings and other line work. Development and stabilization are simultaneous. Monobaths are not discussed here.

In many stabilization processes, developing agents are incorporated in the paper emulsion. Development is achieved by applying an alkaline activator to the emulsion surface. The stabilizer is then applied to neutralize the activator and to convert any remaining silver halide to *relatively* stable, colorless compounds.

Ordinary printing papers cannot be developed by this type of stabilization process, because there is no developing agent present in either the emulsion or the activator. However, a stabilization paper with developing agents in the emulsion can be processed in ordinary print-processing chemicals, if desired. Contrast is likely to be somewhat higher when the paper is tray-processed.

Applications

The use of stabilization processing has increased greatly in the last few years, and it continues to grow as photographers and others who use photography as a tool realize its value.

In stabilization processing, a measure of print stability is exchanged for the following advantages:

1. Stabilization processing is fast; prints are ready for use in a matter of seconds.
2. Speed and simplicity make the process adaptable to uncomplicated systems of mechanization. This, in turn, makes photography a more easily used tool for those who are not experts in photographic processing.
3. Darkroom space and plumbing are greatly reduced. In fact, some applications of the process do not require a darkroom.
4. Stabilized prints do not need washing. This is a significant advantage since water conservation is important in many areas.
5. Most stabilized prints can be fixed and washed to make them permanent. Thus, you can enjoy the speed of stabilization processing and get permanent prints if you so desire.

Here are some of the modern applications for stabilized prints:
Proofing.
Quality deadline work.
Industrial and commercial applications where speed of production is essential.

Phototypesetting and photocomposing.
Medical photography.
Military photography.
Police photography.
Newspaper work.
Immediate enlargements from microfilmed documents.
Instrumentation or recording photography.

Important Points

1. Correct exposure is essential because the development time is constant. Use an on-easel photometer to assist in getting correct exposure.
2. Keep the processor clean. Follow the manufacturer's recommendations as to cleaning and maintenance.
3. Do not overwork the chemical solutions. Observe the manufacturer's recommendations about the capacity and renewal of solutions.
4. Make sure that the processing trays in the machine are dry before loading them with the chemicals, because some stabilization solutions are not compatible with water.
5. Avoid contamination of the activator with stabilizer. This results in chemical fog on the prints.
6. Avoid handling unprocessed paper after handling stabilized prints. Such prints are impregnated with chemicals that easily mark or stain unprocessed material.
7. Stabilized prints must not be washed unless they have been fixed in an ordinary fixing bath. Washing without fixing renders the prints sensitive to light.
8. Stabilized prints must not be heat-dried. The combination of heat and moisture stains the prints an overall yellowish brown.
9. Because stabilized prints are impregnated with chemicals, do not use the same racks or blotters for drying conventionally processed prints. For the same reason, do not file stabilized prints in contact with negatives or any other valuable material.

Processing

For stabilization processing, three elements are needed:

1. Special paper (usually variable contrast) that has incorporated developer in the emulsion.
2. A stabilization processor.
3. Two chemical solutions.

With these elements working together, conventionally exposed prints can be processed and ready for use in a matter of seconds. The prints are of excellent quality and can be used for a great many purposes where permanence is not important. Moreover, the prints can be made permanent, if desired, by subsequent fixing and washing. There are few photographic operations in which this method cannot be used to advantage when the savings in processing time and space are considered. The savings often repays the initial cost of the processor in a comparatively short time. No special skill or lengthy training is necessary to operate most processors.

Typical Processor

The typical two-solution stabilization processor accepts both sheets and rolls of paper.

An $8'' \times 10''$ print is processed and clear of the machine in a matter of seconds. The paper is then in a damp-dry condition, but it dries completely in a few minutes in a normal room atmosphere.

The print must be inserted into the processor according to the manufacturer's instructions and the instructions that accompany the paper being used. In this way, the paper grain will be oriented correctly with the rollers, thus providing proper transport of the paper through the processor.

Solutions in the typical stabilization processor are usually replenished automatically from the original plastic containers by means of solution-level valves. To insure the continuous, smooth operation of a processor and for routine cleaning instructions, refer to the manual supplied with the processor.

Drying Stabilized Prints

Prints are damp on leaving the processor, but they will dry completely, with little curl, in a few moments at room temperature. Accelerated drying by heat is not recommended, nor can prints be ferrotyped on hot drum machines unless they have been fixed and washed.

Mounting

Dry mounting of stabilized prints is not recommended as a normal procedure, but it can be done in the following way if necessary, although there is risk of change in color.

The print (and any card used as an overlay) must be quite dry. The temperature of the press should not exceed 104 C (220 F), and the mounting time should be no longer than it takes for the paper to adhere to the mount—approximately 20 seconds.

Making Stabilized Prints Permanent

At any time before the image begins to deteriorate, a stabilized print can be made permanent by conventional methods. Use any rapid or standard fixing bath.

Do not rinse the print first. Treat it in the fixer for the same amount of time as a conventional print, then wash it thoroughly. As with other materials, a washing aid may be used to increase efficiency and shorten washing time.

• *See also:* PAPERS, PHOTOGRAPHIC; RAPID PROCESSING.

 **Stain Removal**

Stains on Skin

Certain photographic chemicals, particularly developing agents, may cause brownish stains on the fingers or hands. Such stains usually result only after prolonged or repeated contact with the chemicals, and are best prevented by avoiding such contact and washing promptly when contact does occur. Should the skin come in contact with solutions or solid chemicals (especially developers or developing agents), wash at once with an acid skin cleaner. Rinse hands thoroughly after cleaning.

The use of clean rubber gloves, especially for mixing or pouring solutions and cleaning the darkroom, will protect the skin from contact with chemicals and subsequent staining. After use, and before removing the gloves, rinse the outer surfaces of the gloves with acid skin cleaner and water. Keep all working surfaces, such as bench tops, trays, tanks, and containers, clean and free from spilled solutions or chemicals. A typical acetic-acid stop bath makes an effective acid rinse for hands or gloves.

Removing Stain from Negatives

Developer or oxidation stains may be removed by first hardening the film for 2 or 3 minutes in formalin hardener (Kodak special hardener SH-1), and then washing for 5 minutes and bleaching in the two-solution stain remover (Kodak stain remover S-6). After bleaching, redevelopment in a nonstaining developer is necessary.

Kodak stain remover S-6

This solution is used to remove developer or oxidation stain from film.

Stock solution A	
Potassium permanganate	5 g
Water to make	1 litre
Stock solution B	
Cold water	500 ml
Sodium chloride	75 g
Sulfuric acid (concentrated)* . .	16 ml
Water to make	1 litre

Mix the chemicals for the stain remover in the order given. When mixing solution A, be sure that all the particles of permanganate are completely dissolved; undissolved particles may produce spots on the negatives.

When ready to begin the stain removal procedure, mix equal parts of solution A and solution B. This *must* be done immediately prior to use; the solutions do not keep long in combination.

To Use. Harden the film to be treated for 2 or 3 minutes in the formalin hardener, and wash for 5 minutes. (*See:* HARDENING BATHS.) Mix solution A and solution B as directed above, keeping both solutions at 20 C (68 F). Immerse the film in this bleaching solution for 3 or 4 minutes. Next, to remove the brown stain of manganese dioxide formed on the negative in the bleach bath, immerse the film in a 1 percent sodium bisulfite solution (make a

---

*CAUTION: Always add the sulfuric acid to the solution slowly, stirring constantly. Never add the solution to the acid; otherwise, the solution may boil and spatter the acid on the hands or face, causing serious burns.

1 percent solution by adding 10 grams of sodium bisulfite to 1 litre of water). Remove the film, rinse it well, and develop it in strong light (preferably sunlight) with any nonstaining developer (such as Kodak Dektol developer or Kodak developer D-72) diluted 1:2 with water. Then wash it thoroughly.

WARNING: Slow-working developers, such as Kodak developer D-76, Kodak Microdol-X developer, and Kodak developer DK-20, should not be used, since they tend to dissolve the bleached image before the developing agents are able to act on it.

Stains on Clothing

The following formula will remove brownish stains caused by splashing or spilling fixing bath on clothing. The stains are usually caused by silver compounds accumulated in a used fixing bath.

*Kodak silver stain remover S-10**

Water	750 ml
Thiourea†	75 g
Citric acid (anhydrous)	75 g
Water to make	1 litre

To Use. Thoroughly wet the stained part of the fabric with this solution and wait for the stain to disappear. If the stain is old, it may be necessary to repeat the application. Disappearance of an old stain may take longer than disappearance of a new one, so wait several minutes before repeating the application. When the stain has been satisfactorily removed, wash the garment thoroughly. This solution should not be allowed to come in contact with the skin.

---

*CAUTION: Thiourea, which most preparations for removing fixer stains contain, is a powerful foggant of photographic emulsions. Therefore, Kodak silver stain remover S-10, or any formula containing thiourea, must not be prepared or used in close proximity to areas where light-sensitive materials or processing chemicals are handled or used.

†WARNING: Thiourea may, with prolonged contact, irritate the skin. Be sure to acquaint yourself with any necessary handling precautions outlined on the product label. Do not allow thiourea, or any solution containing thiourea, to come in contact with the eyes or skin. Avoid inhaling the dust. Use rubber gloves when preparing and using the solution. Afterwards, decontaminate the gloves by rinsing the outer surfaces with a dilute solution of sodium hypochlorite. The solution can be prepared by adding 30 ml of Clorox, 101, or similar liquid household bleach, to 1 litre of water (about 1 fluidounce to 1 quart). Finally, wash the gloves thoroughly with warm water.

NOTE: Some fabrics may be bleached or damaged by this solution. Before attempting to remove stains, test the chemical on a hidden portion of the garment (such as the shirttail, or a small scrap cut from a seam allowance) and determine whether the material is adversely affected.

Tray Cleaners

Photographic trays can be stained by oxidation products in developers, silver, silver sulfide, and various dyes. The tray cleaners described here can remove most of the more common stains that might be encountered.

Kodak tray cleaner TC-1

Water	1 litre
Potassium dichromate (anhydrous)	90 g
Sulfuric acid (concentrated)*	96 ml

To Use. Pour a small volume of the tray cleaner solution into the vessel to be cleaned. Rinse around so that the solution has access to all parts of the tray; then pour the solution out and wash the tray six or eight times with water until all traces of the cleaning solution disappear. This solution will remove stains caused by oxidation products of developers and some silver and dye stains. It should *not* be used to clean the hands.

Kodak tray cleaner TC-3
Solution A†

Water	1 litre
Potassium permanganate	2 g
Sulfuric acid (concentrated)*	4 ml

Solution B

Water	1 litre
Sodium bisulfite (anhydrous) . . .	30 g
Sodium sulfite (anhydrous)	30 g

---

*CAUTION: Always add the sulfuric acid to the solution slowly, stirring constantly. Never add the solution to the acid; otherwise, the solution may boil and spatter the acid on the hands or face, causing serious burns.

†Store the solution in a stoppered glass bottle away from the light.

Cleaning Trays. To remove stains due to silver, silver sulfide, and many dyes, proceed as follows: Pour a small quantity of solution A into the vessel being cleaned and leave it there for a few minutes; rinse the vessel well, and pour in a quantity of solution B approximately equal to the amount of solution A used. Agitate until the brown stain is completely cleared, and wash the cleaned vessel thoroughly.

Several vessels can be cleaned consecutively without making up new solutions; the solutions should not, however, be stored for repeated use.

• *See also:* FORMULAS FOR BLACK-AND-WHITE PROCESSING; HARDENING BATHS.

Static Marks

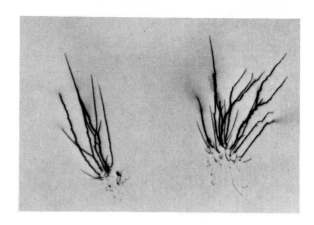

When film is subjected to movements that cause friction, it may become either positively or negatively charged with static electricity. A material in this condition seeks to return to a neutral state by a transfer of electrons to the air, ground, or a nearby object. If this transfer or discharge is abrupt, light is emitted, which produces the familiar static markings often seen on processed negatives. Static charges are also troublesome in that they attract dust particles to the surfaces of processed and unprocessed films.

Although friction is the main cause of static charges, they can be produced by other means, such as intimate contact of film surfaces resulting from pressure or by separation of the surfaces when a roll is unwound rapidly. As a rule, static is most troublesome in conditions of low relative humidity.

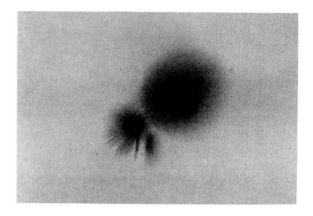

Characteristics

The branch-like markings often seen on sheet-film negatives are easily recognized as being due to static discharge. They are characteristic of a negative charge discharged to a small point or a small object. Static markings, however, take a number of other forms that are not so easily recognized. For example, diffuse spots with dark centers result when a positive charge discharges. A line of bead-like spots down the center of a roll film is often caused when the backing paper is unrolled and the film is passed rapidly between the fingers. An irregular

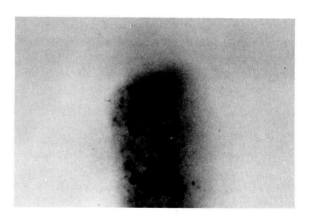

(Top) Branch-like static marks caused by a discharge between a negatively charged film and a nearby object or surface. (Center) Circular spots with a dark center result from a discharge between a nearby object and a positively charged film. (Bottom) A mark characteristic of moisture static, often caused when unwinding a roll of film that has been stored under unusually damp conditions.

Stain Removal

blotch pattern is often caused by unwinding a roll of slightly damp or tacky film. This blotchy pattern is characteristic of moisture static. Another type of marking that occurs in rolls of film is a series of bars of fog at regular intervals across the width of the film. This type of marking takes place at the line of separation as the roll is unwound. Sometimes, forked branches or high-density spots occur along the line of fog, depending on whether the charge was negative or positive. On reversal roll films, static marks often show up as blue streaks.

Prevention

In the manufacture and packaging of films, precautions are taken to avoid the buildup of static charges that may affect the product. In the practical use of films, static will not be a problem if the following steps are taken:

1. In handling film, avoid sudden movements of the material that might cause friction.
2. Whenever possible, maintain the relative humidity at about 45 percent in the work areas where film is handled.
3. Do not wind or unwind rolls of film very rapidly, and avoid winding a roll too tightly.
4. If your film holders have plastic slides, do not withdraw or replace them quickly. In making the exposure, do not place the slide under your arm and then withdraw it quickly for replacement in the film holder. This will induce a static charge in the slide that may discharge to the film surface.
5. Keep the film-loading room and the processing room as free from dust as possible.
6. In preparing negatives for printing, use static-eliminating equipment to remove dust specks and possible static charges that will attract more dust immediately.
7. Strip the backing paper from a roll film carefully, and do not pass the film between the fingers when removing the paper or when unrolling the film to attach the bottom clip or weight.

Stereo Photography

Stereoscopic, three-dimensional (3-D) vision is the seeing of the length, width, and depth of objects, and the distances between objects; it results because human beings have binocular, or two-eyed, vision.

With one eye, the lengths and widths, or area, of objects can be seen. Many of the effects of distance can also be seen because of various depth clues. (*See:* PERSPECTIVE.) However, with stereoscopic vision, a perception of volume as well as distance—the key aspects of the third dimension—is achieved.

Stereoscopic effects can be produced photographically. Images may be recorded by a camera in four ways: (1) with two lenses separated the same average distance as the human eyes, (2) by two separate cameras spaced at a suitable distance, (3) by a single camera moved the necessary distance between two successive exposures, or (4) by a number of specialized means. In every case, special viewers or viewing arrangements are required for the stereoscopic effect to be perceived. Depending upon a number of factors, the three-dimensional effect may seem realistic and lifelike, or it may appear exaggerated or diminished.

The novelty of 3-D photographic images has led to their use in advertising and in theatrical motion pictures at various times. More importantly, stereo photography has found significant applications in education and training, photogrammetry and map-making, medical and industrial radiography (x-ray photography), and other fields.

Stereo Vision

In a human being, the average spacing between the pupils of the eyes (the interpupillary, or interocular, distance) is 63.5 mm (2½ inches). When objects at close to moderate distances are viewed, this separation produces parallax; that is, the objects are seen from slightly different angles. As a result, although the retinal images in the two eyes are similar, there are important differences. The left eye sees more of the left side of a given object, while the right eye sees more of the right side. Furthermore, when one object is behind another, the parallax between the eyes results in the seeing of different portions of the farther object.

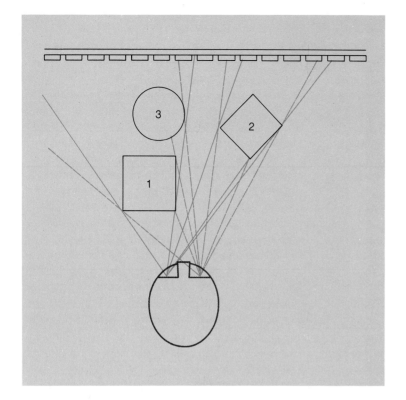

This diagram illustrates the elements of binocular, stereo vision. The different viewpoints of the human eyes reveal slightly different images. For example, the right eye sees the right side of the box (1), but the left eye sees only the front. The right eye sees part of the ball (3) behind box (1), but the left eye does not. Right and left eyes see different parts of the fence behind box (2). The brain fuses the two different images and "sees" the variation as depth, or the third dimension.

The brain fuses the separate images from the eyes and forms a composite perception that includes the sense of the third dimension—volume and distance. It is the parallax differences between the images that produce this perception, and the process is automatic; we only notice the absence of depth perception when we are deprived of the sight of one eye for a period of time.

When objects are close to the viewer, the parallax angles are considerable, but they grow less as the distance to the objects increases. At some distant point, called *stereo infinity,* the parallax angles are so small that true stereo vision ceases. The distance to stereo infinity varies with different people, and it has not been firmly established. Various authorities place it from as close as 51 m (200 feet) up to more than 710 m (2000 feet). Because the decrease in stereo perception is gradual and the increase in the importance of other depth clues is also gradual, stereo infinity is difficult to measure.

The resolving power of the eye also affects this distance. Eye resolution is limited by aberrations of the eye lenses and by the finite size of the cones in the foveal region of the retina. Stereo infinity can be defined as the distance at which the parallax differences in the two retinal images become smaller than the resolving power of the eyes. Although an average can be arrived at, there is great variation from individual to individual.

In addition to the mental comparison of two slightly different images, there are other factors in stereo vision that help create the perception of volume and distance. One of these is the shift in convergence as the eyes view objects at different distances.

The foveal region of the retina in the eye is the region that provides the brain with the sharpest, most detailed, and most colored images. It is a fairly small region, covering only about 2 degrees out of the total oval visual field, which ranges almost 180 degrees horizontally and 125 degrees vertically.

In order to see an object, the eyes converge until the two foveal images are mentally fused. The muscular changes that cause the increased convergence for close objects and decreased convergence for far objects are sensory clues to the distance. In effect, the eyes act as a rangefinder. In addition, the eye lenses change shape to focus images of objects at different distances, providing further sensory clues.

The parallax differences in the two images and the change in eye convergence occur both in viewing real objects and in viewing stereo photographs. However, because each stereo picture has only two dimensions—that is, it is flat and lies in a single plane—the change in focus and eye lens shape occurs only in stereo vision of real objects, not of stereograms.

Principles of Stereo Photography

Stereo photography is the creation of photographic images that, when viewed properly, simulate the parallax images the eyes would see in viewing the original scenes, so that the third dimension is perceived.

Most stereo photography consists of taking pictures from two viewpoints that are as far apart as the two eyes. The pictures can be made either on negative film so that two prints can be made for viewing, or on transparency materials so that two slides can be viewed.

Some arrangement for viewing must permit the eyes to see the two images separately, but in such a way that they can fuse the images into one. The left eye must see the picture taken from the left viewpoint, while the right eye must see the picture taken from the right viewpoint. This is usually done with a stereoscopic viewer, or stereoscope.

Basic Picture Spacing

If each picture is 63.5 mm (2½ inches) wide, or less, the two pictures can be mounted side by side with their centers spaced at the average 63.5 mm interpupillary distance. They can then be viewed through two lenses that permit the eyes to focus them clearly at a close viewing distance. The usual procedure is to use the true perspective principle by providing that the viewing lenses have the same focal length as the camera lenses when the pictures are contact prints or original transparencies. (*See:* PERSPECTIVE.) If the prints or duplicate transparencies are enlarged, the focal length of the viewing lenses is found by this equation:

$$\text{Focal length of viewing lens} =$$
$$\begin{array}{c}\text{Focal length of} \\ \text{camera lens}\end{array} \times \begin{array}{c}\text{Picture} \\ \text{magnification}\end{array}$$

The picture magnification is the enlarging factor, which is found as follows:

$$\begin{array}{c}\text{Picture} \\ \text{magnification}\end{array} = \frac{\text{Print/transparency size}}{\text{Original film (negative) size}}$$

Pictures wider than 63.5 mm can be used for viewing, but their centers will then be farther apart to avoid overlap. (The center spacing of two pictures mounted edge to edge is equal to the width of one image.) The pictures on the stereographs popular in the late nineteenth century were about 76 mm (3 inches) square, and were mounted with their centers that distance apart. These cannot be viewed directly because the eyes cannot diverge to fuse the images. This is overcome by using prismatic viewing lenses; these lenses allow the eyes to be parallel, or to converge slightly—which they can do easily—and still fuse the images. The accompanying diagram shows how this is achieved. Other methods, discussed later, are used when images are even greater than 76 mm in width.

Nonprismatic viewing lenses are used when images are spaced at the standard 63.5 mm (or slightly less to allow some eye convergence). This permits direct viewing and makes it possible to focus the eyes at the distance required for true perspective.

Common Two-Picture Stereo Formats

Most stereo photography has been done with the two-picture arrangement (other methods are discussed in later sections of this article). While any number of formats can be used, a few standard formats have dominated. The two most common in the United States have been the Brewster parlor-size stereo-print format, and the David White color-slide format.

The Brewster format is that of the typical late nineteenth-century stereograph. Two prints about 76 mm (3 inches) square are mounted side by side on a card that is 87 × 178 mm (3⅞" × 7"); the print centers are 76 mm apart. In the period when this format was first used, the tops of the prints were often rounded for reasons of pictorial convention; the shape had nothing to do with creating a stereo effect.

The White stereo-slide format consists of two transparencies in a cardboard, glass, or metal mount measuring 101.6 × 41.3 mm (4" × 1⅝"). The

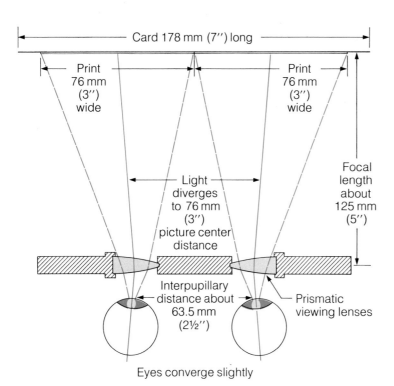

Card 178 mm (7'') long

Print 76 mm (3'') wide

Print 76 mm (3'') wide

Focal length about 125 mm (5'')

Light diverges to 76 mm (3'') picture center distance

Interpupillary distance about 63.5 mm (2½'')

Prismatic viewing lenses

Eyes converge slightly

(Left) The principles of a viewing parlor format stereograph using prismatic lenses are shown in this sketch.

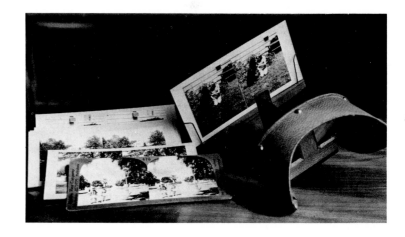

(Right) An old-time stereo viewer with stereographs of the period (now collectors' items). Rounded corners were purely a reflection of contemporary taste. Modern stereographs are seen in the background.

mount apertures are 23 × 24 mm (just under 1 inch each way). The center spacing between the images is 62 mm, slightly less than the interpupillary distance, so that direct, straight-line viewing is possible.

A number of other formats were produced at various times, some of which were popular in Europe but not in the U.S. Each required a matched viewer. A format in widespread use today is that of the Sawyer/GAF Viewmaster system, used for large-scale commercial production of travel pictures, illustrated children's stories, and similar subjects. This format consists of seven stereo pairs of color transparencies mounted on a circular cardboard disc. The images are 12 × 13 mm ($^{15}/_{32}$'' × $^{17}/_{32}$''), and are mounted with a center spacing of about 62 mm for direct, straight-line viewing. The

Stereo Photography

transparencies are produced on 16 mm motion-picture film. Although a camera (the Sawyer Personal) was made and sold at one time for this format, it is not available today. Special equipment is used professionally, or transparencies made on other formats are reduced to 16 mm duplicates during production.

Development of Stereo Cameras

The use of two images to produce stereo effects preceded the invention of photography. The stereoscope (stereo viewer) was invented in England in 1838 by Sir Charles Wheatstone. He had studied the principles of stereo vision, and developed a method of making two stereo drawings that could be viewed in a mirror device to achieve a single 3-D image. Because of reversal in the mirror, each image had to be laterally reversed in its viewing position. An adaptation of Wheatstone's viewer used double mirrors to eliminate the need for image reversal.

When the Talbotype (paper negative) method of photography was announced, Wheatstone had stereo pairs made photographically, probably by shifting the camera position between two exposures of a still-life subject. He also had stereo daguerreotypes made, but these were generally too reflective to be viewed well in his device.

In 1849, Sir David Brewster invented a stereoscope that would view either paper prints or transparencies made on tissue paper (a practical method of glass-plate photography did not appear until 1851, when the collodion wet-plate process was invented). Brewster's stereoscope used lenses of the prismatic type, as described earlier. He also proposed a two-lens stereo camera. The first one was built by J. B. Dancer in 1853, and it established the standard parlor stereo format of the nineteenth century.

As dry plates and sheet films became available, they were used in a variety of cameras for stereo photography. Most such cameras were simply view cameras modified to accept a lens board with two lenses of matched focal length, spaced approximately 63.5 mm apart. A baffle inside the camera divided the interior into two chambers to prevent image overlap.

Eastman Kodak Company pioneered in the use of roll film for stereo photography just after the turn of the century. The earliest models were folding cameras that took six pairs of 89 × 114 mm (3½″ × 4½″) negatives on a roll. There were

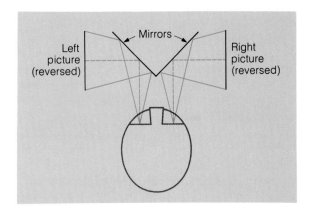

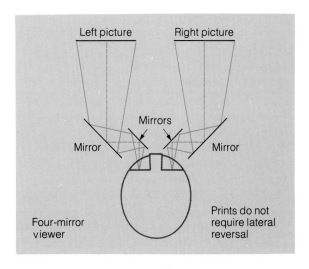

(Top) Wheatstone's original stereo viewer used two mirrors. The images are reversed. (Below) In a four-mirror viewer, the prints do not require lateral reversal.

also stereo Brownie cameras, which were simple two-lens box cameras.

The Rolleidoscope stereo camera, introduced in 1927, took stereo pairs on 120-size roll film. It had a third lens between the two taking lenses, with a mirror and ground glass for reflex viewing and focusing. The first twin-lens reflex planar (2-D) camera, the Rolleiflex, was developed from this popular stereo design.

Although stereo photography on 35 mm film was introduced in 1920 with the Verascope camera, produced by the French firm J. Richard, it was not particularly successful. In large part this was due to poor technical quality—the films and developers of that time did not produce very fine grain or a high degree of sharpness. With the introduction of Kodachrome film in 1936, and a variety of technical advances in materials and equipment during World War II, a successful 35 mm stereo photography system was finally made possible.

In 1947, the David White Company produced the Stereo Realist camera, which revived interest in stereo photography. This system established the White stereo-slide format described earlier. The lens spacing and film-advance mechanism interspersed image pairs in a pattern that made it possible to take 16 pairs of 23 × 24 mm transparencies on a 20-exposure roll of 35 mm film.

The Stereo Realist cameras were precision instruments with two 35 mm $f/3.5$ or $f/2.8$ lenses. The finder lens was placed between the two taking lenses, which eliminated finder parallax. The rangefinder and viewing lenses were placed near the bottom of the camera rather than at the top, and the camera was focused by moving the film plane. A Brewster-type viewer with a built-in illuminator was provided for viewing the mounted transparencies. Stereo projectors were offered later.

The success of the Realist design led to the manufacture of many cameras using the same format—among them, the Stereo Vivid, Videon II, Iloca Stereo, Revere 33 Stereo, and Kodak stereo cameras. These cameras are no longer manufactured, but they may occasionally be found in used-equipment departments and second-hand stores; some have become collector's items among stereo enthusiasts.

The Duplex Super-120 Stereo camera, which is currently available, takes stereo pairs on 120-size film. The images can be mounted in the standard White-stereo format; the method is described in a later section of this article. The inter-lens distance on this camera is somewhat less than the standard 63.5 mm.

Taking Stereo Pictures with Two-Lens Cameras

Conventional exposure and processing methods are used to produce stereo pictures with black-and-white and color films. However, a number of specific procedures will help to produce pictures that are easier to view, that look more natural, and that emphasize the three-dimensional aspect of stereoscopic images.

Camera Angle. The camera should always be laterally level so that the horizon or other horizontal subject lines are horizontal in the images. A slight amount of tilt can be straightened in mounting, but more room is left for proper alignment if the images are straight in the frame to begin with. For special effects the camera can of course be tilted left or right as desired. In addition, it can be aimed at an angle upward or downward. This will result in vertical subject lines converging toward the top or the bottom of the pictures, but this effect is not as objectionable in stereo—which is closer to reality—as it is in planar photography.

The long, textured ground plane serves to carry the stereo vision from the foreground to infinity. Even fine texture suffices to establish distance.

Hypersterno. With stereo cameras that have the standard 63 to 65 mm inter-lens distance, try to have objects at various distances, from as close as 1.5 m (5 feet) to as far away as infinity. Objects closer than about 1.5 m (5 feet) may have an apparent exaggeration of depth called *hyperstereo,* which results from differences in viewing actual scenes and viewing flat images. Objects are regularly viewed as close to the eyes as 254–305 mm (10–12 inches). However, when the eyes are focused at this close distance, backgrounds are blurred so much that their gross displacement by parallax is not seen. Furthermore, human vision seems to provide a relief constant, so that the exaggerated relief of close objects in real life is accepted as normal. In stereo pictures, the backgrounds are not blurred and the exaggerated relief is not readily accepted as seeming normal; both the physiology and the number of reference clues presented are very different in stereo-image viewing.

Hypostereo. Because of the stereo infinity effect, described earlier, objects farther away than about 150 to 300 m (roughly 500 to 1000 feet) will cease to show any stereo characteristics; this is called *hypostereo.* However, if there is a series of objects at various distances up to this point, the maximum three-dimensional effect will be achieved.

In the more general sense, hyperstereo is an increase in stereoscopic effect through an increase in the inter-lens distance beyond that which is normal for the conditions. Hypostereo is just the opposite; it is a decrease in the stereoscopic effect through an effective lessening of the inter-lens distance. Hypersterno makes objects look smaller than life-size, while hypostereo increases their apparent size.

Too great a range of object distances—for example, objects at about 1 to 1.2 m (3 to 4 feet) and objects at infinity—will produce a picture that is almost impossible to view because of excessive differences in parallax. For distant views such as landscapes, try to have at least one object in the foreground, approximately 6 to 15 m (20 to 50 feet) away to give a sense of distance. Use the depth clues discussed in the article PERSPECTIVE to emphasize the distances, especially those at distances greater than stereo infinity. Backlighting is especially effective.

Sharpness. It is usually desirable to have all subjects sharp in stereo pictures. When viewing a subject in real life, the eyes move from point to point; they move left and right, up and down, change convergence depending on the distance of each point, and change lens shape to focus each object with clarity. When viewing stereo pictures, the eyes perform all the same movements, *except that they do not change focus* because all of the stereo picture is at the same distance.

However, if there is an out-of-focus object in the picture, the eyes will try to focus it but will be unable to do so. This may create a discomfort that undermines the illusion of reality and thus makes the picture unsatisfactory. Hence, the aim is to have the entire picture sharp when possible. The use of normal or slightly shorter-focal-length lenses and of small apertures will improve sharpness by increasing

Views like this of the Grand Canyon encompass distances greater than stereo infinity; depth can only be suggested by depth clues. Including foreground objects adds real stereo feeling to the scene.

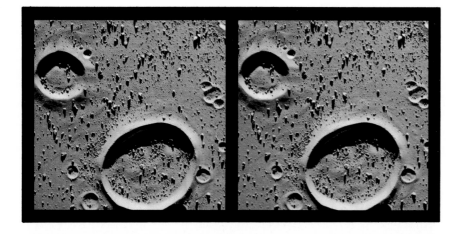

In aerial photos, the interocular distance must be increased considerably if ground detail is to show any depth. Photograph is of a model of the moon.

People make effective subjects for stereo pictures; the reality is increased by adding a third dimension that appears natural.

depth of field. This is a major reason why 35 mm cameras with 35 mm focal-length lenses are often preferred for stereo photography.

There are two exceptions to the need for great depth of field. One is when a plain background without detail is used; this might be a clear, blue sky outdoors, or a plain studio background for a portrait or still-life setup. Because there is no detail, the background can be left out of focus without that fact becoming noticeable.

The other exception is the sharpness of the subject in a portrait. Diffusers can be used over the lenses to slightly soften the sharpness of the subject without causing the eye strain problem. With many portrait subjects, such treatment is flattering; it may also be effective with fashion, glamour, "mood," and similar kinds of pictures. However, generally speaking, portraits are difficult to do in stereo. Full-length figures at distances of 3 m (10 feet) or more are

effective. To get close-up portraits, it is usually necessary to photograph about 1 m (3 feet) from the subject, but at that distance the third dimension is grossly exaggerated. A pair of telephoto afocal converters that attach in front of the camera lenses is very useful; then the head and shoulders will fill the frame at about 2 to 2.4 m (6 to 8 feet), a distance at which the third dimension appears natural.

Wide-angle converters are equally useful stereo devices, but for different reasons. Besides their obvious use to cover greater angles both indoors and out, the depth of field at a given lens aperture is greater than it is with a normal lens.

Taking Pictures with One-Lens Cameras

Various devices are available that make it easy to take two successive pictures with a regular camera from viewpoints 63.5 mm (2½ inches) apart in order to obtain stereo pairs. A manufactured device, the Radex Stereo Parallel accessory, is used atop a tripod. It has a system of levers that quickly position a camera at two points the proper distance apart for successive pictures.

A guide tray can be made to fit on a tripod. A rail at the front holds the camera pointed in the same direction for each picture, so there is no twisting as the camera is shifted. It can be made just long enough and with stops at each end to allow the lens to move 63.5 mm between pictures. However, it is more useful to make it longer and mount a scale on the rail so that various inter-lens distances can be used as required.

A disadvantage of such devices is the time interval between exposures while the camera is being shifted. Moving subjects cannot be photographed;

even a breeze blowing the branches of trees, or the slight movement of a living subject, can cause differences in the two images that will spoil the stereo effect. Two-lens cameras with synchronized shutters do not suffer from this problem.

Two identical cameras can be mounted together on a frame to make a stereo setup. It is important to align the lenses on the same level and to space their centers about 63.5 mm, if normal-focal-length lenses are used. The cameras can be mounted vertically, base to base, or with one camera upside down if that accomplishes the purpose; but proper alignment of the lenses is critical.

Cameras using 126-size film can be used to make slides that crop easily to the 23 × 24 mm standard stereo-slide format. Full-frame 35 mm

(Near right) The tray-type camera holder can be used to make stereo pairs of still objects with a single camera. The scale allows control of inter-lens distance for close and far subjects. (Far right) Another method of making stereo images involves mounting two cameras together. A certain amount of practice is needed when tripping shutters simultaneously to capture moving objects. (Below) A Kodak stereo camera of the 1950's offered photographers a pair of 23 × 24 mm (⅞″ × ¹⁵⁄₁₆″) frames. The mounted pair was shown in the viewer at the camera's right, which was offered in battery-operated and 120-volt models.

cameras can also be used for slides, but considerable cropping is necessary. Any of the common roll-film sizes, such as 6 × 6 cm (2¼″ × 2¼″), can be used to take color or black-and-white negatives. Standard 3S and 3R size color prints from processing labs are 89 mm (3½ inches) wide. They can easily be trimmed to 76 mm (3 inches) square and mounted on Brewster format cards for viewing in any parlor-stereo viewer that may be available.

Various mirror devices have been made to present two side-by-side images within the standard frame area of any size camera. There is at least one such device available today. With 35 mm cameras, it makes two images about 24 × 17 mm, but some overlap between the two images reduces the effective picture width. Similar devices can be made using thin, front-surface mirrors for use with any camera, even instant-picture models.

Inter-Lens Distance

Changing the Inter-Lens Distance for Close-ups. While it is true that human beings see the world at a constant 63.5 mm (2½-inch) interpupillary distance, that is not always the best inter-lens

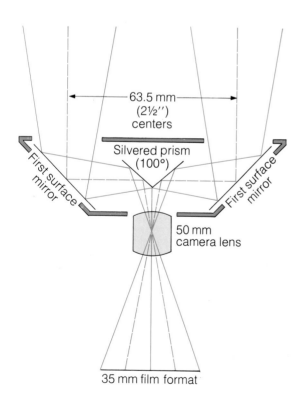

distance for taking stereo pictures. When taking close-ups, for instance, it is far too great—the pictures have such parallax that it is nearly impossible to view them—and when the images are fused, the third dimension is grossly exaggerated. In addition, the effective background is also much closer than normal in close-ups. At the usual inter-lens distance, parallax is so great that the left and right lenses record significantly different portions of the background, severely reducing the common area and thus the usable picture width.

These problems can be overcome, and very acceptable close-up pictures can be taken, if the inter-lens distance is reduced. This is readily accomplished when taking successive pictures with a one-lens camera by adjusting the distance the lens is moved. The tray device described in the previous section is a very useful accessory for taking such pictures. Some two-lens stereo cameras have a coupling system that permits firing each shutter individually, rather than together, if desired. This makes it easy to shift the camera position between exposures with the left and the right lens.

Two-camera setups can be used for stereo close-ups if the inter-lens distance can be reduced sufficiently. Moving subjects can be photographed if both shutter releases can be reached simultaneously with the fingers of one hand, or if a coupling device such as a pressure bar can be improvised. Pocket cameras using 110-size film are particularly easy to mount together at close distances because of their small size. When mounted base to base, inter-lens distances as small as 25 mm (1 inch) can be obtained with some models. This is appropriate for subjects about 500 mm (20 inches) from the cameras. Plus-2 diopter supplementary lenses can be used to focus a fixed-lens camera at this distance.

Determining Inter-Lens Distance. As a general rule, the proper inter-lens distance for stereo close-ups taken with normal-focal-length lenses can be found by this equation:

$$\text{Inter-lens distance} = \frac{\text{Object distance}}{20}$$

Therefore, if a subject is being photographed about 600 mm (23½ inches) away, the two successive lens

The mirror device shown can create a split-frame stereo pair on a standard 24 × 36 mm 35 mm film. The system can also be used on other formats.

Stereo Photography

positions should be $600 \div 20 = 30$ mm ($1\frac{3}{16}$ inches) apart.

A more exact equation, for use when there are a number of objects at various close distances, is:

Close-up inter-lens distance =

$$\frac{\left(\dfrac{F - N}{3} + N\right) \times V}{24 \times C}$$

where F is the far object distance, N is the near object distance, V is the viewer lens factor, and C is the camera lens factor. All measurements must be in the same units. The two lens factors are:

$$\text{Camera lens factor} = \frac{\text{Focal length used for picture}}{\text{Normal focal length for format}}$$

$$\text{Viewer lens factor} = \frac{\text{Viewer lens focal length}}{\text{Focal length used for picture}}$$

Obviously, when the focal length used for the picture and the viewer-lens focal length are normal for the format being used, these factors are both one.

The following example illustrates the use of this equation:

Near object distance:	600 mm
Far object distance:	900 mm
Normal focal length for format:	35 mm
Focal length to be used for picture:	50 mm
Viewer lens focal length:	40 mm

Camera lens factor = $50 \div 35 = 1.43$
Viewer lens factor = $40 \div 35 = 1.14$

$$\begin{aligned}
\text{Inter-lens distance} &= \frac{\left(\dfrac{900 - 600}{3} + 600\right) \times 1.14}{24 \times 1.43} \\[2mm]
&= \frac{(100 + 600) \times 1.14}{34.3} \\[2mm]
&= \frac{700 \times 1.14}{34.3} = \frac{798}{34.3} \\[2mm]
&= 23.3 \text{ mm } (0.92, \text{or } {}^{15}\!/_{16} \text{ inch})
\end{aligned}$$

Inter-Lens Distances for Far Subjects. With objects at greater-than-normal distances, it is best to increase the inter-lens distance in taking stereo pairs.

Although objects beyond stereo infinity do not show any relief when viewed stereoscopically, stereo infinity increases as the inter-lens distance is increased. Therefore, excellent stereo relief of objects at great distances can be obtained by using an appropriately greater inter-lens distance.

The standard separation of 63.5 mm provides some stereo relief at distances of up to about 150–210 m (500–700 feet) when there are closer objects at various distances as well. When all of the subject is at a considerable distance, the accompanying graph shows suggested inter-lens distances when the camera is used at eye-level.

The lower shaded portion of the graph shows a range of inter-lens distances at which various degrees of acceptable stereo relief will be obtained. For example, when the closest object is 6.2 m (20 feet), inter-lens distances from the standard 63.5 mm (2½ inches) to about 178 mm (7 inches) can be used for acceptable results. As indicated, the graph is drawn for lenses of normal focal length. When using telephoto lenses, divide the inter-lens distance shown on the graph by the camera lens factor (Telephoto focal length ÷ Normal focal length). It is important in taking distant views with increased inter-lens distances to avoid close foreground elements; in many cases the pictures will exhibit such excessive hyperstereo that they cannot be fused into a single image.

The upper shaded portion of the graph shows how the distance to stereo infinity increases with the additional inter-lens distance. For example, if the closest object is 30 m (about 100 feet), and the inter-lens distance is 380 mm (15 inches), the distance to stereo infinity becomes almost 1 mile.

When taking stereo pictures downward, as from a mountain or a very tall building, there is no foreground or middle-distance detail. As a result, all ground detail at the subject plane is likely to show no relief unless hyperstereo is used. This can be achieved by increasing the inter-lens distance more than would be appropriate in an eye-level situation. The following equation can be used to calculate the inter-lens distance for various degrees of stereo relief in downward-angle pictures:

$$\text{Inter-lens distance} = \frac{\text{Distance to closest ground detail}}{\text{Hyperstereo factor}} \times \frac{}{\text{Camera lens factor}}$$

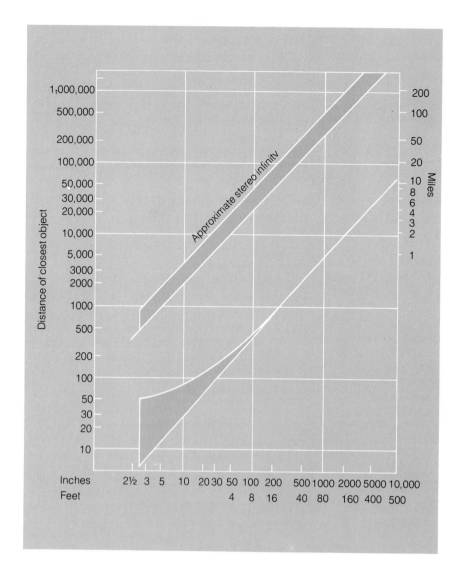

Given in this graph are suggested inter-lens distances for far distant subjects.

HYPERSTEREO FACTORS

Degree of Hyperstereo	Approximate Inter-Lens Angle*	Hyperstereo Factor
Moderately low	5	10.0
Moderate	10	5.0
Moderately high	20	3.0
High	30	2.0
Very high	40	1.5

*The normal minimum stereo angle is about 3 degrees, which is equivalent to the angle established by a 63.5 mm (2½-inch) inter-lens distance at a subject distance of 1200 mm (48 inches).

Example: Distance to closest ground detail: 914 m (3000 feet); degree of hyperstereo: moderate; lens focal length: 105 mm; normal lens focal length: 35 mm.

Camera lens factor $= 105 \div 35 = 3$

Inter-lens distance $= \dfrac{914}{5 \times 3} = 61$ m (200 ft)

As this example shows, when the entire subject is a great distance away, a very large inter-lens distance is required to produce a satisfactory stereo effect. Taking pictures of such a subject with a single-lens camera is usually satisfactory because visible movement of the subject is undetectable at great

Stereo Photography

distances, except perhaps for clouds. If clouds are moving rapidly, the only way to achieve success in photographing them is to have two cameras with matched lenses and radio-controlled shutter releases, or two photographers communicating by portable radios. By whatever means the two views are taken, the subject must be framed by eye, and the edges of the pictures should be matched to the same close-distance part of the subject rather than to a far-distance part.

Stereo Micrographs

Stereo pictures can be taken through a microscope, using the basic techniques described in the article PHOTOMICROGRAPHY. With monocular microscopes, two techniques are used to obtain stereo pictures. One displaces the subject slide laterally; the other displaces it with rotary or tilt movement.

For lateral displacement, a guide bar is clamped to the stage to provide one-directional movement. An alternative is a movable stage with two-directional controls. The stages of micrometer microscopes are ideal, because the lateral displacement can be controlled both directionally and in degree by the micrometer controls. The required amount of lateral movement depends on the subject depth and the degree of magnification, so success becomes a trial-and-error matter. It is often a time-saving procedure to use "stereo bracketing" by taking a series of exposures at various lateral displacements. The pair that best exhibits the desired degree of stereo effect can be chosen by comparative inspection after processing.

Tilt- or rotary-displacement stages have been made that rotate the slide in its surface plane by screw controls. A good starting angular displacement is 5 degrees—2½ degrees left and 2½ degrees right.

The best subjects for stereo photomicrography are those viewed by reflected light. Except for crystals, most subjects that are thin enough for transmitted-light photography are so thin that they exhibit little relief in stereo.

There are various kinds of binocular microscopes. A true stereo microscope consists of two monocular microscopes mounted together at an angle that superimposes their fields in the plane of focus. Each of the two eyepieces can be fitted with a camera, as in conventional photomicrography, and

simultaneous pictures can be taken. This is the only way living subjects such as tiny insects can be photographed in stereo.

Mounting Stereo Pictures

Once stereo-pair images have been made, the key to satisfactory viewing lies in mounting them correctly and accurately. Because lenses invert the image, stereo pairs made on a single piece of film or plate are transposed right for left, as shown in the accompanying diagram. This must be corrected when transparencies are mounted or prints are made. In the case of prints it is a simple matter to cut out the images, trim them, and mount them in correct relationship. If the images are printed onto a single piece of paper to avoid cutting, the print paper as well as the negatives must be shifted between exposures.

Stereo viewing is like looking at a scene through a window. The edges of the image act as the window frame, and the relationship of objects in the picture to the edges is all-important. In nearly all cases, the pictures are trimmed and aligned so that the window appears to be the same distance from the viewer as

Because lenses invert the image, stereo pairs on a single piece of film are transposed right for left.

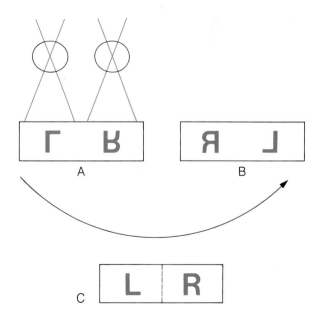

the closest object, and all other objects appear to be "through," or farther away than the window frame. In some rare instances—mostly for effect—a single object will be allowed to appear closer than the apparent window. Or, when only distant objects are included in the picture, the pairs may be mounted slightly farther apart than usual so that the window appears closer than the closest object, to harmonize with the sense of great distance.

A common method is to make all measurements and trimming decisions in terms of the left image, and to trim and mount the right image to match. The first step is to trim the tops and bottoms accurately, and parallel to the horizontal elements or the horizon line in the picture.

The vertical size is not as critical as the horizontal size of the images. If important subject matter would otherwise be lost, the height can be a little greater than normal for the format; on the other hand, if the composition will be improved, the vertical dimension can be less than normal. In the case

of transparencies, the cropping is usually determined by shifting the image within the precut mount opening. With prints, it can be determined by using strips of paper or a cropping mask. The left print should be marked and trimmed, using a razor blade and steel ruler, with the print supported on a piece of scrap cardboard to insure cleanly cut edges.

To match the vertical trimming of the right image, use a magnifying glass and a finely divided ruler to measure the distances of several objects from the top and bottom edges in the trimmed left print. Transfer these measurements with pin pricks onto the right image print, and trim it accurately.

The width of the images can be less than the required center-to-center distance for the format in use, but not more, or the images will overlap. Working with the left image, tentatively decide where the side edges should be, using masking strips. Identify the closest object in the images, and in the left print measure the distance from some easily identified point in the object to the left edge. Trim the print to

The two-camera arrangement shown on page 2333 was used to make this pair on negative film. The 3S prints were mounted on a 3½" × 7" card for viewing in a Brewster-type stereoscope.

Stereo Photography

that distance, making sure that the side is at accurate right angles with the top and bottom edges. Do the same to establish the right edge of the image, making sure that it is both vertical and not too wide for the mounting format.

Transfer the left-edge measurements to the right image print, using the magnifying glass and ruler, and trim it accurately. Then trim the right print to exactly the same width as the left print. If there is not enough image in the right picture, trim the right edge of both pictures the same amount. The background detail at the edges of the two pictures will almost always be slightly different—the left picture shows more detail on the right side, while the right picture shows more detail on the left side.

NOTE: The critical factor is having the nearest object *exactly* the same distance from the left edge in both pictures. That is what places the "window" at the same apparent distance when the pictures are viewed.

After the prints are trimmed, mount them on heavy card stock with a dark gray or black surface. Center the prints vertically and horizontally on the card. If the prints are the same width as the required center-to-center separation for proper viewing, their center edges will touch. If they are narrower, there will be a space between them. In any event, they must be mounted so that the distance between any two corresponding points—left edges, central object, centers, or right edges—is exactly the proper interpupillary distance.

To make an object appear in front of the viewing window, choose an object slightly behind it to establish the left-edge and interpupillary spacings. If all objects are at a great distance, use the nearest object to establish a greater-than-normal spacing so that everything will appear to be located behind the window frame.

Prints can be mounted with a good adhesive, or with dry mounting tissue. Transparencies are mounted in masks according to the same principles. However, the mount openings are precut and alignment is established by moving the transparencies around in the mask before taping them in place. Masks with narrower openings are available for mounting close-up pictures taken with two-lens stereo cameras. In this kind of image pair, the image

will not fill the openings of a standard stereo-slide mount.

Whatever the format, the principles are the same:

1. Find the picture center distance.
2. Place the images level and equal distances from the top and bottom edges.
3. Place the closest objects so they will be equal to the required center-to-center spacing.

Other Methods of Viewing Two-Picture Stereo

The basic principle of stereo viewing is that the left eye should see the picture taken by the left camera lens, and the right eye should see the picture taken by the right camera lens (or position). Viewers using straight-line and prismatic lenses and various mirror arrangements have already been described. Lens-type viewers are standard, but there are other ways in which the eyes can receive separate image impressions.

Anaglyphs. The anaglyph system superimposes the two images and uses color separation to insure that each eye sees only the proper image. Black-and-white negatives are used to make the prints. One image is printed in cyan (blue-green), and the other in magenta (reddish-blue); they are printed or projected with a great degree of overlap and are viewed through "glasses," with which one eye sees through a strong red filter, and the other eye sees through a strong green filter.

The red filter causes the white background to appear red, and the magenta image blends into it so that it cannot be seen. However, the red filter causes the cyan image to appear black, so that it is seen with maximum contrast. Similarly, the green filter causes the cyan image to remain invisible against a green background, but makes the magenta image appear a strong black. In this way, each eye sees a different image, and the brain combines them to produce the perception of three dimensions. The anaglyph principle has been used for book and magazine illustrations, and for a number of motion pictures. It has the disadvantage that without proper glasses, the image is a meaningless garble in which neither image can be clearly distinguished.

Vectographs. A system similar to that of the anaglyph was developed by the Polaroid Corporation, but it used the crossed-polarizer principle of viewing, rather than that of color separation. Vectographs were made from black-and-white stereo negatives. Each image was printed on a dye-transfer matrix in order to deposit a dye that crystallized into a polarized image on a special base material. The base material caused the transferred images to be polarized in directions at 90 degrees to one another. When viewed with polarizing glasses in which the lenses had a corresponding 90-degree difference, the left eye could see only one image, and the right eye could see only the other. Vectographs were used for the most part in medical and military applications.

Stereo Projection. Special projectors have been made to project standard stereo slides. They have two bulbs, two condenser systems, and two projection lenses. The lenses are mounted so that the distance between them and their vertical alignment can be adjusted. There is a polarizing filter in each light path arranged so that their angles of polarization are at 90 degrees to one another. The two images are projected on a metallic-surface screen and are aligned using the lens adjustments.

The projected images are viewed with polarizing glasses that have filters in 90-degree opposition, just as in viewing a Vectograph. The metallic screen surface is necessary because only metal will not depolarize the light it reflects. Aluminum-painted screens are satisfactory, but a screen such as the Kodak Ektalite is preferred because of its high levels of reflectivity. This is a distinct necessity, because the polarizers in the projection system reduce the image brightness by an average factor of $2.5\times$.

If the slides have been taken and mounted with the proper inter-lens distances, the proper distance from the screen for viewing natural-appearing stereo relief is equal to the diagonal of the projected screen image. This distance can easily be achieved when a small group is viewing the slides. With a larger group, most people will have to view from a greater-than-optimum distance, with the result that the stereo effect will appear exaggerated.

Stereo pairs taken with two cameras can be projected in the same way, using two ordinary projectors equipped with properly oriented polarizers in front of their lenses. The screen must have a metallic surface, and appropriate polarized viewing glasses must be used.

Motion-Picture Stereo. The polarizing system of projection has been used for 3-D motion pictures. It has an advantage over the anaglyph system in permitting images to be seen in full color. In the most common system, a mirror attachment is used in front of the camera lens to record two images in the frame. A similar device (or a divided lens) and polarizers are used at the projector to throw two images on the screen. They are viewed through polarizing glasses.

Although both motion- and still-projected stereo images have enjoyed brief popularity from time to time, they have three major drawbacks:

1. Image mounting and projector-screen alignment must be precise.
2. The viewer must maintain a constant position for maximum effect from any given viewing position.
3. Each viewer must wear a suitable pair of glasses.

Generally speaking, the limitations are more trouble than the 3-D effect is worth.

Free Viewing of Illustrations
Many stereo illustrations are printed with a center spacing of 60–65 mm (about 2½ inches). With practice, it is possible to learn to see these illustrations in 3-D without a viewer. However, a simple viewer makes them easier to see.

When focused on distant objects, the eyes have nearly parallel axes of vision; when focused on close objects, the axes converge. The free viewer learns to keep the eyes nearly parallel while focusing on images held about 300 mm (12 inches) away. If the pictures are held perpendicular to the line of sight, and squarely in front of the face, each eye can see only its "own side" image, and the brain can fuse them for a stereo effect. Sometimes a piece of cardboard held between the eyes to block crossover viewing helps to develop the knack of free viewing.

The accompanying diagram shows how to make a small viewer that will simplify the viewing of printed stereo images. Four small +5 supplementary lenses are required. They are mounted in pairs, with their concave sides facing one another, to form two magnifying lenses of about 100 mm focal length. A frame to hold them can be cut from a small piece of wood, or it may be possible to tape them into a cardboard frame. Their centers should have the standard spacing of 63.5 mm. When held in front of the eyes, the viewer focuses the images with the eyes parallel, as if viewing an object at infinity.

Bar-Type Stereo

Special two-picture, large-size stereo transparencies can be made on a single plate or film through a bar-type grid. The grid consists of alternate opaque lines and transparent spaces. It is mounted about 12 mm (½ inch) in front of the image plane in a large view camera that has a long-focal-length lens with a diameter greater than 50 mm (2 inches). A special diaphragm with two small holes in it is located behind the lens. When a picture is taken through this arrangement, the bar screen causes the two images to be recorded on the film in alternating strips from each diaphragm aperture. The geometry of the system insures that the alternate image strips do not overlap.

After the transparency is processed, it is placed on an illuminator, and a bar screen is placed in front of it with the same orientation as in the camera. When the eyes are placed at a distance equal to the diaphragm-to-film distance (or a multiple of that distance equal to the degree of image enlargement), the eyes see the two images separately and they are fused into a stereo relief image.

A simple viewer for free-viewing stereo pairs is easily made. Details are given in the text.

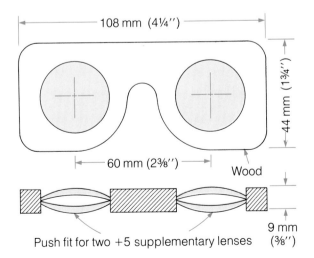

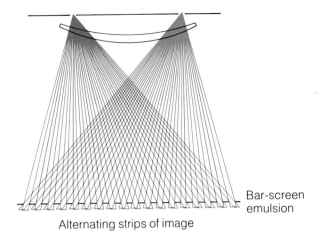

Alternating strips of image

Bar-screen emulsion

This diagram illustrates the geometry of the bar-type grid used to make large-size stereo images on a single plate or film. The design of the system assures that the alternate image strips do not overlap.

Lenticular Stereo

A similar principle is employed in lenticular stereo, but with greatly improved results. Instead of a bar grid, a lenticular screen is placed in contact with the emulsion, both in the camera and in the viewing arrangement. The lenticules of the screen are long, cylindrical lenses molded in transparent plastic. Each lenticule forms long, narrow images of the apertures behind the lens. If only two apertures are used, the transparency can be viewed from only one position. However, if multiple apertures are used, a stereo image can be seen from a number of viewing positions.

A variation of this process employs a moving lens to scan the scene in front of the camera while the exposure is being made. This provides a continuous image behind the lenticules.

These methods have been used to make stereo images for reproduction by halftone printing methods with lenticular screens embossed in a thin plastic coating. Magazine and book covers, postcards, advertising displays, and a variety of novelty items have been produced in this manner, all showing 3-D images. (*See:* Lenticular Systems.)

Aerial Stereo Photography

Most maps are now made from aerial stereo photographs. The procedure is called *photogramme-*

Stereo Photography

2341

try. The aerial camera is aimed straight down and pictures are taken at intervals so that they overlap about 60 percent of their width. Glass or film positives are made from the negatives, and the overlapping areas are viewed in a stereo plotter. By following a greatly enlarged hyperstereo image of the terrain, contour lines of ground height can be drawn, along with the shapes of features of interest.

Another use of aerial stereo photography is in reconnaissance work. A plane is equipped with two strip cameras: one aimed down and forward, and the other aimed down and backward. A strip camera makes a long, continuous exposure through a fixed slit that is similar to the opening in a focal-plane shutter. The film moves behind the slit at a rate proportional to the plane's ground speed. The result is a continuous, unblurred picture of the ground below, with every point recorded from exactly the same angle. The same principle is used to photograph the completion of races. (*See:* PHOTO-FINISH PHOTOGRAPHY.)

The plane makes a pass over an area of interest, exposing a roll of film in each camera. When the film is processed, continuous hyperstereo views, with an enormous amount of three-dimensional detail, are obtained. The films are viewed by polarized stereo projection.

Other Applications

Stereo photography is not confined to conventional materials and techniques. Stereo radiographs can be obtained by using x-rays or other wavelengths to penetrate materials for separate views from two appropriately separated angles. By proper selection of energy levels and focus, stereographs can be obtained at any desired distance within a living subject or industrial sample. These techniques produce highly valuable information for medical diagnosis and treatment, quality control, flaw detection, and similar purposes.

• *See also:* LENTICULAR SYSTEMS; PERSPECTIVE; PHOTO-FINISH PHOTOGRAPHY; PHOTOGRAMMETRY; PHOTOMICROGRAPHY.

Further Reading: Darrah, William C. and Richard Russack. *An Album of Stereographs, or, Our Country Victorious and Now a Happy Home.* Garden City, NY: Doubleday & Co., 1977; Hubbard, Geoffrey. *Cooke and Wheatstone and The Invention of the Electric Telegraph.* Fairfield, NJ: Augustus M. Kelley Publishers, 1965; Jones, John. *Wonders of the Stereoscope.* New York, NY: Alfred A. Knopf, 1976; Okoshi, T. *Three-Dimensional Imaginary Techniques.* New York, NY: Academy Press, 1976; Valyus, N.A. *Stereoscopy.* Belmont, CA: Pitman Publishing Corp.

 ## Stop Bath

A stop bath is a weak acid rinse used between the developer and the fixer in black-and-white film and print processing. A plain water rinse is used instead of a stop bath in most color film processing. A stop bath may or may not be used in color print processing, depending on the chemical solutions used and the processing method. It is important to check color processing instructions carefully on this point.

The primary reasons for using an acid rinse or stop bath between development and fixing are to check development instantaneously by neutralizing the developer carried over, and to maintain fixing bath acidity and capacity. The capacity figures given for fixers usually apply only when a stop bath is used. An acid stop bath also minimizes the formation of dichroic fog, removes calcium scum that may have formed in the developer, and tends to prevent the formation of alum scum and sludge in the fixing bath. The use of a hardening stop bath is desirable in developing films and plates in very hot weather, because such a bath prevents excessive swelling of the gelatin and protects the softened emulsion.

The use of a stop bath is particularly recommended with paper prints, which often tend to stain when transferred directly from the developer to the fixing bath without thorough agitation in the fixer.

Composition of a Stop Bath

A stop bath is a simple solution of an acid or an acidic compound in water. Acetic acid is almost universally used, although citric acid or potassium metabisulfite may be substituted in equal concentration. Generally, a fresh acetic-acid stop bath has a pH of approximately 3.5; a used or exhausted bath, a pH of about 5.5.

Prepared stop-bath concentrates may be purchased. These usually incorporate an indicator chemical that gives the diluted solution a yellowish tint when fresh, but turns a deep purple when the acidity is exhausted. Under a printing safelight, the solution in a tray will look either colorless or black. It is usually not convenient to include an indicator when mixing a stop bath from a formula; however, the bath can be tested from time to time, as described in a later section of this article.

Some formulas include other chemicals to help protect film emulsions during unusual processing. The most common are potassium chrome alum, which toughens ("hardens") gelatin, and sodium sulfate, which retards undue swelling.

Using a Stop Bath

The film or print is lifted from the developer and drained (or the developer is poured out of the tank) and is immersed immediately in the stop bath. The stop bath should be the same temperature as the developer in order to avoid reticulation or distortion of film emulsions. With constant agitation, the stop-bath action is complete in 15 to 30 seconds. The material is then drained and transferred directly to the fixer.

Stop-Bath Formulas

Most stop-bath formulas call for 28 percent acetic acid. The acid may be purchased in this strength, or as 99 percent (glacial) acid. It is a simple matter to prepare the weaker solution from the glacial concentration:

28% (approx.) acetic acid
Glacial acetic acid	3 parts
Water	8 parts

Pour the acid slowly into the water while stirring. Handle the glacial acid with care; it can cause burns.

Kodak stop bath SB-1
Water	1 litre
28% Acetic acid	48 ml

This is a general-purpose stop bath. Rinse films for 15 to 20 seconds, or prints for 5 to 10 seconds, with agitation.

Kodak stop bath SB-1a
Water	1 litre
28% Acetic acid	125 ml

This bath is recommended for use after highly alkaline developers, such as those employed with line materials.

Kodak hardening bath SB-4

This solution is recommended for use in conjunction with developers containing sodium sulfate.

(*See:* HIGH-TEMPERATURE PROCESSING.) It is used at temperatures above 24 C (75 F).

Water	1 litre
Potassium chrome alum crystals (dodecahydrated)	30 g
Sodium sulfate (anhydrous)* . . .	60.0 g

Agitate the negatives for 30 to 45 seconds when they are first immersed in the hardener, or streakiness will result. Leave them in the bath for at least 3 minutes between development and fixing. If the temperature is below 29.5 C (85 F), rinse the negatives for 1 to 2 seconds in water before immersing them in the hardener bath.

The hardening bath is a violet-blue color by tungsten light when freshly mixed, but it ultimately turns a yellow-green with use; it then ceases to harden and should be replaced with a fresh bath. The hardening bath should never be overworked. An unused bath will keep indefinitely, but the hardening power of a partially used bath decreases rapidly on standing for a few days.

Kodak stop bath SB-5
Water	500 ml
28% Acetic acid	32 ml
Sodium sulfate (anhydrous)* . . .	45 g
Water to make	1 litre

This is a nonhardening bath for use up to 26.5 C (80 F). Treat the films or plates in this bath for about 30 seconds with agitation at 18.5 to 21 C (65 to 70 F) between developing and fixing. This bath should be replaced after approximately 13 rolls have been processed per litre (quart).

Kodak stop bath SB-5a

For photofinishing, use double the above quantities of 28 percent acetic acid.

Testing Stop Baths

Kodak test solution SBT-1 for print stop baths provides a quick and accurate method for determining when such a bath should be revived or discarded. An acid stop bath or fixing bath should not be overworked, since the use of an exhausted bath fre-

---

*If crystalline sodium sulfate is preferred to the anhydrous form, use 2¼ times the quantity listed.

quently leads to stains and markings in the prints. When produced by a fixing bath, such stains show up only after a period of time.

Since the appearance of an acid stop bath without an indicator changes very little during its useful life, some means of determining when it is unfit for further use should be employed. This solution permits a quick check on the acidity of the stop bath.

Kodak stop bath test solution, SBT-1

Water (distilled or demineralized)
   at 26.5 C (80 F) .... 750 ml
Sodium hydroxide .... 6 g
With stirring add:
   Bromocresol purple
   (*Eastman* organic chemical
   No. 745) .... 4 g
Mix for 15 to 20 minutes; then
   add phosphoric acid (86%) ... 3 ml
Water to make .... 1 litre

CAUTION: The stop-bath test solution contains chemicals that can be hazardous. Sodium hydroxide is caustic and is capable of causing severe burns in all tissues. Special care should be taken to prevent contact with skin or eyes. A face shield or goggles should be used when handling the solid compound. Phosphoric acid is a strong, nonvolatile inorganic acid. It is corrosive to tissue and can cause severe skin or eye burns. Impervious gloves and goggles should be worn when handling the concentrated solution. In case of contact with either of these chemicals, immediately flush affected areas with plenty of water; for eyes, get prompt medical attention.

How to Test a Print Stop Bath. Fill a clean, empty 30 ml (1 oz) vial about three-quarters full

with the acid stop bath. To this add two drops of the SBT-1 solution. An acid stop bath that is still useful will remain yellow. When the acid has been neutralized, the bath will turn purple.

Under a light amber safelight, the yellow color is not noticeable, but the purple color appears dark.

The SBT-1 test solution can also be added to the tray containing the stop bath. Add the test solution directly to the stop bath, while stirring, as recommended in the accompanying table.

Again, if the liquid darkens under safelight illumination or turns a light purple in room light, the bath is exhausted and should be discarded. Prints should not remain in the stop bath containing the test solution much longer than 2 minutes; otherwise, slight yellow stains may result.

• *See also:* DEVELOPERS AND DEVELOPING; FIXERS AND FIXING; FORMULAS FOR BLACK-AND-WHITE PROCESSING; HIGH-TEMPERATURE PROCESSING.

Stop-Motion Photography

Stop-motion cinematography consists of photographing an inanimate object a frame at a time with a motion-picture camera, moving the object a small amount between frames, so as to give the effect that the object is moving of its own volition. Thus, in television commercials, product packages may move to or from the camera, rotate to show the back of the label, or, in more fanciful productions, fly off into space like rockets.

The equipment for stop-motion cinematography is a standard motion-picture camera that is fitted with a motor and clutch to allow exposure of single frames at absolutely uniform speed. Cameras

RATIO OF TEST SOLUTION TO STOP BATH						
Solution	Metric			U.S. Liquid		
Acid stop bath	1 litre	2 litres	4 litres	1 qt	2 qt	1 gal
SBT-1	1 ml	2 ml	4 ml	20 drops	40 drops	80 drops

having spring motors often have a single-frame release, but they do not run at accurately governed speeds when used in this mode, and the result is usually a severe flicker in the finished film.

In addition to the motor and clutch, the camera should have a device permitting accurate focusing through the lens at any time without fogging the film. A very sturdy tripod camera stand is an absolute essential; the camera must not accidentally move in the middle of a sequence, or the entire job will have to be done over.

Exposure

A motion-picture camera with a 170-degree shutter, running at 24 frames per second, will have an exposure of 1/50 sec. per frame. However, for stop-motion work, the camera is usually run at a much slower rate; a 24-frame speed would put a great strain on the clutch and possibly damage the camera because of the repeated starting and stopping. Stop-motion and animation are commonly done with the same type of clutch, and its speed is generally around 4 frames per second if it is allowed to run steadily. Thus, with a 170-degree shutter, the exposure per frame will be about 1/8 sec., and either the light on the set may be greatly reduced, or the camera shutter may be used at a smaller opening if the light cannot be reduced. This, of course, can be done only with cameras having shutters that can be adjusted to different angles; in this case, reducing the shutter angle to, say, 30 degrees will give an exposure of 1/48 sec., just about the same as a camera with a 170-degree shutter at 24 frames per second.

Timing

It requires only a little simple arithmetic to determine the amount of movement to be given the subject in order to get a desired rate of speed on the screen. Suppose that a toy automobile is to cross the screen (hence the area of action being photographed) in 5 seconds. Assume that the size of the car demands that it be photographed from such a distance that the width of the camera field is just 4 feet. At 24 frames per second, 5 seconds of screen time is 120 frames of film. Then, the car must go 4 feet in 120 frames, or 1 foot in 30 frames, which means it must move $2/5$ of an inch in each frame. If the car crosses the field at a steady speed, this is all that you need to know in order to make the shot.

However, sometimes a scene begins with the object already in the picture area, and it begins to move after a certain period of time. In this case, of course, the stationary period is taken care of by running the camera steadily for the required number of frames. Then the motion needed is divided into frames, just as the above. However, if the motion is fairly rapid, it will appear to start too suddenly. This is taken care of by what is known to animators as "fairing." Fairing consists of making the first few moves very small, and gradually increasing to the calculated amount for the greater part of the move. If the movement is to stop with the object still on the screen, then the procedure is reversed; the movements are made smaller and smaller toward the end of the move. The final effect on the screen is a gradual start and stop, which looks much more natural.

Great precision is not needed in this. One may simply figure the desired rate of movement, then make the first 10 frames of the move gradually increasing size and the last 10 frames diminishing. If the total time of the move must be maintained, the intermediate movements are all made a little bigger to compensate.

Other Uses of Stop Motion

Stop-motion photography can be used for purposes other than simply moving objects from one place to another. By stop motion, objects can be made to either appear (simply by placing them in the scene at the right time) or disappear. Words can spell out by themselves, through the use of cutout block letters, or erase themselves, by removing the letters one by one between frames. The principle of exposure and timing is the same in all cases.

In general, objects to be animated should be kept simple. It is exceedingly difficult, for instance, to animate a doll walking, because it is not just the movement of a single object from one place to another. The legs have to move rhythmically and at the right rate for the forward progression of the doll, the arms must swing in a natural manner, and the whole body must sway as a person does in the act of walking. This demands a high degree of skill and experience on the part of the animator. In addition, it requires a specially built puppet that is capable of making all desired motions and also capable of staying in each position by itself while being photographed.

For amateurs, it is best to avoid trying any pseudonatural effects of this sort. It is, however, seldom necessary. Even in theatrical films, it has been found possible to simplify matters by striving for fantasy rather than naturalness. In a once popular series of animated films, *Puppetoons,* made by George Pal, the characters were all wooden figures in the forms of cubes, spheres, and cylinders. No attempt was made to imitate human appearances or motions. With appropriate sound, the resulting films were quite interesting. There is a fertile field for experiment in this direction.

• *See also:* ANIMATION; CLOSE-UP MOVIES; MOTION-PICTURE PRODUCTION; TABLETOP PHOTOGRAPHY.

Storage of Sensitized Materials and Processing Solutions

Light-sensitive photographic materials are perishable products that are subject to damage by excessively high temperature, high relative humidity, harmful gases or vapors, and x-rays or other forms of radiation.

Films and Papers

Storage Temperature. Black-and-white materials and color films intended for sale to the general public can be stored at 21 C (70 F) or lower. Professional color films should always be stored under refrigeration at 13 C (55 F) or lower. Low-temperature storage retards the effects of keeping; it does not arrest them completely.

Relative Humidity. High relative humidity is very detrimental to all sensitized photographic materials. To protect the sensitometric characteristics of the material, relative humidity in storage areas should be kept between 30 and 50 percent.

Kodak films are packaged in equilibrium at 50 percent relative humidity in sealed foil envelopes, snap-cover plastic containers, and taped metal or plastic cans. This packaging protects the film against moisture (high relative humidity) until the packages are opened for use. Partly used packages of film should be resealed in the foil envelope or returned to the original container and sealed until required—a procedure that is particularly necessary if the film is to be returned to cold storage.

Moisture Condensation. To avoid condensation on film or paper that has been refrigerated, allow the material to warm up to room temperature before opening the sealed packages. The best practice is to remove the packages from cold storage the day before use. Otherwise, follow the warm-up directions given in the instruction sheet packaged with the material.

Storage of Exposed Material. To minimize changes in the latent image, and color-balance shifts caused by these changes, keep the interval between exposure and processing as short as possible. If the exposed material cannot be processed within a few hours, store it at 10 C (50 F). If the delay in processing is to be 24 hours or longer, store it at −18 C (0 F). Note that refrigerated exposed material must be brought to room temperature in the same way as described for unexposed material.

Use of a Desiccant. When no other method of humidity control is available, the desiccant silica gel is a valuable absorber of moisture. If, for example, exposed films are to be mailed or shipped over a long distance in unpredictable climatic conditions, prepared silica gel drying units can be enclosed with the films. These drying units are available from camera stores. Silica gel lasts indefinitely and it can be reactivated by heating in a vented oven. The amount of silica gel required depends on the amount of film and packaging, and on the climatic conditions, but a useful rule of thumb is 28.5 g (1 ounce) of silica gel to 0.68 kg (1½ pounds) of film and packaging combined for a drying period of 2 weeks.

Protection against Harmful Gases. Gases or fumes such as formaldehyde, hydrogen sulfide, sulfur dioxide, ammonia, motor exhaust, solvents, cleaners, fungicides, and mercury can seriously damage all photographic emulsions. The foil envelope or other type of moisture barrier gives protection against most vapors and gases, but some of them slowly penetrate some types of packaging material. Consequently, it is good practice to store all sensitized materials as far as possible from the sources of contamination.

Protection from Radiation. Just as light affects a photographic material, so does short-wave radiation such as x-rays and those from various kinds of radioactive material. Lead-lined containers can be used to protect sensitized material from radiation, but again, the safest method of storage is to keep the material as far away as possible from the sources.

Protection from Physical Damage. Backed-up storm sewers and burst water pipes are frequent causes of water damage in storerooms, particularly those located in basements. Store material at least 150 mm (6 inches) above the floor and provide a floor drain wherever a water hazard exists. Do not store material near hot water pipes or radiators, and maintain the temperature and relative humidity at the levels suggested earlier.

Too many heavy packages stacked on top of one another may cause damage to the lower ones due to weight or excessive pressure. Be sure that cartons or large rolls of photographic paper are not stacked in such a way that the stack may fall over. Such falls can damage a considerable amount of paper or other material.

Photographic Solutions

Storage of Photographic Solutions. Under proper conditions, prepared photographic solutions remain in good condition for weeks or months depending on the particular solution. Most solutions keep indefinitely in the original sealed containers.

Large quantities of prepared solution are kept in storage tanks made of stainless steel or a plastic material. Oxidation is the main enemy of photographic solutions, particularly developers. Floating lids in large tanks are a valuable aid to reducing the effects of oxidation, and suitable dust covers prevent contamination by airborne chemical dust and other foreign particles.

Small volumes of prepared processing solutions are best stored in almost-full, tightly stoppered bottles. A small air space should be left in a glass bottle to allow for expansion of the contents. Completely filled *glass* bottles may burst if subjected to an elevated temperature. Note that this precaution is unnecessary with plastic bottles. When some solution has been used from a large bottle, transfer the remainder of the solution to a smaller bottle, so that it is always practically full.

If possible, do not use metal closures or caps, corks, or glass stoppers. Plastic screw caps are the most suitable.

Storage Temperature for Solutions. The maintenance of a proper storage temperature for photographic solutions is important. A storage tempera-ture of about 18.5 C (65 F) is ideal. Developers oxidize at high temperatures with a loss of activity and a tendency to stain the processed material. Low temperature is also undesirable, because some chemicals in solution crystallize at or below 13 C (55 F) and are very difficult to redissolve.

• *See also:* ARCHIVAL PROCESSING; COMMERCIAL PROCESSING; DISPOSAL OF PHOTOGRAPHIC SOLUTIONS; DUPLICATE BLACK-AND-WHITE NEGATIVES; EMULSIONS; FILMS AND PLATES; REGENERATION; SILVER RECOVERY.

Stroboscopic Photography

Stroboscopic photography is defined subjectively by the appearance of the image rather than the method of obtaining it. A stroboscope is a means of observing and, if desired, recording successive phases of motion by means of periodically interrupted light. Stroboscopic photography is best described as an *effect* that takes place because of rapid imaging.

The stroboscopic effect is often seen in motion pictures when spoked wheels or fan blades seem to be running very slowly or in reverse. And, since conventional electric lights vary their brilliance in phase with the oscillations of 60 Hz household current (in the United States), many audio turntables incorporate stroboscopic rings as indicators of turntable speed. These examples represent two ways of creating a stroboscopic effect: either a mechanical device that periodically interrupts observation, or some type of pulsed illumination.

History

As early as 1850, William Henry Fox Talbot experimented with stroboscopic photography by using pulsed illumination. He opened the shutter of a camera in a darkened room and discharged successive flashes of light—actually sparks—from charged Leyden jars (a forerunner of the electrolytic condenser). Ernst Mach, the Austrian physicist, also used successive flashes to photograph bullets as they sped from the muzzle of a gun. Incidentally, Mach's stroboscopic photographs were the first photographic images of sound waves. He is largely

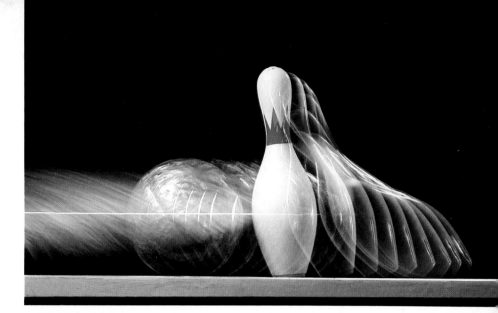

(Right) Bowling pin falling. The image was made by one main electronic flash from the left and in front of the subject. Multiple stroboscopic flashes from the right served to rim-light the bowling pin as it was toppled. Photo © 1978, Ben Rose. (Below) This image, while resembling a stroboscopic picture, was made with electronic flash. While electronic flash units are sometimes called strobe lights, this is incorrect.

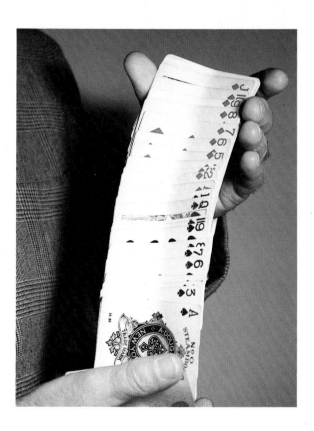

remembered today for the "Mach number" associated with the speed of sound, or objects moving relative to the speed of sound.

Two other great figures experimenting with stroboscopic photography before the turn of the century were the painter Thomas Eakins and the physiologist Etienne Jules Marey. Unlike Talbot and Mach, Eakins and Marey interrupted light mechanically, using high-speed solenoid shutters.

Harold E. Edgerton is almost universally credited with bringing stroboscopic recording from the laboratory to the world of photography. He was one of the first to unite electronics with photography. He had a special interest in motion analysis, and in 1931, while still a graduate student in electrical engineering, he developed the electronic flash tube, which is the ancestor of the electronic flash. While electronic flash units are sometimes called strobe lights, this is incorrect. Electronic flash units as customarily supplied to photographers do not have the capability of emitting flashes with the frequency that would allow observation of the successive phases of periodic motion—the essence of stroboscopic photography.

◄ For this exposure, the car was placed on a turntable. The camera was moved in such a way as to describe a circle on the film. As the turntable rotated and the camera panned, the lens zoomed and a number of stroboscopic lights flashed. Photo © 1975, Ben Rose.

Edgerton's development of the flash tube stimulated Gjon Mili, who was then an engineer with Westinghouse Corporation, to begin his career as a photographer. Mili and Edgerton collaborated on a famous series of stroboscopic photographs that appeared in *Life* magazine in the late 1930's.

Modern Stroboscopic Photography

With few exceptions, stroboscopic photography today utilizes the flash tube pioneered by Edgerton. All flash tubes operate on the same principle. They consist of a tube of heavy-duty glass with an electrode at each end. The tube is emptied of air and a small amount of xenon gas is pumped into the tube. The xenon is made conductive—normally the gas is a poor conducter—by energizing a coil wrapped around the glass tube. With the discharge of a condenser, the xenon is heated violently in order to produce a brilliant and very brief flash of light.

The flash tube in conventional electronic flash units operates on this principle. However, flash units for stroboscopic photography can give flashes as brief as one billionth of a second; flash duration of ordinary units is about a thousandth of a second.

Another difference between electronic flash units and lights for stroboscopic photography is the recycling time—the ability of the flash to recycle and fire the tube again. Electronic flash units may take several seconds to recycle; stroboscopic lights can fire several times a second, with a useful rate of perhaps 50 times a second.

The penalty for high-speed recycling of stroboscopic flash units is relatively low light output—perhaps 10- to 15-watt-seconds. Large-capacity condensers of ordinary electronic flash units cannot be

In stroboscopic photography, the interval between flashes is a factor in the spacing of the images on the film. Relatively slow flashes (above) produce a much different photograph than repeated, rapid flashes (left). Photos by Neil Montanus.

charged in the time required for stroboscopic work. The answer to high-speed recharging is very small capacitors, often only about 15 microfarads (μF).

One useful stroboscopic design uses 950 volts with either the 15 μF condenser or—for more light output—15 μF units in parallel. The duration of the flash in such a configuration is about 1/40,000 sec. Shorter flash duration and faster recycling is obtained as the charging voltage is raised and the size of the condenser is reduced. But, as explained, the power output of the flash suffers.

A Caution

Lights for stroboscopic photography are often custom-built by the photographer. The duration of the flash desired, the recycling time, and the general configuration of the units depend heavily on the photographer's desires. Mass marketing of such units is impractical. Anyone interested in working with this very specialized kind of photography must be knowledgeable in electrical theory and electronics. Voltages are very high in high-speed flash, and a capacitor can store an electrical charge for an amazingly long time. With stroboscopic lights, or with any electronic flash unit, one cannot assume that the condenser is discharged. Careful practice requires that any condenser be discharged by connecting a 1000-ohm, 10-watt resistor across the terminals with jumper wires; the resistor should be left in place for 10 to 15 seconds. A fully charged condenser holds a voltage and current that can be fatal.

Applications of Stroboscopic Photography

Stroboscopic lights can be connected to, and synchronized with, both still and motion-picture cameras. This kind of photography is useful in the analysis of motion. It can give images a feeling of a third dimension by making a record in space of where an object has been and where it is going. It offers a broad area of experiment in which to find the unexpected happening. The human eye can absorb roughly ten images a second. Stroboscopic photography knows no such limits.

• *See also:* EDGERTON, HAROLD; ELECTRONIC FLASH; HISTORY OF PHOTOGRAPHY; MAREY, ETIENNE JULES; MOTION STUDY; MULTIPLE FLASH; TALBOT, WILLIAM HENRY FOX; WATT-SECOND.

Studio Planning

In large photographic establishments, the studio may be thought of as just the camera room where entire pictures are taken. In small portrait businesses, the premises are often referred to as the studio—meaning the camera room, the sales office, the business office, the darkroom, and the finishing areas. Another kind of studio might be a small store in a shopping plaza, an establishment perhaps 16 feet by 75 or 80 feet. This type of operation uses darkroom and finishing services *off* the premises—either a central laboratory, a commercial processor, or a custom laboratory.

This portrait studio reveals careful planning and a design for simplified day-to-day operation. Note the absence of wires and cables on the floor.

Size

In addition to the photographer's own preferences, two considerations dictate the optimum size of a studio. First, the kinds of work assignments—portraits, weddings, commercial, industrial—are a factor in studio size. Obviously, a large wedding group or a massive industrial product will occupy more space in a studio than less-imposing subjects. The type of film formats used will also affect the size of the studio. Photography with small formats, such as 35 mm, can generally be accomplished in less studio space than would be required for view camera work with the 8″ × 10″ format. More than one photographer calls for more space, but the considerations of format and photographic subject will determine how much more space is needed.

The subject typically photographed in the studio will affect ceiling height as well as required floor area. A full-length photograph of a bridal party requires getting lights up high and at some distance from the subject. A 9-foot ceiling may not be enough, a 12-foot ceiling is typical, and 16-foot ceilings are found in the larger studios. A 24-foot ceiling is not uncommon in a large studio devoted to photography of automobiles or similar-sized industrial products. For this kind of studio, a 9-foot overhead door is probably a minimum, and a 16-foot door may sometimes be required.

Utilities

Regardless of dimension, the photographic studio must have a "dedicated" electrical supply; this is simply an electrical line that comes directly from the power supply to the breaker box or fuse box and is used only for the studio. Sharing power with another business could seriously affect both the brightness of the photographic lights and their color temperature. A large refrigeration/cooling unit in an adjacent property, for example, might cause a voltage drop of 5 volts when it is operated. This small drop in voltage will cost the studio about three times that much in brightness of lights. The intensity of lights would drop to 85 percent of the brightness at maximum voltage. Color temperature would also be affected by a change in voltage.

To determine the amount of electrical current needed, simply add the total wattage of the lights and other electrical equipment and divide that number by the voltage of the power supply. The studio might require 15,000 watts. This number divided by the nominal voltage of 120 volts would call for about 125 amperes of electrical service.

There are two other important factors in planning for electrical service for the studio. Determine with the power company *who* will pay for installing the dedicated power line and *how much* it will cost. Some areas may require that the line for the studio

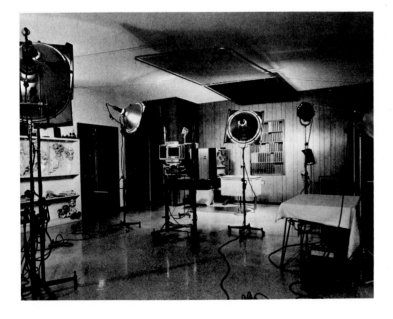

This spacious studio is· flexibly planned and could be used for a wide variety of assignments.

Modern darkrooms are painted in colors that reflect safelight illumination. A helpful addition to this room would be black surfaces behind the enlargers to prevent image degradation.

be brought a considerable distance, and this will result in a considerable expense.

A second factor to explore with the electrical supplier is a margin of surplus electrical service for expansion of the studio in the future. Twenty-five percent extra power is a fairly safe figure to consider. It may be more expensive initially to purchase this extra capacity, but it will no doubt be less expensive and troublesome to plan for expansion than to be limited by power inadequacies in the future.

Location

Before renting studio space, buying a studio, or securing vacant land to build upon, make a critical examination of the site. Among the issues to be considered are those of access, utilities, waste disposal, and vibration.

Is there good access for personnel and for clients, and are there facilities for getting the photographic subjects to and from the studio? Can the local power company supply abundant electrical power at a reasonable rate? For some studios, high-quality, low-hardness water at good pressures is an important factor; and these studios should be planned with regulations about waste disposal and sewer facilities in mind.

We can become used to many kinds of vibration, particularly in the low frequencies in the range of

5 to 20 Hz. However, vibration affects the quality of the photographic image; and quality that is missing from the image at the time the photography is made cannot be restored.

There have been instances of photographic studios located near busy and well-traveled highways, near railroad lines, and even near gravel-pit operations. These are obviously poor locations because of the heavy vibrations that are generated. Such sites are plagued with dirt and dust as well.

Another source of vibration is heavy equipment: fan rooms, air-conditioning units, large pumps, and boilers. If this kind of equipment is to be a part of the studio, make sure the camera room and enlarging and copying equipment are isolated from ambient vibration.

General Studio Illumination

When planning, the non-photographic lighting for the studio should be considered; that is, the ordinary lighting for darkrooms, hallways, and the camera room. Recent developments in fluorescent lighting tubes have restored this kind of light to favor in the photographic studio.

Older fluorescent lights had two qualities that kept them out of the studio and darkroom despite their economy and cool operating features. In the studio, or in viewing and evaluating photographs, the color characteristics of fluorescents were seldom capable of correct rendition of color. In the darkroom, switched-off fluorescents exhibited an afterglow that fogged certain films and papers.

Modern fluorescent lights are available for correct color emission across the spectrum. These are specially constructed and coated. If you intend to use fluorescents in the studio, specify those that have a Color Rendering Index (CRI) of 90+. For darkrooms, most major manufacturers produce a "nonafterglow" tube that extinguishes more rapidly than a 300-watt tungsten bulb. Fluorescents will reduce the total heat-load, and this is often valuable in a darkroom.

Painting the Studio

Modern studios use light, warm, unsaturated colors both in the camera room and in darkrooms. Ceilings of both areas are often painted with a titanium-oxide white, which has a reflectance of between 90 and 95 percent. Paints are being reformulated to meet EPA and OSHA requirements; and lead compounds as a base or drying agent are fast disappearing. This is beneficial to the studio, for lead-based paints in the presence of sulfides and other pollutants tended to gray or yellow in time.

Darkroom walls are being painted in colors that will reflect safelights, and this is true of countertops as well. A safelight at the correct distance with the proper bulb should be reflected as much as possible by walls and ceilings. (*See:* SAFELIGHTS.) There are epoxy-based and acrylic-based paints that are highly resistant to both fumes and solutions, and these should be considered for darkroom use.

The black-painted darkroom is largely gone from the contemporary scene, except for black surfaces behind projection equipment such as enlargers, where it helps prevent degradation of the image due to reflected light from the projector lamp.

Other Facilities

For discussion of darkroom, mixing room, and other studio facilities, see DARKROOM, PROFESSIONAL.

• *See also:* BUSINESS METHODS IN PHOTOGRAPHY; COLOR TEMPERATURE; COMMERCIAL PHOTOGRAPHY; COMMERCIAL PROCESSING; CUSTOM LABS; DARKROOM, PROFESSIONAL; DISPOSAL OF PHOTOGRAPHIC SOLUTIONS; ENLARGERS AND ENLARGING; MIXING; PRODUCT PHOTOGRAPHY; SAFELIGHTS; STORAGE.

Subtractive Color Synthesis

Color synthesis means the making of colors by the use of a set of primary colors. Additive synthesis of color starts with the primary colors of light—red, green, and blue—which, when added together in the right proportions, can create nearly any color.

Subtractive color synthesis starts with white light, which is an approximate even mix of all wavelengths. For the purposes of color synthesis, white light can be thought of as being composed of equal parts of red, green, and blue light, as white light is achieved by additive synthesis. Subtractive synthesis achieves color by taking away (subtracting) some of the white light. The subtractive color primaries are yellow, magenta, and cyan, and they are in the form of transparent layers of color that are, or act like, filters when used to synthesize colors. A full-strength cyan filter, for example, subtracts all of the red light from the white light, leaving the green and blue. The eye adds the green and blue light to see blue-green, or cyan.

A cyan filter is said to control red light because it subtracts it from the white light. It does not control blue or green light. Rather, a magenta filter controls green light, and a yellow filter controls blue light.

The subtractive filter can be made in different strengths—to absorb or control only part of the light. A half-strength cyan filter, for example, absorbs only half the red light, allowing the other half to pass through. In the following examples, different strengths of magenta, yellow, and cyan filters are combined to synthesize various common colors from white light.

$$0M + 0Y + 0C = White$$
$$Full\ M + Full\ Y + Full\ C = Black$$
$$\tfrac{1}{2}M + \tfrac{1}{2}Y + \tfrac{1}{2}C = Gray$$

$$Full\ M + 0Y + 0C = Magenta$$
$$0M + Full\ Y + 0C = Yellow$$
$$0M + 0Y + Full\ C = Cyan$$

$$Full\ M + Full\ Y + 0C = Red$$
$$0M + Full\ Y + Full\ C = Green$$
$$Full\ M + 0Y + Full\ C = Blue$$

Studio Planning

½M + Full Y + 0C = Orange
½M + 0Y + Full C = Violet
¾M + Full Y + ½C = Brown
0M + Full Y + ½C = Chartreuse

Color film is made and processed to produce varying strengths of the three subtractive color dyes in three layers in order to reproduce a full range of colors.

Printing inks cannot be printed in any but full strengths. Process inks used to print full-color reproductions are transparent inks in magenta, cyan, and yellow colors (called process red, process blue, and process yellow by printers). Partial strengths are achieved by the halftone process. A half-strength printing of magenta, for example, looks like a checkerboard of magenta and white squares when magnified. If this is printed along with a solid printing of cyan ink, the resultant color is violet.

½M + Full C = Violet

Because printing inks must be applied to the paper rapidly and in a thin layer, they do not have the same degree of filtering action as a full layer of dye in a color film. As a result, dark colors and black cannot be readily achieved. To compensate for this, a black image is printed along with the three process colors—hence the term "four-color halftone reproduction."

Printing ink and dye layers in color prints are on white paper. The white light illuminates the paper. It is filtered twice by the ink or dye: once as it passes through to the paper, and once when it is reflected back to the eye through the colorant. For this reason, a lesser amount of colorant acts as a full-strength filter than in transparencies where the light goes through only once.

• *See also:* COLOR THEORY; HALFTONE; PROCESS COLORS.

Sulfuric Acid

Oil of vitriol, battery acid

Used as a preservative of pyro. It is the main acid used in chrome alum fixing baths, in bleaching baths for reversal processes, in some reducers, and in many tray cleaners.

Formula: H_2SO_4
Molecular Weight: 98.08

Heavy, oily-looking, colorless or slightly grayish liquid.

When sulfuric acid is mixed with water, a great deal of heat is emitted; if the water is poured into the acid, the generation of heat is sudden and sometimes almost explosive, often spattering the liquid in all directions. To prepare diluted sulfuric acid safely, start with the required amount of *cold* water in an open glass or plastic container. Measure out the required quantity of sulfuric acid in another container. Then, start stirring the cold water, and very slowly pour the sulfuric acid into the water a little at a time. Allow the final solution to cool before using. Do not use metal containers or stirrers.

DANGER: Sulfuric acid is corrosive to skin, and to most metals and other materials. It is also highly poisonous.

Sun, Photography of

Some of the most fascinating and awe-inspiring products of astronomical photography have been pictures of variations on the surface of the sun, prominences of flaming gas extending into space, and other solar phenomena. Many aspects of the sun can be photographed at times of eclipse with ordinary cameras and telescopes; the techniques for this kind of work are covered in the articles ASTROPHOTOGRAPHY and ECLIPSE PHOTOGRAPHY.

Direct photography of the sun at times other than eclipse is most rewarding for the individual photographer when the sun is low in the sky and the intent of the picture is pictorial appeal. (*See:* SUNRISE AND SUNSET PICTURES.) Direct sun photography at other times or for other purposes is generally not practical and can be dangerous. The risk of damage to equipment or injury to the eyes is high, and results—if any—are likely to be disappointing.

The following points should be noted for their application at those times when photography of the sun is practical. They are discussed in more detail in the articles previously mentioned.

1. The size of the sun's image on the film is equal to: Focal length of lens (mm) ÷ 110. Focus the lens at infinity.

2. Do not point an unfiltered lens at the sun unless you can look at the sun comfortably and without squinting (and without sunglasses). Generally, that is only at sunrise or sunset, and on overcast days. At all other times, the camera must be protected by neutral density filtration, as explained in point 3. Otherwise, the sun's rays focused at the focal plane can cause damage. Even a properly filtered lens should not be left pointing at the sun any longer than is necessary. Put on a lens cap, or point it away from the sun.

3. The average luminance of the sun at sea level is 4840 million lumens per square metre. This is so intense that even at times of partial eclipse it must be reduced 10,000 to 100,000 times in order to bring it within the exposure range of modern films. A 5.0 neutral density filter provides a reduction of 10,000× (13⅓ stops); a 6.0 neutral density filter provides a 100,000× reduction (16⅔ stops). The degree of light reduction required depends on the degree of eclipse and the speed of the film.

4. *Protect your eyes at all times.*
   a. *Never* look through the ground glass of a view camera or the viewing system of a single-lens reflex camera that is pointed at the direct sun, even when the lens is suitably filtered for photography. Neutral density filters reduce light intensity, but they do not remove the infrared radiations that can burn or permanently injure the eyes.
   b. *Never* look at the direct sun through neutral density filters, sunglasses, or layers of blackened color films—none remove infrared radiations.
   c. *Use only* exposed and developed black-and-white film to filter the sun for direct viewing. Expose a medium-speed film (such as Kodak Verichrome pan or Plus-X film) directly to strong light and develop it for maximum density—twice the normal time or longer. Use a sandwich of *two layers* of the blackened film to obtain a filter of 6.0 density, which also provides infrared protection. (The dyes of color-film emulsions do not do this.) Place the filter in front of your eyes, or the camera lens, *before* looking at the sun.

• *See also:* ASTROPHOTOGRAPHY; ECLIPSE PHOTOGRAPHY; SUNRISE AND SUNSET PICTURES.

Sunrise and Sunset Pictures

Good photographs of sunrises or sunsets are among the easiest pictures to take because exposure is not too critical. Overexposure makes the sunset appear lighter and earlier, while underexposure gives deeper, richer colors, making the sunset look more advanced.

When an exposure meter is used, the reading should be based on the brightness of the sky and clouds. This will render the foreground dark and the sun slightly overexposed, with rich colors in the clouds. Any objects such as trees, buildings, or peo-

TYPICAL EXPOSURES FOR SUNRISE AND SUNSETS*		
ASA	**f/stop**	**Shutter Speed (sec.)**
25	f/5.6	1/60
64	f/5.6	1/125
200	f/8	1/250
400	f/11	1/250

*Bracket exposures to make sure the desired effect is achieved.

matter on the lens increases flare considerably and may ruin your pictures. Even the finest lenses are subject to flare when pointed directly at a bright object like the sun. A photographer using a reflex camera, or any other type of ground-glass focusing, will usually be able to see and control flare before taking the picture. A lens hood is often a great help in avoiding lens flare.

• *See also:* SUN, PHOTOGRAPHY OF.

Superadditivity

Various developing agents are used in photography because their characteristics are different. Metol produces shadow detail rapidly, thus affording good film speed, but it builds density rather slowly. Hydroquinone, on the other hand, is slow to bring up shadow detail but in time can develop very great density in the more heavily exposed areas. To secure the benefits of both characteristics, photographic chemists years ago compounded developers containing both developing agents in varying proportions.

It would be expected that the character of a developer containing both developing agents is a sum of the properties of the two. That is, it would have the detail-rendering quality of Metol and the density-building ability of hydroquinone. It was learned rather early that the combination of the two developing agents was, in fact, superior to either alone. A Metol-hydroquinone formula has all of the speed of a Metol developer and exhibits even greater density-building power than one containing only hydroquinone. The total rate of development is greater than the sum of the rates of the single-constituent developers. This synergistic effect is referred to as superadditivity.

In most formulas, a superadditive combination is produced when the Metol is present to an amount approximately equal to ¼ the weight of the hydroquinone. A newer developing agent, Phenidone (1-phenyl-3-pyrazolidone), forms superadditive

ple appearing in the foreground will be silhouetted against the sky to form a dramatic frame for the subject. Try a series of pictures showing the progression of a sunset by making an exposure every 5 minutes or so. To photograph the afterglow immediately following a sunset, try 4 to 6 stops more exposure than for a normal sunlit scene, or 2 or 3 stops more than your sunset exposure.

In photographing sunsets, the use of a long-focal-length lens is often desirable to make the flaming ball of the sun appear larger. The narrow angle of view provided by such a lens also simplifies eliminating unwanted foreground objects.

To avoid lens flare when photographing sunsets (or any backlighted subjects), the camera lens must be extremely clean. Dust particles or other foreign

Despite the dramatic visual effects seen here, sunsets and sunrises are perhaps the easiest pictures to achieve. This is because the exposure of these subjects is not critical; underexposure simply makes the time of day appear earlier and overexposure makes it look more advanced.

combinations with only $\frac{1}{40}$ the weight of the hydroquinone in a given formula. Thus, a Phenidone developer requires only $\frac{1}{10}$ as much Phenidone as the same formula would require of Metol. There are, however, problems with Phenidone, such as keeping characteristics, which prevent it from completely displacing Metol in many formulas. Metol-hydroquinone combinations are still popular.
• *See also:* CHEMISTRY OF PHOTOGRAPHY; DEVELOPMENT.

  ## Supplementary Lenses

A supplementary lens is a simple lens added to a camera, projector, or enlarging lens to change its focal length. Usually this practice causes some decrease in image quality, but the results are often economical and practical.

The most common use of a supplementary lens is to shorten the focal length of a camera lens in order to obtain large images at very close distances. This use is discussed in detail in the article CLOSE-UP PHOTOGRAPHY. Shortening the length of a projector lens makes it possible to project a larger image without changing the distance to the screen.

Increasing the focal length of a lens makes it possible to obtain larger images at longer distances with a camera, or to project over a longer distance to a standard-size screen with a projector.

Focusing

In the case of a camera, if infinity focusing is required when a supplementary lens is used, a bellows-type camera is required to move the camera lens to a distance equal to the new focal length from the film. Thus, infinity focusing cannot be obtained when the focal length of a lens on a rigid-body camera is shortened. For example, when the focal length of the lens has been increased, the lens-to-film distance necessary for infinity focusing with a single-lens reflex camera may require the use of extension tubes or accessory bellows. To focus objects at closer distances, it must be possible to move the lens combination farther from the film than the infinity-focus position.

When the camera-lens focus control is set to the infinity position, focus will be at a distance equal to the focal length of the supplementary lens, measured from the supplementary lens. As explained in the next section, the focal length can be determined from the power of a supplementary lens.

Shortening the focal length of a camera lens reduces its format coverage. You cannot shorten the focal length of a normal lens by using a supplementary lens and expect it to cover like a wide-angle lens. This is seldom a problem in close-up photography or when using view-camera lenses, which have extra coverage to allow for camera movements. However, it may become evident when photographing more distant subjects with other lenses. The image on the camera ground glass should be examined carefully. Increasing the focal length of a camera lens does not create a coverage problem.

Power and Focal Length

The power of a supplementary lens is expressed in diopters. A supplementary lens with a positive (+) power will shorten the focal length of a prime lens; one with a negative (−) power will increase the focal length.

Power is determined as follows:

$$\text{Diopters, D} = 1000 \div \text{Focal length of supplementary lens, } F_S, \text{ in mm}$$

Example: The focal length of a supplementary lens is 250 mm; its power is:

$$1000 \div 250 = 4 \text{ diopters.}$$

To determine focal length, terms are exchanged in the formula:

$$F_S \text{ (mm)} = 1000 \div D$$

To determine what power supplementary lens is required to convert to a different, combined focal length:

$$D = \frac{F \pm F_C*}{F \times F_C}$$

where F is the focal length of the camera lens, and F_C is the desired combined focal length.

*When F_C is larger than F, subtract; the resulting power will be minus (−). When F_C is smaller than F, add; the resulting power will be plus (+).

To Convert From:	To:	Multiply By:
Inches	Metres	0.0254
Feet	Metres	0.3048
Metres	Inches	39.37
Metres	Feet	3.281
Metres	Millimetres	1000
Millimetres	Metres	0.001

In order to work with this and the following formulas involving D, all quantities must be expressed in metres. See the accompanying conversion table.

Example: What supplementary lens is required to change the focal length of a lens from 6 to 6½ inches?

Conversion to metres: $6 \times 0.0254 = 0.152$
$6½ \times 0.0254 = 0.165$

$$D = \frac{F - F_C}{F \times F_C} = \frac{0.152 - 0.165}{0.152 \times 0.165} = \frac{-0.013}{0.025} = -0.52$$

Thus, approximately a $-½$ diopter supplementary lens is required.

To determine the focal length of a lens combination:

$$F_C = \frac{F}{1 + (F \times D)}$$

Example: What is the focal length of a combination of a 100 mm camera lens and a -2 supplementary lens?

Conversion to metres: $100 \times 0.001 = 0.1$

$$F_C = \frac{0.1}{1 + (0.1 \times -2)} = \frac{0.1}{1 - 0.2} = \frac{0.1}{0.8} = 0.125 \text{ m} = 125 \text{ mm}$$

NOTE: The results obtained with the above formula will be affected by the separation between the supplementary and camera lenses. A formula that takes this factor into account is included in the article CLOSE-UP PHOTOGRAPHY. A graph showing the combined focal length of a number of prime and positive supplementary-lens combinations is included in the same article.

Exposure with Supplementary Lenses

When positive supplementary lenses are being used for close-focusing purposes, no exposure change is required; the effective f-numbers of the combination are the same as the marked f-numbers of the camera lens. When either a positive or negative supplementary lens is used to change the focal length of a view-camera lens, an exposure adjustment is always necessary. It can be determined as follows:

$$\text{Stops change} = F_C \div F$$

When the focal length is shortened, stop down from the marked value by the required amount of change. When the focal length is lengthened, open up by the indicated number of stops change.

Example: An 8-inch lens used with a -1 supplementary lens has an effective focal length of 10 inches—a change of 2 inches. The correction is:

$$\text{Stops change} = 2 \div 8 = ¼ \text{ stop}$$

The lens should be opened up by ¼ stop.

Using Supplementary Lenses

A supplementary lens has one concave and one convex side. Often, an arrow is marked on the lens mount pointing toward the convex side. Better image quality usually results when the convex side faces *away from* the camera lens.

The supplementary lens should be mounted as close as possible to the camera lens. Increased separation reduces the effect of the supplementary lens as calculated by the preceding formulas.

Supplementary lenses may be combined for increased power. A $+2$ lens and a $+3$ lens have a combined value of $+5$; a -1 lens and a -2 lens have a combined value of -3. The supplementary lens with the highest power should be mounted closest to the camera lens. Image quality will be seriously degraded by using more than two supplementary lenses together.

Supplementary Lenses

Even a single supplementary lens will degrade definition when the camera lens is set at maximum aperture. Stopping down to a medium or small aperture will minimize the effect, but will never equal the optimum quality obtainable from the camera lens alone.

Definition may be improved by mounting the supplementary lens on the rear of the camera lens, with the convex side facing toward the film. The supplementary lens mount should be painted flat black for use in this position in order to prevent flare from reflections.

When two supplementary lenses are used, one may be mounted in front of, and one behind, the camera lens for improved results.

• *See also:* CLOSE-UP PHOTOGRAPHY; LENS CONVERTERS; LENSES.

Surveillance Photography

Photographic surveillance techniques are used for the detection of crime, for motion studies, and for scientific investigation. The surveillance may be *passive* with the camera rigidly mounted and triggered by a remote switch, or the camera may be used as a continuous or intermittent recording device. *Active* surveillance requires a photographer to aim, focus, and continuously control the camera.

Passive surveillance relies upon proper setup of camera trips, or installation of continuous or intermittent surveillance cameras, to capture the required pictures. Without operator control, initial detailed analysis of the photographic detection system must be done to provide, with reliability, a record of the required information or identification.

Active surveillance may be overt or covert. In observation of demonstrations or fire scenes, there may be little need or opportunity to hide the camera or operator. Where observation of suspected criminal activity is concerned, however, concealment of the photographer and cameras may be vital to obtain the required evidence.

Passive Surveillance Cameras

Passive surveillance cameras generally fall into two categories: demand cameras and continuous-surveillance cameras.

Demand Cameras. Demand cameras remain inactive until they are triggered by a switch or other actuating device. The camera then runs at either a continuous frame rate or at a rate such as one frame every two seconds.

The demand camera is useful in situations where a constant filming of an occurrence is desired. Thus, the camera is often installed to cover customers at the check-out counter of all types of stores—large chain stores, small grocery stores, and liquor stores. The camera is operated when a robbery is threatened and a photographic record is made to aid in the identification of the suspect. In addition, this camera can be used for surveillance of building entrances during the hours when the building is closed. Unauthorized entrance would trigger the camera, and a photographic record would be made of the intruder.

Continuous-Surveillance Cameras. Continuous-surveillance cameras are used in situations where a photographic record of movement or events is required over a particular period of time (usually hours). This type of camera photographs the scene at an intermittent rate (such as one frame every minute) that compresses time and provides a rapid review of the activity when the processed film is viewed at a normal rate. This type of photography is known as time-lapse photography.

The continuous-surveillance camera can be used for a wide range of applications. The time-lapse mode of operation of the camera is useful in applications where filming *all* the action is *not* necessary, but where a sequence of pictures at regular intervals will suffice. One of the advantages of this mode of operation is that a roll of film lasts for a longer period of time. The camera is useful for:

1. Providing pictures of activity on a loading dock during an 8-hour day to determine if a more efficient traffic pattern can be developed.
2. Providing an indication of the use of a plant gate for a period of a week.
3. Making a permanent record of dial readings on a control panel to determine daily fluctuations.
4. Identifying the cause of a traffic-snarled intersection.
5. Studying the motions of a machine operator.

Passive surveillance cameras are frequently used in stores to monitor customer activity for instances of shoplifting. The camera will run at either a continuous frame rate or at a rate such as one frame every two seconds.

6. Recording the progress of the construction of a building.

Camera Placement. One of the most important considerations in setting up a photographic-surveillance system is the placement of the camera or cameras. If the camera is to be used for the identification of individuals, it should be located so that a facial view can be obtained. Important locations to be considered are exits, tellers' cages, cash registers, and elevator doors. The camera should be placed as close to face level as practical, keeping in mind the security of the camera.

If the camera is to provide a record of traffic flow in an area, a location must be found that will provide the necessary coverage.

The following steps will help in making a survey to determine the location and number of cameras needed to fill surveillance requirements.

Step 1. Obtain or draw a floor plan of the area to scale. Items included should be doors, counters, machine placement, wall sockets, lights, windows, pillars, desks, and cabinets. This is necessary to help plan the location of the camera and its coverage.

Step 2. Determine the field of coverage of the camera lens from various positions in the room. The best positions are those that cover all of the areas of interest. Field of coverage is dependent on the focal length of the camera lens. As the focal length of the lens decreases, the area of coverage widens.

Step 3. Determine the distance from the camera location to the subject area. This distance must be set on the focusing ring on the camera. The important considerations here are that the camera's field of view contain only the area of interest and that the image of the subject on the finished film be large enough to provide the information required. This latter consideration is important when the film will be used for identification purposes. In general, a subject image size of about ⅛ inch on the film is required to enable good identification of the subject.

Step 4. If a camera is available, it is a simple matter to check the calculations of the preceding steps by actually shooting a few feet of film from the locations determined in Step 2. A stepladder can be used to simulate the height at which the camera will be mounted.

Step 5. Have the test films processed and view them to confirm that the chosen locations will provide the desired results.

Step 6. When mounting the camera in its final position, be sure the wall or support to which the mounting bracket will be attached is sturdy and that the camera is secured firmly to the bracket. This will prevent any building vibrations from causing camera movement during exposures.

Lighting. The lighting available in the area under surveillance is of great importance. There must be enough light to provide sufficient exposure. The best way to determine the adequacy of the lighting is to use a photographic exposure meter at the camera location, pointing it in the direction of the camera's view. Set the shutter speed and film exposure index controls on the exposure meter for the camera and film being used.

Many passive surveillance cameras are equipped with an automatic exposure control that controls the lens opening by light reflected from the scene to the electric eye on the front of the camera when a film cartridge is in the camera. It is important that the electric eye is not obstructed and that the camera does not point directly at the sun or other unusually bright light source. In either case, poor exposure of the subject will occur. Pointing a camera in the direction of a strong light source such

as a window or large reflecting surface can result in the subject being underexposed, since the electric eye will cause the lens opening to close down in order to compensate for the large light area. The result is loss of important detail in the final picture.

If there is not enough light for proper exposure, supplementary illumination will have to be added to the area. Such a situation may be found in storerooms, on loading docks, or in supply yards, especially at night.

In cases where poor lighting exists and supplementary lighting is not possible, a poor photographic record may still be better than no record at all. Occasionally, adjustments in processing can be made to overcome this problem.

If the area of interest is outdoors or in a room with a large window area, the level of lighting will change during the course of a day. Automatic exposure control will adjust the exposure according to the changing conditions within limits. If the area to be covered is rather large, evenness of the illumination is also important. If a portion of the area is lighted with subdued illumination, this portion should be "filled in" with supplementary lights only if significant action may occur in it.

Detector Devices. There are two ways of triggering a passive surveillance camera. One way is for a person such as a teller, clerk, or guard to press a button or actuate some type of a switch. The other method requires the use of a device (called a detector) that can sense an intruder and start the camera. Detectors come in all levels of complexity. The following paragraphs describe the operation of some of these devices.

Photoelectric Detectors. Photoelectric detectors are among the oldest and most widely used types of detectors. One type of photoelectric detector relies on a beam of light falling on a photosensitive detector. When the light beam is broken by a person entering a room, for example, the interruption causes the camera to operate.

Another type of photoelectric detector relies on the use of sensitivity to infrared radiation. The detector senses an increase in infrared radiation such as that radiated from the body of an intruder, and through electronic circuitry, causes the camera to operate.

Audio Detectors. This system relies on a microphone detector that detects only unusual or out-of-

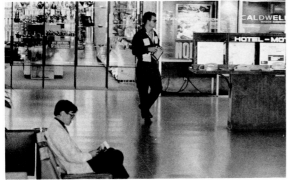

A

B

C

D

E

A surveillance sequence should cover the subject thoroughly, even though some of his actions may appear insignificant. (A) Subject enters an airport waiting room. The apparently innocent traveler in foreground will turn out to be his contact. (B) Talking on the phone, subject is off guard. (C) Subject pauses at the lobby entrance. (D) He appears to see the photographer; at such times, the photographer should freeze. (E) Faces are not identifiable, but hairline, glasses, or clothing may help establish identity. (F) A package changes hands. Action is recorded and subjects can be identified.

F

Surveillance Photography

the-ordinary sounds such as those made by a person moving items in the protected area.

Vibration Detectors. These are very sensitive detectors of any movement in the protected area. They are generally employed in areas in which there should be no personnel during particular hours.

Multi-Use Devices. Multi-use devices are primarily switches that can be used in a variety of locations. They can be actuated either manually or automatically. These devices include overhead door contacts, magnetic door contacts, floor mats, vibration contacts, shunt locks, foot rails, lead foils, cash-drawer pressure pads, mercury contacts, and holdup buttons.

Capacitance Detectors. A capacitance field is established around the area. A person entering the area disturbs the balance of this field; this imbalance is detected by the unit and the camera is then actuated.

Ultrasonic Detectors. The area is filled with ultrasonic sound waves having a frequency above 20,000 Hz. A frequency this high cannot be heard by the human ear. However, movement by a person in the area will cause a disturbance in the sound-wave pattern monitored by the detector, and the detector will activate the camera.

Active Surveillance

Active surveillance implies the direct use of a camera by someone such as a police investigator observing a suspect, or a scientist collecting data on the activities of humans or animals. The investigator must bring to bear all of the observational techniques that he or she would normally use and combine them with photography.

With fast films, infrared films and flash, or low-light-level scopes, the surveillance photographer can overcome many of the limitations imposed by darkness. The lighting on the subject will govern, to a large degree, the choice of film and camera equipment for a surveillance task. The use of a high-speed film or infrared film can be a relatively inexpensive way of obtaining surveillance photographs without alerting the subject. Surveillance scopes can detect activities at a much lower light level and allow photography of a subject.

Camera Position. Choice of the camera position can be critical to obtaining useful surveillance photographs. The camera must be positioned to get a useful image size on the film. When the camera cannot be located near the subject, telephoto lenses must be chosen to provide the needed magnification. Usually, concealment of the camera or camera operator is required so that the subject is not aware of being photographed.

When choosing the camera position, try to evaluate the effect that the shutter noise, the red glow of infrared flash, the movement of the photographer, or light reflections from the lens will have on the subject. If any of these factors could cause the subject's attention to be attracted, change the camera position, conceal the camera or photographer more effectively, or choose an alternative photographic technique.

Equipment. The need for photographs taken at very low light levels dictates the choice of equipment and films. Fast lenses and high-speed film are necessary to record scenes with low illumination levels. For still photography, the most versatile camera system is a 35 mm camera with interchangeable lenses. Fast lenses of all focal lengths allow the camera to be adapted for almost any situation.

In addition to the camera system for surveillance, the photographer must consider what accessories will be needed. For telephotography, a firm tripod is a *must*. Proper use and interpretation of an exposure meter can mean the difference between success and failure in many surveillance situations. Supplementary lighting will usually involve infrared lamps or electronic flash equipped with infrared filters.

Films. Films for surveillance are either moderate- to high-speed panchromatic materials, or special-purpose films sensitive to infrared radiation. To achieve the required subject identification, the photographer must choose the film that will yield good definition with speed adequate for the lighting conditions at hand.

Film definition is influenced by the graininess and resolving power of the emulsion. The sharpness of a film image is determined by the quality of the image reaching the film, the degree of exposure, and the method of development.

Photographic materials can be sensitized to record radiation that is not visible to the human eye.

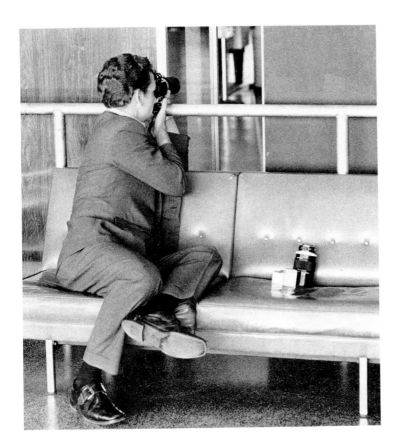

Correct choice of camera position can be critical, as the camera must be positioned to get a useful image size on film. Here, the camera position was chosen to cover an airport waiting area. The photographer is concealed by two advertising display cases.

The photographer should steady his camera on any convenient support when he cannot set up a tripod; here, he uses the back of a bench. To avoid attracting attention, the photographer preaimed and prefocused his camera on an open door. He then partially concealed the camera with a newspaper and squeezed off the release without bringing the camera to his eye.

This fact is of great importance for surveillance photography. If an area is illuminated with infrared radiation, a subject can be observed and photographed with little likelihood of being alerted.

In relatively confined areas, suitably filtered, continuously burning tungsten lamps will usually provide all of the infrared radiation needed for either still- or motion-picture photography with high-speed infrared films. In places such as theaters, nightclubs, or bars, where there is already some visible light, supplemental infrared lamps will allow still- or motion-picture records to be made. If an

Distant street lamps, low-wattage tungsten lamps, and late evening twilight combine to give this scene adequate illumination. The photographer was careful to avoid the underexposure indicated by his light meter when it was pointed toward the many light sources.

observer looks directly at an infrared lamp, a dim red glow may be visible, but it will not be noticeable if the lamp appears to be part of an exit light, a neon sign, or other display lighting.

Infrared Surveillance Scopes. Several manufacturers provide infrared surveillance scopes that allow continuous observation of a subject without detection. These devices use an image converter to translate the infrared into a visible image that is displayed on a screen. The screen is observed through an eyepiece and can also be photographed through this eyepiece. The infrared scope can be used to direct a camera that can photograph the subject with the ambient infrared radiation or with infrared flash.

Light-Intensifier Scopes. Even in relatively dim light, high-speed films can usually capture the subject if the photographer can see clearly enough to focus a camera. For still lower light levels, developments in electronics provide a means for seeing and photographing subjects where even the eye cannot discriminate objects. Unlike the devices that convert invisible infrared radiation to visible light, these image-intensifier systems require no external radiation source. Instead, the light provided by a distant streetlight, moonlight, or even starlight that is reflected by the subject is captured and amplified elec-

tronically. The output of the electronic amplifier is converted to a bright image that can be observed with the eye or that can be photographed.

Most image-intensifier systems have a high-speed, long-focal-length lens that forms the low-light-level image on an image-converter tube. This tube converts the light image to electronic signals that are amplified several thousand times. The signal is transmitted to a screen that produces a visible display of the amplified image.

Observation and photography of the display can be done with a 35 mm single-lens reflex camera or with a reflex-viewing movie camera placed at the eyepiece.

• *See also:* AVAILABLE-LIGHT PHOTOGRAPHY; BAD-WEATHER PHOTOGRAPHY; BINOCULARS, TAKING PICTURES THROUGH; CRIME PHOTOGRAPHY; DOCUMENTARY PHOTOGRAPHY; EVIDENCE PHOTOGRAPHY; EXISTING-LIGHT PHOTOGRAPHY; FIRE AND ARSON PHOTOGRAPHY; INFRARED PHOTOGRAPHY; LEGAL ASPECTS OF PHOTOGRAPHY; RAPID PROCESSING; TIME-LAPSE PHOTOGRAPHY.

Further Reading: Siljander, Raymond P. *Applied Police and Fire Photography.* Springfield, IL: Charles C. Thomas Publishers, 1976;———. *Applied Surveillance Photography.* Springfield, IL: Charles C. Thomas Publishers, 1975.

Surveillance Photography

Synchronization

Shutters do not open instantly; they take a measurable amount of time to go from fully closed to fully open. Similarly, flash sources take a measurable amount of time to reach peak output. The first problem of photography with bulb-type flash is to synchronize these two timings so that the light is at full intensity when the shutter opens and closes; with electronic flash, the problem is to be sure that the shutter is fully open before the flash fires.

To achieve this, camera and lens shutters have built-in synchronizing circuits to close the contacts that fire the flash at the proper instant in relation to the shutter action.

Types of Synchronization

In equipment that permits the use of more than one kind of flash, the choice of synchronization depends on the type of shutter and the type of flash. The various kinds of synchronization are designated by letters. The designations and major uses are:

M—Provides a time delay of approximately 17 milliseconds from flash triggering to fully open between-the-lens shutter. Utilizes peak output of Class M flashbulbs.

X—Provides flash triggering when the between-the-lens or focal-plane shutter has just become fully opened. Suitable for electronic flash.

FP—Provides appropriate time delay from flash triggering to shutter opening to synchronize slow-burning "focal-plane" bulbs. Shutter design dictates the actual delay time.

The accompanying table summarizes data for synchronization, type of flash, and usable shutter-speed range.

On some cameras and lenses, synchronization is selected by moving a lever to a marked position; on others there are separate terminals to which the flash unit may be connected. The letters "X," "M," and "FP" may be used, or the types of synchronization may be marked by symbols—a lightning bolt for X-sync and a bulb for M- or FP-sync.

Some simple cameras accept only one kind of flash, usually flashcubes, magicubes (a kind of flashcube that does not require battery power), or flip-flash (strip flash). Other models accept only electronic flash. With such equipment, synchronization is automatic. All that may be necessary is to set the camera to the flash mode, or to set a required shutter speed. Check the camera instructions carefully. (Note that magicubes will not fire in flashcube-type cameras, and that flashcubes may damage magicube-type cameras.)

SHUTTER SPEEDS AND FLASH SYNCHRONIZATION

Shutter Type:	Blade		Focal Plane	
Type of synchronization:	M	X	FP or M	X
Flash Source				
Class M bulbs*	All speeds	1/30	—	—
Class F bulbs†	—	1/30; 1/60	—	—
3; 50 bulbs	—	1/30	—	—
6B, 26B bulbs	—		All speeds	—
Electronic flash	—	All speeds	—	All speeds

*Class M bulbs: M3B; 5 and 5B; 25 and 25B; 11; 40; 2 and 2B; 22 and 22B.
†Class F bulbs: flashcube: magicube; AG-1, AG-1B, M2B.

Synchronization and Shutter Speeds

As the table shows, blade shutters will synchronize at all speeds with many types of flash. A maximum shutter speed of 1/500 sec. is available with most small-diameter lenses; larger lenses have slower maximum speeds. Speeds slower than 1/30 sec. may cause overexposure or the appearance of ghost images. If in doubt with a blade shutter, use 1/30 sec. and X-synchronization with any flash.

Focal-plane shutters will synchronize at all speeds with class FP bulbs at the FP setting. These bulbs have a peak duration long enough to remain at full intensity throughout the travel of the shutter slit across the film plane.

With the very short duration of electronic flash, a focal-plane shutter must be fully open before the flash fires. This limits the top speed to 1/60 sec. in most cases, or 1/125 sec. in some small-format cam-

The picture on the top illustrates cutoff of part of the image by using a focal-plane shutter at the wrong shutter speed for electronic flash. The image below resulted from using the correct shutter speed. Photos by John Menihan.

eras. The maximum X-sync speed is usually marked in color or by a symbol on the speed selector of cameras with focal-plane shutters. As explained in the article ELECTRONIC FLASH, using a higher speed results in part of the picture being unexposed because the shutter curtains form a moving slit. Slower speeds also permit X-synchronization with focal-plane shutters. However, if the ambient light level is high, the film may receive enough exposure in the interval between the end of the flash and the closing of the shutter to create overexposure or to record a ghost image of a moving subject. Unless this effect is desired, it is safest to use the maximum permissible X-sync speed.

Unsynchronized Flash

Before the invention of the flashbulb, photographers used the "open flash" technique with flash-powder units. The shutter was opened, the flash fired manually, and the shutter closed. The same technique can be used with modern equipment simply by setting the shutter to "B" or "T." It is useful when flash must be fired from a position away from the camera, or when a single unit must be moved and fired repeatedly to cover a large area. (*See:* PAINTING WITH LIGHT.) This technique is successful only when the ambient light level is low enough not to expose the film significantly during the intervals between flashes.

Synchronization Connections

Almost all flash units connect to the camera or lens-shutter sync terminal by means of a cord with a pin-coaxial (PC) tip. This kind of connector occupies very little space, but it may pull out of the terminal easily if worn. Some camera manufacturers provide locking devices to provide a permanent connection. It is a good idea to secure a nonlocking PC connector with a piece of tape, especially if the camera and flash are to be hand-held without a connecting bracket.

The PC cord tip should be inspected frequently because its outer sleeve can get pinched out of round, making proper connection difficult or impossible. An inexpensive tip-conditioning tool is available to correct sleeve distortion and pin misalignment if they are not too severe. Sync cords should also be tested for electrical continuity before use. A simple way to do this is to fire the flash unit by shorting

between the tip pin and sleeve with a paper clip or other small piece of metal.

Many small-format cameras have "hot" accessory shoes that make electrical connections for synchronization through contacts in the mounting foot of an appropriate flash unit. To prevent short circuits, it may be necessary to insert an insulating strip in the shoe when mounting flash units without a "hot foot," or when using hot-foot units in other mounts. Refer to the equipment instructions to determine whether this is required.

Remote Synchronization

Flash units placed at a distance from the camera can be synchronized by means of a suitable extension cord. The cord must be equipped with the proper connectors at each end, usually PC male and PC female. A single unit can be connected directly to the shutter circuit. Multiple units can be connected one after another, in series, or to a multiple connector, which in turn is connected to the shutter.

A far more convenient method of synchronizing remote or slave electronic flash units is by means of "magic eye" sensors. These are light-sensitive diode switches no larger than flashcubes, which connect directly to the firing circuits of flash units. No cords back to the camera are required, which makes it easy to place units in hard-to-reach locations or places where cords would be visible in the picture. It also eliminates the danger of people tripping over the cords and damaging equipment. The only necessity is that each sensor be able to see the light from a unit that is synchronized with the shutter; when it fires, each sensor will fire its unit instantaneously.

Most such sensors are usable up to about 25 feet under all light conditions; some high-sensitivity sensors can be used at greater distances if the ambient light is not too bright. A few have a high/low sensitivity selector for use under a wide variety of conditions. There is one potential drawback to this method of remote synchronization. When several photographers are working in the same location, the flash of one may set off the remote units of another at unexpected and unwanted moments.

• *See also:* ELECTRONIC FLASH; FLASH PHOTOGRAPHY; MULTIPLE FLASH; PAINTING WITH LIGHT; SHUTTERS; SLAVE.

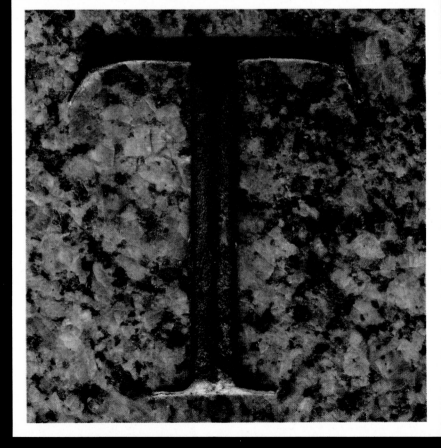

Tabletop Photography

In its simplest form, tabletop photography consists of arranging a scene on a table or other suitable surface and photographing it. Popular subjects include model trains, ships, planes, and boats; figures made of clay or pipe cleaners; kitchen utensils, fruits and vegetables adorned with cartoon faces; flower arrangements; tools, machine parts, and gears; and toys and puppets.

Lighting

With two or three photolamps, a variety of lighting arrangements can be created. By just changing the position of the lights, any mood can be created on a tabletop. Shining the lights on the background instead of on the subject itself, for example, will silhouette the subject. This approach can produce striking results, making models look more realistic because their minor imperfections are not visible in the silhouetted image.

It is often effective to use a light source such as a candle within a scene so that it seems to be providing the illumination for the picture. When photolamps are providing the main illumination, get a rough approximation of the exposure by using the photolamp guide numbers supplied by photolamp manufacturers. For flexible and varied lighting arrangements, an exposure meter will prove more accurate.

Backgrounds can be created for sets from enlarged photographic prints, framed pictures, calendar illustrations, or tapestries. The wall of a room can also be used as a background.

The most familiar household articles assume a new and exciting air when illuminated by colored lights. Spotlights with colored theatrical gelatin filters add a new dimension to any subject. Colored lights projected on glassware or statuettes are especially striking. When more elaborate equipment is

Dramatic lighting from sunlight and an unusual viewpoint produced this striking photograph of a toy car. Photo by Fred Prate.

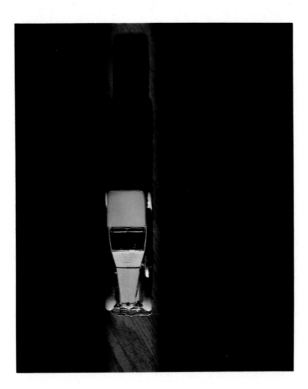

A back-projected beach scene adds to the illusion of reality in this still-life arrangement of glass objects. Textured cloth was used for the "sand" effect.

not available, colored cellophane held over the lens of a slide projector with a rubber band will make a satisfactory colored spotlight.

If the camera is capable of making double exposures, fascinating multiple exposures can be made by photographing the same subject in three or four different positions, illuminating it each time with a spotlight of a different color. Colored candle flames can be created by using different colored filters over the camera lens for each exposure on the same frame. Be sure the filters are perfectly clean and free from fingerprints, otherwise the flames will look fuzzy.

(Left) A single light positioned on the left side illuminates this figurine. The light is aimed so that it will not strike the background. (Right) A slide projected from the rear onto a matte-acetate background completes the oriental theme. Photos by Keith Boas.

Tabletop Photography

An elaborate setting on the theme of the Four Seasons was used for this display of fine china. The edge of the table is deliberately shown in this picture to illustrate the full set-up, which includes real autumn leaves and a square of turf. Photo by Michael Waine.

Table

A folding card table makes an excellent base for many tabletop setups. If a hole about 1 foot square is cut through the center of such a table, and a piece of opal glass placed over the hole to hold the subject, spotlights can be positioned to shine up from beneath the table for special lighting effects.

Special Effects

Familiar household items can be used to add special effects. For example, snow can be made from baking soda or salt, convincing water from crumpled cellophane or pebble-surfaced glass, and realistic-looking clouds from tufts of cotton. Rain can be simulated by smearing a pane of glass with petroleum jelly, and then spraying the greasy surface with a spray-type window cleaner to simulate beads of water. (Real water will not work.)

To create the effect of Christmas ornaments and other subjects photographed through a frosty windowpane, dab rubber cement around the corners of the glass pane and sprinkle powdered sugar on the cement.

There are relatively few technical problems in tabletop photography. Use slow shutter speeds and small lens openings if depth of field is needed. There is no need to work in haste, because there is no live model fidgeting, and no need to hurry before the

light changes. If the pictures do not come out the way you intended, they can easily be remade.

• *See also:* CLOSE-UP PHOTOGRAPHY; EXPOSURE; LIGHTING; MODEL AND MINIATURE PHOTOGRAPHY; PRODUCT PHOTOGRAPHY.

Talbot, William Henry Fox

(1800–1877)
English chemist, archaeologist

Talbot is generally credited with inventing the negative-positive system of photography. In his earliest experiments he used silver nitrate to sensitize paper; he later found that silver chloride was more sensitive. In 1835, he made his first photograph on sensitized paper, a photograph of his home, Laycock Abbey, near Chippenham in Wiltshire. After Daguerre announced his invention, Talbot described his system, which he called *photogenic drawing,* to the Royal Society in January of 1839.

His further experiments led to his discovery of the greater sensitivity of silver bromide as compared with silver chloride; he also adopted Herschel's discovery of the solvent powers of sodium thiosulfate to fix his images. In his investigations of the sensitivity of silver iodide, he discovered that a latent image

A Talbotype image: The Chess Players, by W. H. Fox Talbot. Photo courtesy of the International Museum of Photography, Rochester, NY.

was produced that could be developed in a solution of gallic acid; the exposure required to produce an image was reduced to about $\frac{1}{100}$ of that required for a silver chloride paper. By waxing the resulting negative, it could be printed on silver chloride-sensitized contact papers; this process he named "calotype." He patented an improved version in 1841 as the Talbotype. In 1844–1846, he published *The Pencil of Nature,* which was the first book with photographic illustrations and which showed many applications of photography, such as document copying. In 1852, Talbot patented a system of photoetching on steel and copper plates, which he named Photoglyphy; this was the forerunner of halftone image reproduction methods.

• *See also:* CALOTYPE.

Tanks

The development of film in tanks has been a preferred method of processing for many years. Trays are now seldom used for processing film except for some large sizes. Many different types of tanks are used by amateurs, hobbyists, and professionals.

Sheet-Film Tanks

The sheet-film tank is the outgrowth of the earliest form of plate tank. Since glass plates are rigid, the original plate tank consisted merely of a plastic or glass box with grooves in its walls. The tank was filled with developer, and the plates were inserted into the grooves one by one. Very dilute developers were usually used to allow time to insert and remove the plates. The basic fault with such tanks was that it was practically impossible to agitate the plates in the developer. Agitation of the entire tank accomplished little because the developer was trapped between the plates and had no place to go.

More modern tanks, for small sizes of glass plates, included an all-metal tank made by Kodak and a similar metal tank made by David Allan in England. In these, a separate cage was provided for the plates, which could be loaded and then dropped into the tank that contained the developer. In the "Dallan" tank, there was a lighttight spout at one end. The plates could be loaded into the cage, and the cage placed in the tank. With the lid on, the tank was both lighttight and watertight, so the developer could be poured in through the spout. After covering the spout, the tank could be agitated by turning it upside down at intervals.

With the growing popularity of sheet films and the decline of glass plates, the Dallan tank was supplied with a set of single sheaths made of metal, each holding one sheet of film. After loading the sheaths with film, the operator dropped them into the grooves of the cage and then dropped the entire cage into the tank.

A similar tank on a small scale is currently being made by Nikor. It differs in that the cage is made with grooves that hold the films in a slightly cupped form so they will not drop out of the cage. This is used in an ordinary round stainless steel tank exactly the same as that used with the Nikor rollfilm reels.

The modern method of processing sheet films in tanks is to use a plain hard-rubber or steel tank for each solution. Films are inserted into hangers, which are simple frames that hold one sheet of film each and have a long bar at the top so they can be suspended in a tank of any reasonable size. The most popular size of tank for this purpose holds 14 litres (3½ gallons) of solution and will accept hangers with films up to 20 × 24 cm or 8″ × 10″ in size. Some special hangers holding four 4″ × 5″ films in the same area as one sheet of 8″ × 10″ film are also available. For convenience in handling, the hangers are usually inserted into a hanger rack, which then drops into the tank as a unit. This makes it possible to agitate the entire batch of films by raising and lowering the entire rack as a unit. Smaller-capacity tanks are also widely used for sheet-film processing.

Roll-Film Tanks

The earliest form of daylight tank for processing roll film was produced by Kodak. It consisted of a wooden box containing two spindles, a reel, and a roll of black celluloid apron with rubber spacers along the edges. Also part of the outfit was a metal cup with a lighttight and watertight lid.

Modern apron-type tanks, which include the Kodacraft and the German Correx tank, are not daylight-loading. They use a transparent apron that is dimpled on both sides and suspends the film by its edges between turns of the apron in such a way that the solution can get to both sides. Thus, they may be used with any type of film, including those having antihalation dyes on the back side. They are made in sizes for 35 mm film and roll films up to 120-size.

Spiral Reel Tanks

With the advent of 35 mm film for still cameras, a new type of tank became popular; this is the familiar spiral reel and cup. The first of these was probably the Reelo, which was made by E. Leitz for use with the Leica camera. In the Reelo, the reel itself was molded of Bakelite and was not adjustable. The spiral grooves were made so the film had to be started from the middle of the reel and wound in from outside by cupping the film between the fingers and turning the reel. After loading in the dark, the reel was placed in its cup, also made of Bakelite, and the lid was attached. Solutions could be poured in and out through a light-trapped funnel in the cover,

and agitation was done by rotating the tank on the tabletop. It could not be inverted without spilling the solution.

A great many plastic tanks of the same general type were offered over the following years. Some had grooves of different shapes to permit loading by pushing the film in from outside. Some even had little mechanical gadgets in the reels to allow semi-automatic loading by twisting the ends of the reels.

At least two tanks using plastic reels were made for room-light operation: the Agfa Rondinax tank and the Kodak day-load tank. In the latter, the exposed film was placed in a separate compartment, the end of the film threaded through into the reel, and then both compartments covered. Turning a knob wound the film into the reel. Closing the compartment in which the film cartridge was contained automatically cut off the film and permitted the end to be wound into the reel. The tank was filled through a funnel in the lid. The remainder of the process was much the same as with any other tank.

Modern Roll-Film Tanks

Modern roll-film tanks are all made in much the same way. They are basically stainless steel cups containing one or more reels made by coiling up stainless steel wire and welding it to spacers to form the reel ends and hub. These reels are light, easy to load, and are made in a variety of sizes for films from 16 mm wide (the 110-size roll) through 35 mm and on to several sizes of roll films. The wider films are usually loaded with the assistance of a simple film-loading device that keeps the film properly cupped and guides it into the reel.

Special reels are made for larger amounts of film. There is a Nikor tank for 15 metres (50 feet) of 16 mm film, and several for different lengths of 35 mm film up to 30 metres (100 feet). For ordinary film types, standard reels are used. Where a larger quantity of work is being done, there are tanks that hold up to four (or even more) reels in a single cup. There is also a variety of reel racks to allow processing 35 mm films and roll films on stainless steel reels in the same 14-litre (3½-gallon) tank as is used for sheet films.

Agitation

With small tanks, agitation is most easily carried out by inverting the tank at intervals and rotating it gently. Large sheet-film tanks, and those using a rack full of reels in the 14-litre (3½-gallon) tank, usually call for agitation by raising and lowering the rack at intervals.

A modern and more efficient method of agitation is used in these larger tanks. A stainless steel tube, perforated with numerous small holes, is placed in the bottom of the tank and connected to a device that contains a timer and a tank of nitrogen. At intervals, it releases a burst of nitrogen bubbles that rises through the tank to the solution surface and stirs up the developer quite efficiently. Use of nitrogen gas is necessary with developers in order to avoid oxidation. However, in the fixing and washing baths, oil-free air is just as useful and cheaper. In some color-processing bleach baths, air is essential to oxidize the bleach and maintain its activity.

Chemical Mixing Tanks

Chemicals should not be mixed in the vessel used for processing. Generally, small amounts of chemicals are mixed in plastic or stainless steel buckets. In large plants, stainless steel tanks are used for mixing and storing solutions. These usually contain a motor-driven stirrer to reduce the labor of mixing. Such a stirrer must be properly designed to avoid causing vortices in the solution. These may produce areas that are not completely mixed, and may introduce air into the solution, which causes oxidation. Commercially available equipment is designed to reduce this problem.

Color Film Processing

Color transparency films (and black-and-white reversal films as well) used to require re-exposure to white light partway through the process. Modern processing solutions have eliminated this requirement by the use of chemical fogging agents. Earlier plastic tanks had a reel made especially for reversal work, in which one end flange was made of transparent plastic. The re-exposure could be made right through the end of the reel.

• *See also:* COLOR FILM PROCESSING; DARKROOM, AMATEUR; DARKROOM, PROFESSIONAL; DEVELOPERS AND DEVELOPING; DIRECT POSITIVE PROCESSING; FILMS AND PLATES; GASEOUS-BURST AGITATION; MIXING; PROCESSING LONG ROLLS; REVERSAL PROCESSING; WASHING.

Tanning Developer

A tanning developer is a developer that has the property of hardening soft gelatin while developing a silver image. Since the hardening or tanning action occurs only where a silver image is developed, it is possible, in the case of a film originally coated with soft gelatin which is soluble in warm water, to wash away all the non-image gelatin and leave a gelatin relief image exactly corresponding to the silver image. The film is exposed through the base so that the developed, hardened gelatin adheres to the base during the wash-off procedure. This process is used in making matrices for the dye transfer process and also with certain drafting-room copying films.

Formulas for tanning developers are not available, but they generally utilize either pyrogallol or pyrocatechin as the developing agent, with a moderate amount of sodium carbonate, and little or no sodium sulfite. Since the tanning action depends upon the oxidation of the developing agent while it is reducing the silver bromide to silver, it is obvious that anything that hinders this oxidation will also diminish the tanning action. Only enough sodium sulfite is used to prevent aerial oxidation for the short time needed to develop the film. Such a developer, of course, does not keep and must be mixed fresh for every film or batch of films developed at one time.

• *See also:* DEVELOPERS AND DEVELOPING; DYE TRANSFER PROCESS.

Taylor, Harold Dennis
(1862–1943)
English lens designer

H. D. Taylor is famed for his 1893 lens design known as the "Cooke Triplet." He had patented several triplets where various of the three lens elements were cemented doublets. However, when he announced the design of the "Triplet," which was manufactured by the firm of Taylor, Hobson, Cooke (the Taylor was no relation), he created lens design history. For the first time, it was shown that all the major aberrations could be well-corrected in a lens having just three elements. His lens could be made

lens into the bag, aim, and make the exposures. The drawback with this kind of support is that you need a surface, at a level you can sight from, on which to rest the bag. When photographing from a car, the bean bag works well if rested on a window ledge, provided, of course, that the vehicle's engine is not running during the exposures.

Shoulder Support. Another support that may be useful in the field consists of a shoulder support similar to the stock of a rifle. The device is used in much the same way. It is excellent for recording birds in flight.

Handy Objects. Buildings, rocks, or trees can be used if they are in the right location for the desired shot. Simply brace the camera against the object and make the exposure.

Chainpod. If there are no convenient supports available for bracing the camera, a chainpod may be used. A chainpod consists of a standard tripod screw attached to a length of chain. After attaching the tripod screw to the camera, hold the camera at eye level, step on the chain, and pull against it to create tension to steady the camera.

Hand-Held Lens. If you are forced to hand-hold the telephoto lenses, follow this rule of thumb in selecting the best shutter speed: Use a shutter speed no slower than the one closest to the focal length of the lens being used. For example, with a 135 mm lens, 1/125 sec. would be the slowest shutter speed to use when hand-holding the lens. Using a 200 mm lens would call for a shutter speed of 1/250 sec.; a 400 mm lens, 1/500 sec.

When hand-holding telephoto lenses, always remember to cradle the lens barrel with one hand, tuck your elbows to your sides, and hold your breath (halfway through the exhale) when making the exposure.

Accessories

Lens Hoods. Lens hoods for long lenses are generally much longer than those used with shorter focal-length lenses. Because telephoto lenses are narrow-angle lenses, longer lens hoods are required for effective glare reduction. They are especially useful when photographing distant scenes in which aerial haze already reduces the image contrast.

Filters. When using telephoto lenses to photograph over great distances, filters can be used to further combat the effects of aerial haze. With black-and-white film, a red filter maximizes contrast. With color film, ultraviolet filters or skylight filters limit the blueness of the haze. Of course, other filters may be appropriate for other effects. (*See:* FILTERS.)

Filters for telephoto lenses can be quite expensive because they are generally of a larger diameter than filters for normal lenses. Some long lenses will accept small-diameter glass filters over the rear lens element; these are relatively inexpensive. Gelatin filters can, of course, be used with telephoto lenses. One method of using gelatin filters is to attach a small piece of filter over the rear lens element. Care should be taken to make sure that the gelatin filter does not detach itself from this position as it could jam the mirror mechanism and result in a costly repair bill.

Special Problems

Mirror Lenses. Mirror lenses, also known as catadioptric lenses, are characterized by short physical length, large diameter, and a small mirror mounted in the center of the front element. By "folding" the path of light rays, mirror lenses can have long focal lengths and yet be very short physically. A 500 mm (20-inch) mirror telephoto lens may be only 200 mm (8 inches) long. Mirror lenses are compact and convenient, but there are drawbacks in using them. First, they have no diaphragms to control exposure. Exposure is controlled by varying shutter speeds, by using neutral-density filters, or by doing both. Second, the fixed aperture for these lenses is generally $f/5.6$ or $f/8$. They are not very fast, so using slow-speed, fine-grain film is often a problem. A more serious drawback is the way in which these lenses render an out-of-focus background. Details tend to multiply and remain fairly sharp, instead of going completely out of focus as with other lenses. Generally, mirror lenses tend to yield images that have lower color contrast and less color saturation than those of comparable all-glass design. (*See:* MIRROR LENSES.)

Extenders. A lens extender is simply a Barlow lens that is fitted between the camera body and the prime camera lens. An extender increases the focal length of the prime lens so that a normal lens can become a short telephoto lens, or a short telephoto can become a long one. Extenders come in several powers: 1.5, 2, 3, or Zoom. With a $2\times$ extender, a 50 mm lens becomes a 100 mm lens, a 135 mm lens

This photograph, taken with a catadioptric lens, shows a typical background as rendered by this mirror lens. The reflection of the central spot is seen in the background as crater-like "doughnuts."

fixed lenses, such as most twin-lens reflex cameras. Telephoto afocal converters are usually more limited in range, usually increasing one focal length by a 1.5 factor. Like extenders, converters usually lower the image quality of the prime lens, although some rather costly ones designed for specific camera lenses can produce high-quality results. (*See:* LENSES.)

Monoculars, Binoculars, Telescopes. Devices designed for distance viewing can be made to work for photography, but results are usually less satisfactory than with telephoto camera lenses. The only

becomes a 270 mm lens, and so forth. But the extender also reduces the transmitted light, so that with a 2× converter, an $f/2$ lens becomes an $f/4$, an $f/2.8$ an $f/5.6$, and an $f/5.6$ an $f/11$. Image quality suffers to some degree depending on the quality of the extender, and for best results you may have to stop down considerably. To improve quality, some manufacturers are optically matching extenders with a prime lens and marketing the two items together.

Afocal Converters. Afocal converters serve the same purpose as extenders, but they are used on the front of normal lenses instead of behind them. This makes afocal converters useful for cameras with

Two images that show the apparent alteration of perspective with telephoto lenses. The normal photo (top) will assume the same perspective as the telephoto view (bottom) if it is held to the eye so the image of the cables is the same size as that in the telephoto view. Photos by Peter Gales.

exceptions are with really long focal lengths such as 800 mm or longer. In these cases, using a catadioptric telescope designed for photographic purposes can save money in the long run. Of course, telescopes designed especially for astrophotography are exceptions.

Perspective

Perspective seems to be altered when telephoto lenses are used. But in reality, perspective does not change, as the accompanying photographs illustrate. The "stacking" of objects or the "compression of space" is not "distortion" or "false perspective." The perspective is quite correct; it just appears to be false because of the viewing distance of the two-dimensional final photograph. See the article PERSPECTIVE for a full explanation of this phenomenon.

• *See also:* BINOCULARS, TAKING PICTURES THROUGH; BIRDS, PHOTOGRAPHY OF; CAMERA SUPPORTS; FISHEYE LENS; LENSES; MIRROR LENSES; PERSPECTIVE; TELESCOPES, PHOTOGRAPHING THROUGH; VISION; WIDE-ANGLE PHOTOGRAPHY; ZOOM LENS.

Telescopes, Photographing through

A telescope is a very long-focal-length optical system. When the need arises for images of great magnification and narrow angle of view, a telescope can be coupled to a camera.

The most common use of a camera-telescope combination is to make astronomical photographs (see the article ASTROPHOTOGRAPHY), but the technique can also be applied to photography of terrestrial subjects with good results. Big "close-up" images, taken without the subject's awareness, can have a great deal of impact in candid and illustrative photography. Wildlife and surveillance photography are just two of many specialized areas in which the use of telescopic systems is often essential.

The primary problems in photographing terrestrial subjects through a telescope are maintaining steadiness and providing proper exposure. The extreme focal length of such a system means that even the slightest vibration can have a serious effect on image sharpness. Because of the system's· focal

Coupling your camera to a telescope can extend not only the range of your camera, it can greatly expand your photographic horizons. Photo by Michael Fairchild.

length, the basic lens speed (maximum aperture) is quite small compared with that of most camera lenses—typically $f/8$ or $f/10$, or smaller. If further light reduction is needed, the camera lens diaphragm cannot be used; in fact, the camera lens is not used in the most efficient setups. That means there must be some provision for inserting neutral-density filters between the telescope and the camera, where the diameter of the system is smallest; this placement is a matter of optical quality as well as economy. Some terrestrial telescopes have an internal diaphragm, or fixed-stop plates that can be inserted; others have an adjustable-diaphragm sunshade. The f-values these devices provide may have to be recomputed when a camera is used. A camera with an internal metering system simplifies exposure greatly.

In the last twenty years, mirror lenses of great focal length but quite short physical length have been produced especially for photographic use. These have been derived from mirror-plus-lens telescope designs, but have features that make them especially convenient to use with cameras. (*See:* MIRROR LENSES.) For the most part, such lenses are quite expensive. The photographer who already has a telescope, or who wishes to make a moderate investment in order to achieve very long-focus photography, can be guided by the following information.

Types of Telescopes

Telescopes are classified according to whether they use lenses, mirrors, or both to form a prime image. All telescopes use eyepiece lenses to focus and magnify the prime image for viewing, but the eyepiece may or may not be used for photography.

Refracting Telescopes. Lens-type instruments are refracting telescopes. They are essentially like telephoto and long-focus camera lenses, but are usually larger and of longer focal length. The simplest type is a tube with a very long-focus objective lens at the front and an eyepiece lens at the rear. (Collapsible versions of this simple design resulted in the name of the instrument—which means "distant seeing device"—also becoming a verb, "to telescope.")

In this kind of design, the tube length must be essentially the same as the focal length of the objective. This is not a particular disadvantage in astronomical work, but it is highly impractical in many other applications. To overcome the problem of physical length, most terrestrial reflecting telescopes incorporate prisms to "fold" the optical path without shortening the focal length. Typically, a 20×

(magnification) scope is about 355 mm (14 inches) long, but the image size is equivalent to a 1000 mm (39⅜-inch) lens on a 35 mm camera. If the scope has an interchangeable or a variable-power ("zoom") eyepiece, the equivalent focal length can be extended to 2500 mm (100 inches) or more with no change in physical size. Many such scopes incorporate internal focusing, accomplished by a mechanism that moves one of the prisms. These features make this kind of refracting telescope highly suitable for photographic use, up to a power of about 40×. Beyond that point, there is so much light loss, and the effects of heat waves or other atmospheric disturbances are magnified so greatly, that image quality is usually unacceptable.

Reflecting Telescopes. As the name indicates, reflecting telescopes use mirrors. In the basic design, the Newtonian telescope, a concave parabolic mirror—the objective—collects light from the subject and reflects it to a focus. The objective mirror is at the rear, or bottom end, of the telescope body, the tube. A small angled mirror, or a prism, is suspended in the tube to intercept the path of the re-

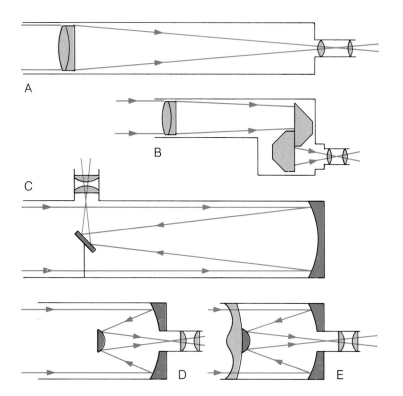

Types of telescopes. (A) Straight-tube refracting, the long focal length of which requires a long tube length. (B) Prismatic refracting, in which prisms reflect light over a long internal optical path so that a short tube accommodates a long focal length. (C) Newtonian reflecting, which has very large-diameter objective mirrors that are easier and far less costly to produce than lenses of equivalent size and quality, but which also has a long focal length that requires a long tube. (D) Cassegrain reflecting, in which mirrors shorten the physical length while maintaining a long focal length and all the advantages of reflection image-forming. (E) Catadioptric, in which a corrector-plate lens element greatly improves the image quality by counteracting mirror aberrations. In modern designs of the latter type, the eyepiece may extend into the tube with additional lens elements for greater magnification at no increase in tube length.

flected light and direct it to an eyepiece. The secondary mirror is so small that it does not obstruct a significant amount of the light entering the tube.

The Newtonian design is eminently practical for astronomical work because it provides greater focal length, light-gathering power, and image correction at much less cost than a comparable refracting telescope. However, physical size greatly limits its practicality for terrestrial use. The tube length must be the same as the focal length of the objective (within a few centimetres or inches). The thought of coupling a camera to a 1219 mm focal-length optical system becomes less exciting when it is realized that this means a device 4 feet long. Also, the eyepiece is located at the forward end of the tube, which makes handling awkward. Although it can be used, the Newtonian telescope is usually the last choice for terrestrial photography in any situation where convenience of setup and ease of adjustment—as well as speed of working—are important considerations.

The Cassegrain design provides much shorter physical length with no loss in focal length in a reflecting telescope, in much the same way as prismatic-design refracting telescopes. The image path is folded by a convex secondary mirror that directs the converging light rays back through a hole in the center of the primary, objective mirror; the eyepiece is located at this point. The Cassegrain design makes possible highly compact telescopes of great focal length and quite wide aperture. Modifications of the Cassegrain design incorporating lens elements provide the most widely used kind of telescope employed for terrestrial photography.

Catadioptric Telescopes. Mirror-plus-lens, or catadioptric, telescopes are basically Cassegrain designs; usually the name of the inventor of a modification is added to distinguish the design. The fundamental addition is a corrector lens that bends entering light rays to compensate for aberrations induced by the objective mirror. The improvement in image quality obtained this way has led to extensive use of quite large catadioptric telescopes for astrophotography. Smaller models are excellent for terrestrial use. A typical telescope for this purpose has a 1.8 m (6-foot) focal length in a tube only 200 mm (8 inches) long, with focusing from infinity to 3 m (10 feet). Many such telescopes are supplied with adapters for direct coupling to a small- or medium-format camera.

The catadioptric design is so practical and performance is so excellent that many lens manufacturers use it for very long-focal-length camera lenses, usually identified as mirror, reflex, or "cat" lenses. The design concentrates the mass (weight) into a small volume, which helps to damp vibrations. In some situations it is possible to hand-hold the equipment for photographic use, although solid mounting is always preferable. The small size makes it quite readily portable. Because of these factors, a catadioptric telescope or lens is easily the first choice for terrestrial photography whenever extreme focal length is required.

Telescope Specifications

The basic specifications given for medium- and small-size telescopes are usually simply power and objective diameter in millimetres. Thus, 40×75 indicates that the telescope in question magnifies the visual size of an object 40 times, and that the objective lens or mirror is 75 mm in diameter. With larger telescopes, specifications usually include the focal length and diameter of the objective, the power obtained with a stated eyepiece, and the aperture, or basic f-value.

The focal length of a telescope is the focal length of its objective lens or mirror. The aperture is the focal length divided by the diameter of the objective. Some terrestrial telescopes have an internal iris diaphragm, or accept stops, to change the f-value; an external iris diaphragm is incorporated in the sunshade of some medium-size and small-size refracting telescopes. Apertures are identified by f-numbers, just as they are with lenses.

The power, or magnification, obtainable with a telescope is determined by the eyepiece. It is calculated in this way: objective focal length ÷ eyepiece focal length. Thus, the shorter the eyepiece, the greater the power. Most telescopes offer various powers by means of interchangeable eyepieces—sometimes mounted on a turret—or a variable-focal-length zoom eyepiece. The best-quality eyepieces are called "orthoscopic."

Power can also be manipulated by inserting a Barlow lens—a negative or afocal lens—in the eyepiece mounting tube to relay the image from the objective to the eyepiece lens. The effect of the Barlow lens is to increase the focal length of the objective, which results in greater power with a given eyepiece.

Telescopes designed for astronomical use have no distance focusing capability because the subject is always at infinity; they do have critical focusing at the eyepiece for the sharpest image. Terrestrial telescopes must allow focusing on subjects at various distances. Some models have internal focusing, accomplished by shifting a prism, secondary mirror, or lens element. Otherwise, focusing is usually accomplished by changing the distance between the eyepiece and the objective. A variety of focusing movements—rack-and-pinion, sliding tube, helical thread—are used.

Equipment for Telescope Photography

The combinations described in the next section require some means of coupling the telescope and camera, and of supporting them firmly. Many manufacturers of terrestrial telescopes supply adapters so that properly aligned direct coupling with a camera (usually a 35 mm single-lens reflex camera) is easily accomplished. A variety of accessory adapters and couplers are also available from photographic dealers. The accessory devices are usually some kind of bracket that screws into the camera's tripod socket and attaches to the telescope either by a second tripod screw or by an adjustable clamp. There are also tubes or mounting rings that screw or bayonet directly into the lens mount on the camera body. Beware of any device that screws into the filter threads of a lens barrel and offers no other support to the camera. The lens is not designed to support the weight of the telescope or the camera body—depending on which is mounted on a tripod—and can easily be damaged in such an arrangement.

With small cameras the most solid support is usually obtained by mounting the telescope itself on a tripod. Many instruments have a tripod socket, which may be on an adjustable collar to permit balancing the setup as well as to turn the camera between horizontal and vertical formats. If a coupling bracket is used between the camera and the telescope, it should have a sliding/locking tripod bushing for balancing.

With larger equipment it may be necessary to use separate tripods for the telescope and the camera; this is a bit cumbersome to set up, but provides excellent support.

Any arrangement should be protected from cross breezes, if only by the photographer's body.

The telescope greatly increases the amount of surface that offers wind resistance and consequently increases the danger of vibration. Wait a moment or two after stepping into a shielding position before releasing the shutter, in order to let any vibration subside.

The only practical kind of camera to use for high-quality results is one with through-the-lens viewing and focusing. The most common choice is a 35 mm single-lens reflex model, because it offers small size, light weight, large film capacity, and ease of operation and reloading. A medium-format SLR or a view camera may also be used to excellent effect, sacrificing only some convenience in handling. A bellows-type camera has the greatest susceptibility to externally caused vibration.

The most flexible telescope-camera combinations do not use the camera lens. Therefore, not only must the camera permit lens removal, it must have a self-contained shutter. A camera with an internal metering system will provide accurate exposures. If the telescope does not have an internal (or accessory) f-stop control, light transmission can be reduced by using neutral density filters. Most catadioptric systems provide for filters to be inserted at the eyepiece tube. If the telescope does not have an integral hood, a deep lens shade is important to reduce flare in large-diameter equipment.

A major source of vibration in a mirror-reflex camera can be eliminated if the mirror can be locked out of position before the exposure, or if the shutter has a delayed release after the mirror moves. The slow-speed or self-timer settings on some cameras provide the second feature. A cable release will also help to prevent vibration.

Telescope-Camera Combinations

There are four ways in which a telescope and camera can be combined for photography.

1. Eyepiece-Camera Lens. The normal lens of the camera is aligned with the eyepiece of the telescope. The camera lens is used at maximum aperture and at its infinity focus setting. Image sharpness is adjusted with the telescope focus control. The effective focal length of this combination is equal to the camera-lens focal length multiplied by the telescope power. The magnification is the same as the telescope (eyepiece) power. To make the setup, the only thing required is a bracket to keep the two units aligned. A loose-fitting tube between the eyepiece and lens may help exclude stray light; it can be improvised from black paper, although flexible plastic or rubber tubes are available for this purpose. The system has two major deficiencies: It reduces the light reaching the film more than any other combination, and it involves the greatest number of lens elements, which may induce aberrations in the image.

2. Eyepiece, or Positive, Projection. The camera lens is not used. The camera is coupled directly to the telescope eyepiece, which projects the image onto the film. The focal length of the system is that of the telescope; the magnification of an object at infinity is equal to the telescope power. Larger images can be obtained by moving the film plane farther from the eyepiece. To accomplish such an adjustment, an extendable coupling is required (some manufacturers supply an adjustable extension tube calibrated for various increases in magnification), or a camera with an adjustable back. This system provides more light than the first, and has only one set of lens elements to induce aberrations. However, as the film is moved farther from the eyepiece, the overall image brightness decreases. Focusing is controlled by the telescope.

3. Prime Focus, or Direct Objective. Neither the camera lens nor the telescope eyepiece is used.

Telescope-Camera System

F_o = focal length of telescope objective
F_e = focal length of eyepiece
F_c = focal length of camera lens
F_s = focal length of telescope-plus-camera system
P = power (magnification)
f = f-number of effective aperture
D = diameter of telescope objective

L = distance from eyepiece to film plane
A = distance from eyepiece to normal focus point of telescope objective
B = distance from Barlow lens to normal focus point of telescope objective
C = distance from Barlow lens to film plane

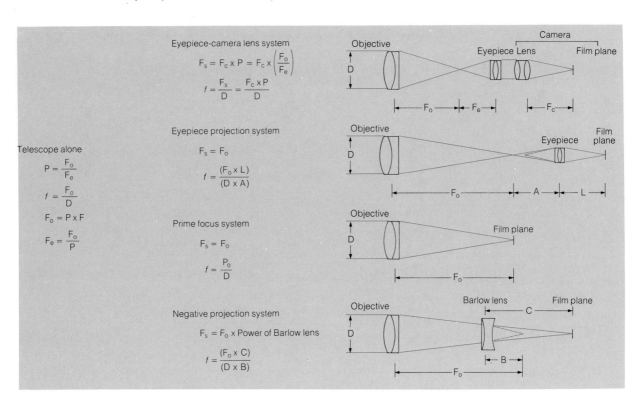

Telescope alone

$$P = \frac{F_o}{F_e}$$

$$f = \frac{F_o}{D}$$

$$F_o = P \times F$$

$$F_e = \frac{F_o}{P}$$

Eyepiece-camera lens system

$$F_s = F_c \times P = F_c \times \left(\frac{F_o}{F_e}\right)$$

$$f = \frac{F_s}{D} = \frac{F_c \times P}{D}$$

Eyepiece projection system

$$F_s = F_o$$

$$f = \frac{(F_o \times L)}{(D \times A)}$$

Prime focus system

$$F_s = F_o$$

$$f = \frac{F_o}{D}$$

Negative projection system

$$F_s = F_o \times \text{Power of Barlow lens}$$

$$f = \frac{(F_o \times C)}{(D \times B)}$$

The image from the objective is focused directly on the film. The effective focal length of the system is that of the objective. Magnification is equal to the objective focal length divided by the focal length of the normal lens for the camera. If the telescope does not have internal focusing, focus is adjusted by moving the film plane. This system provides maximum light transmission with minimum aberrations, but cannot achieve the magnifications possible with combination 2 or 4.

4. Negative Projection. A Barlow lens is used between the objective and the camera; the eyepiece and camera lens are not used. This is the same as prime projection; greater magnification is achieved because the Barlow lens increases the effective focal length of the objective, typically by $2\times$ or $3\times$.

The effective *f*-value of the system differs according to which of these combinations is utilized. The accompanying illustrations and equations show how *f*-values are computed, and summarizes other factors.

For further details in setting up combinations, see the section "Focusing Procedure and Camera Alignment" in the article ASTROPHOTOGRAPHY.

• *See also:* BINOCULARS, TAKING PICTURES THROUGH; LENS CONVERTERS; MIRROR LENSES; TELEPHOTOGRAPHY.

Television Screen, Photographing

Images can be photographed in color or black-and-white with still or motion-picture cameras.

Film Requirements

TV images are quite dim compared with average subjects in daylight. Therefore, to avoid using large lens openings and very slow shutter speeds, a high-speed film that is balanced for daylight exposure in the ASA 200 to 400 range can be used. However, medium-speed daylight-balanced films can also be used in the ASA 64 to 100 range. See the exposure table on p. 2391 or use a reflected-light exposure meter to determine proper exposure. To prevent camera motion at shutter speeds slower than 1/30 sec., mount the camera on a tripod or other firm support.

(Top) High-speed, daylight-balanced color films are best for photographing pictures on a TV screen. This photo was taken on Kodak Ektachrome 200 film (daylight), 1/30 sec. at f/2.8. (Bottom) For best results, adjust the TV brightness control so that both highlight and shadow areas of the image show detail.

Adjusting the Television Set

To obtain the best-quality photographs, adjust the TV set so that the contrast of the television picture is slightly lower than normal. Adjust the brightness control so that both the highlight and shadow areas of the TV image show detail. The shadows should not be a light tone or completely black. Adjust the controls on a color set for a pleasing color picture on the screen.

Sometimes in order to get enough exposure, depending upon the camera and film, it may be necessary to adjust the TV set for maximum brightness.

Room Lighting

To help eliminate reflections on the face of the television tube, turn off most or all of the room lights. Reducing the light in the room also helps to make the area surrounding the TV image appear black in photographs. This is usually more pleasing than a lighter area showing part of the room or the border around the picture tube.

Do not use flash or photolamp lighting to photograph television images. These light sources are much brighter than the TV image, and the pictures will show a blank television screen.

Taking the Picture

For best results, move in close to the television screen with the camera. If the minimum focusing distance for the camera will allow it, move in until the TV screen fills the picture area in the viewfinder. If the TV screen is small, a close-up lens can be used to get a larger image in the photographs.

If a single-lens reflex (SLR) camera with through-the-lens viewing is used, what is seen through the viewfinder is exactly what will result in the picture. But if the viewfinder on the camera is separate from the lens, it may not show exactly what will be included in the picture. To center the TV screen on the film with a camera of this type, use the close-up framing device described in the accompanying table.

If the camera can focus on subjects as close as 2 feet, TV screens that have a diagonal picture size of 14 inches or larger can be photographed and a satisfactory image size can be obtained without using a close-up lens. If the closest focus setting on the camera is 3 feet, TV screens that are 18 inches in size or larger can be photographed without a close-up lens.

Shutter Speed. Television images are composed of 525 straight horizontal lines called scanning lines. The image is formed in the TV set by a moving electron beam that scans the picture in two sections. All the odd-numbered lines are traced in 1/60 sec. to produce an image. As soon as this cycle is completed, the picture is scanned again in 1/60 sec., this time tracing the even-numbered lines. Therefore, it takes 1/30 sec. to make a complete picture on the screen. That is why a shutter speed of 1/30 sec. or slower must be used to record at least one complete picture cycle; otherwise, a dark band may appear across the photograph.

If the camera has a focal-plane shutter, a shutter speed of 1/8 sec. or slower should be used to obtain uniform exposure.

When shutter speeds slower than 1/30 sec. are used, put the camera on a tripod or other support, like a table. Use the fastest shutter speed possible, up to 1/30 sec. (1/8 sec. with a focal-plane shutter), in order to minimize subject motion in the pictures. For sharp pictures, make the exposure when the subject on the screen is not moving.

Automatic Cameras. Fill the picture area in the viewfinder with the TV image so that the exposure

CLOSE-UP LENSES FOR STILL CAMERAS WITH NORMAL LENSES

TV Screen Size*—Picture Diagonal (inches)	Close-up Lens	Distance from Lens to TV Screen† (inches)	Camera Focus Scale Setting at (feet)
22, 23, 25	+1	39	Infinity
20, 21	+1	34¾	25
18, 19	+1	32¼	15
14, 15, 16	+1	25½	6
11, 12	+2	19½	Infinity
9	+2	15½	6

*The nominal size of a television screen refers to the diagonal of the picture area.
†Measure the distance from the front rim of the close-up lens to the TV screen.

At shutter speeds faster than 1/8 sec. with a focal-plane shutter, or faster than 1/30 sec. with a leaf shutter, a dark band may appear in the picture. Photo at left was taken at 1/125 sec. with a focal-plane shutter.

meter in the camera "sees" only the TV screen. If the camera is too far away from the TV screen, the exposure meter sees too much of the dark area surrounding the TV image, resulting in overexposure of the film.

If the minimum camera-to-subject distance for the camera (without a close-up lens) will not allow a close-up that will fill the viewfinder with the TV image, it may be necessary to make a close-up exposure-meter reading. With some automatic cameras, the exposure setting determined by the camera can be maintained by partially depressing the shutter release and holding it in that position. Thus, the exposure can be set with the camera close to the TV screen. Continue to hold the shutter release partially depressed until the camera is moved back to take the picture. See the camera manual to determine whether your camera has this feature.

When taking pictures, the low-light indicator may appear in the camera viewfinder. This warning can usually be ignored and pictures can be taken anyway. The results will probably be satisfactory, but the pictures may appear dark. By comparing the exposures suggested in the following table, using the largest lens opening and the slowest shutter speed marked on some automatic cameras or given

in the camera manual, it is possible to determine whether the camera is capable of making properly exposed pictures.

Some automatic cameras determine the exposure by automatically selecting the shutter speed after the lens opening has been selected. To photograph TV images with this type of camera, focus the camera on the TV image, and adjust the lens opening until the shutter-speed control automatically selects a speed of 1/30 sec. (1/8 sec. or slower with a focal-plane shutter).

Pictures of color television taken with some color films may look somewhat blue-green. With most daylight color films, a Kodak color compensating filter, CC40R, over the camera lens will help to bring out the reds in pictures.

If the CC40R filter is used to improve color rendition, and the built-in exposure meter in the camera makes the reading through the filter over the lens, the camera should automatically increase exposure to compensate for the filter. But if the automatic camera has an exposure meter separate from the lens, it will be necessary to cut a small piece of the gelatin CC40R filter and tape it over the exposure meter. Then the camera should automatically adjust for proper exposure when the filter is used.

An overall blue-green color was avoided in this picture by using a CC40R (red) filter over the camera lens; exposure was increased by one stop. This photo was taken with Kodak high speed Ektachrome film (daylight), 1/8 sec. between f/2 and f/2.8.

Adjustable Cameras. With an adjustable camera that has a built-in exposure meter, when the meter reading is taken, be sure the TV screen fills the picture area as recommended for automatic cameras. If the camera does not have a built-in meter, a separate reflected-light exposure meter can be used to determine the exposure. Hold the meter close to the TV screen so that it reads only the screen. Position the meter to read approximately equal parts of light and dark areas of the TV picture. If you do not have an exposure meter, set the camera as suggested in the accompanying table.

Some exposure meters may indicate incorrect exposure for photographing TV because of the way the meter reacts to the TV image. Compare the exposure indicated by the meter with the exposure suggested in the table. If the exposure is much different, make some trial exposures with the camera to determine a correction factor for the exposure meter.

The camera settings in the table were derived from practical picture tests. These exposures are good starting points, but exposure can vary because the brightness of TV images varies with individual differences in the way the TV controls are adjusted, with the age of the TV set, and with differences in make or model. To be sure of getting a properly exposed picture of an especially important subject, bracket the exposure.

Movie Cameras. To make good-quality movies of television images, it is necessary to use a special camera synchronized with the television set to record successive picture cycles on successive frames of movie film. This is not practical for the amateur moviemaker; however, satisfactory results can still be obtained with an ordinary super 8 movie camera that has an f/2.8 (f/1.9 for 8 mm cameras) or faster lens.

Operate the camera at the normal camera speed for 16 or 18 frames per second. Since the movie camera is not synchronized with the TV picture cycle, the projected movie will show a slightly uneven flicker or banding effect.

With a super 8 camera that has an f/2.8 or faster lens, movies of color or black-and-white TV images can be made when a high-speed color film (ASA 160) is used. With a conventional super 8 camera not designed for existing light, the TV brightness control should be turned up as high as possible without losing too much detail. Adjust the contrast control to restore the contrast so that it appears slightly lower than normal. With a camera that has manually adjustable lens openings, set the lens at f/1.9, if possible. If the maximum lens opening on the camera is smaller than f/1.9, movies can be made at the maximum opening, but they will be somewhat dark.

Medium-Speed Film. With cameras designed for existing light, movies of television images can be

SUGGESTED CAMERA SETTINGS FOR PICTURES OF COLOR TELEVISION IMAGES*

Film Speed (ASA/ISO)	Leaf Shutter	Focal-Plane Shutter
400	1/30 sec. f/4	1/8 sec. f/8
200	1/30 sec. f/2.8	1/8 sec. f/5.6
64–100	1/15 sec. f/2	1/8 sec. f/2.8

*With leaf shutters, use a shutter speed of 1/30 sec. or slower. With focal-plane shutters, use a shutter speed of 1/8 sec. or slower to avoid dark bands in pictures. With shutter speeds slower than 1/30 sec., use a tripod or other camera support.

made with the TV set adjusted normally. With these cameras, better sharpness and exposure can be obtained when a medium-speed film (ASA 40–64) is used rather than a faster film. The flicker or banding effect in movies made of television images is less noticeable with super 8 cameras that feature large shutter openings for existing-light moviemaking.

High-Speed Film. High-speed film (ASA 160) can also be used in existing-light cameras for photographing TV images, but it will require a little extra effort to obtain good exposure. At the minimum recommended camera-to-subject distance for these cameras, the automatic exposure control sees the dark area surrounding the TV screen and causes overexposure, or washed-out movies, on high-speed films.

One way to obtain correct exposure with high-speed films is to use a close-up lens so that the camera can be positioned close enough to the TV set for the exposure meter in the camera to make the reading of the TV image only.

Some cameras have an exposure-meter lock or similar device that allows a close-up reading to be made on the TV screen. After the reading has been made, the camera can be moved back to the minimum camera-to-subject distance in order to film the TV image. If the camera has this feature, see the camera manual for instructions on using it.

Another way to obtain proper exposure on high-speed films without using close-up lenses is to use a neutral density filter over the camera lens to reduce the amount of light reaching the film. A 0.40 neutral density filter should give the correct exposure for high-speed films.

Since the lens on the movie camera will probably be at its maximum opening, accurate focusing is necessary. Use the rangefinder if the camera has one, or measure the distance carefully from the TV screen to the film plane in the camera. The location of the film plane can be judged by observing where the front edge of the super 8 cartridge is located when it is in the camera; or, if an 8 mm camera is used, where the film is located behind the lens.

Sound Movies. Sound movies of television programs can be made with a movie camera that records sound. To make sound movies, it is necessary to use sound movie film in the camera. Plug the microphone into the camera microphone jack according to the instructions for the equipment. Point

the mike toward the TV speaker and keep the mike at least 6 feet from the TV set so that an audible hum will not be recorded in the sound track. If an on-camera microphone is used, point it toward the TV set. When using a camera with this feature—the camera must be closer than 6 feet to the television set—plug a separate microphone into the camera. This will deactivate the on-camera mike and allow positioning of the active mike 6 feet or more from the set.

To minimize the possibility of recording extraneous noise or other unwanted sounds, set the volume control on the TV set slightly higher than normal.

• *See also:* Cathode-Ray Tube Recording.

 Television, Slides for

Color slides give commercial and public television stations and cable television operators a useful and versatile method for supplementing local programming. Slides can be made by photographing scenes or sets, illustrative materials, or specially prepared artwork.

Programming

Slides serve many purposes in television programming. A local advertiser can superimpose pricing information or a store's location over a film or videotape commercial. This can be done by setting up a live television camera in the studio and placing a card with the desired information in hot-press lettering or hand lettering on an easel in front of the camera. To avoid the inconvenience and expense of having the studio crew standing by until the "super" is called for, a slide can be made by simply copying the information on the card with a film camera, and then placing the slide in the telecine projector, ready to be called whenever it is needed.

Slides can be very effective in creating inexpensive commercial spots for local advertisers. A photographer can go to the advertiser's premises and, with a camera, a roll of color film, and a modest amount of lighting equipment, bring back a selection of pictures to produce a commercial presentation of any desired length. Loaded in the telecine projector, the slides can be brought up one after the other in a rapidly changing sequence.

With a complicated slide series, a transfer to videotape may be desirable. This method of production also offers the opportunity to introduce such special effects as fades, mixes, or "supers."

Many television producers use color slides to supplement programs on film or videotape. For example, a gardening show could use slides to show close-ups of flowers. Slides can be shown for any length of time, enabling viewers to study picture details.

Exposure

Calculating the correct exposure for television slides requires a different procedure from that used by photographers who make slides for direct projection on a screen. This is because the white level video signals must be considered. For example, suppose that the first scene to be photographed for a series of slides has a large sky area with white clouds, while the second has to be taken on a hazy day. A scene-averaging light meter may indicate that the film should be given the same exposure in both cases. However, when these slides are projected into the telecine camera, the peak white signal levels are likely to be quite different—the slide with the white clouds could give a signal 15 or 20 IEEE units higher than the one made under hazy conditions (because there is no true white in the latter scene).

Spot Meter. To get around the problem of variations in peak white signal levels, the film must be exposed so that the lightest areas in scenes will always be reproduced at approximately the same density in the film images. This can be done by using a spot meter.

When a spot meter is used to calculate the exposure for a scene, a measurement is made of the lightest area in the scene, and the camera lens is then adjusted to obtain a specified value of density in the film image. Recommended Practice RP46-1972 of the Society of Motion Picture and Television Engineers specifies the density corresponding to television white level* should be 0.3 to 0.4 (except for specular highlights and other small areas where details need not be reproduced). To set up an exposure-control system based on the use of a spot meter, a

---

*Television white level preferably corresponds to a fully lighted object in the scene having a reflectance of approximately 60 percent. This results in the reproduction of fully lighted human faces that give reflectances of 35 to 15 percent at film densities 0.2 to 0.5 greater than the density corresponding to television white.

series of test exposures must be made on the film selected for use in the camera. This is needed to find the spot-meter reading that will give a density within the recommended range, at given settings of the camera lens aperture and shutter speed. For these tests the gray scale test chart used in the studio for setting up television cameras can be used.

Working with the television engineer, the photographer can determine the spot-meter reading for the lightest step of the test chart, which represents the correct exposure conditions for the camera film used. Field tests are also required to determine adjustments that might need to be made in exposure level. Consistency of exposure level is the real key to making good television slides.

The light-integrating method of determining exposure has the advantage that scenes with widely varying contrast ratios can be accommodated, but this is achieved at the expense of varying maximum and minimum densities in the images. When the exposure is being calculated with a spot meter to give uniform minimum densities in the images, scenes with different contrasts will have varying degrees of black compression. This can be avoided by using artificial illumination (fill light) to reduce scene contrast. (*See:* EXPOSURE TECHNIQUES.)

Copy Stand Exposure

For slide-making with a copying stand, a modification of the basic exposure-control system is needed to accommodate the special conditions encountered in photographing flat artwork and illustrative materials. A special test chart should be prepared from commonly used artist's materials—for instance, a small patch of white sheeting used for hot-press lettering mounted in the middle of an 8″ × 10″ section of black art board.

The test chart should be placed on the copying surface and uniformly illuminated. Then a series of exposures should be made. After the film has been processed, the slides should be run through the telecine to find the exposure level at which the most favorable video waveforms are obtained.

Slide Framing and Registration

Accurate registration of picture information within the television raster requires:

1. A slide projector capable of precisely positioning the slide mounts in the optical system of the telecine camera.

2. Slide mounts giving a snug fit in the slots of the projector magazine or slide-changing mechanism.
3. A means for properly locating the film frames in the slide mounts.
4. A camera with the capability for correctly positioning the film perforations relative to the exposure aperture (mask) in the film plane.
5. A means for locating picture information in the desired position in the film frames during exposure in the camera.

Professional-quality slide projectors meet the first requirement—precise positioning of the slide mounts in the telecine optical system. However, if the information is not correctly positioned in the slides, there is nothing the telecine operator can do to correct the fault, since these projectors are designed to hold slides rigidly in place.

To conform with the second requirement, the slide mounts must be the right size to give a close fit in the projector mechanism. SMPTE Recommended Practice RP9-1966 specifies that slides for precise applications in television should be 50 ± 0.025 mm (1.984 ± 0.001 inches) square. This is a significant improvement over the slide mounts intended for amateur use, which may be as much as 0.80 mm ($\frac{1}{32}$ inch) undersize.

The third requirement, a means for accurately locating the film frames in the slide mounts, is also provided for in the above-mentioned SMPTE Recommended Practice RP9. According to these specifications, the slide mounts should have registration pins to engage the film perforations.

The fourth requirement, a camera that will accurately locate the film perforations relative to the edges of the mask at the film exposure plane, is not so easy to meet. The film-advancing mechanisms in 35 mm single-exposure cameras are designed only to move sufficient film over the aperture at the exposure plane to accommodate the next exposure. Exactly the same advancement for each frame is not a requirement. Therefore, the location of each exposure relative to the film perforations can (and usually does) vary slightly depending on the degree of slippage in the film-advance mechanism of the camera.

If exact registration is needed, a special copy camera with registering pins is available. Production houses specializing in making slides and filmstrips are likely to be equipped with animation stands with complete registration capabilities.

Correctly locating the picture information in the film frames during exposure—the fifth requirement—can be achieved in several ways. One method is to utilize standard-sized cards for the artwork, with holes punched in the upper edge to fit over registering pins embedded in the copying table. Another method, giving artists more freedom in the preparation of artwork, makes use of a field chart for setting up the camera.

A field chart consists of a sheet of transparent plastic with a series of evenly spaced rectangles ruled on it. As the distance of the camera above the copying surface is increased, successive fields inscribed on the chart will be seen at the film plane in the camera, coinciding with the edges of the exposure mask. Marks placed on the camera support column of the copying stand and numbered to correspond with the fields ruled on the chart can then be used to set the camera at the proper height above the copying surface, thus accommodating a wide range of sizes in the cards used by the artists. When the artwork is being prepared, a field chart laid over it should be used to indicate the field at which the copying camera can be set when the exposure is being made. This number may be marked on the edge of the card as a guide for the photographer.

Safe Title Area for Television Transmission

In the production of slides for television, important picture information, such as lettering and commercial messages, should be held within the area of the television picture that will be reproduced by the majority of home receivers. The accompanying illustration shows the safe title area specified in SMPTE Recommended Practice RP27.3-1972, "Specifications for Safe Action and Safe Title Areas Test Pattern for Television Systems."

The illustration shown here can be used as a guide in the preparation and scaling of artwork and the location of the artwork under the copying camera when slides are being made. A grease pencil could be used to outline the safe title area on a television picture monitor, as an aid in the evaluation of slide production. The test slide can also be projected on a viewing screen to facilitate checking slides before they are used in television programs.

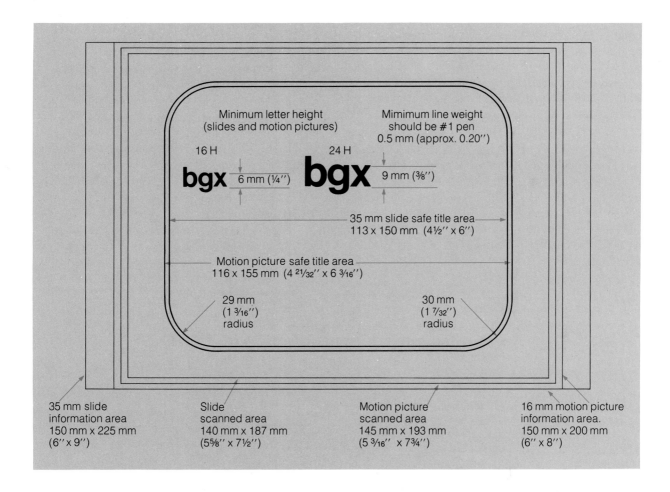

Dimensions of artwork templates for materials used in the television system. This illustration, which is drawn to scale, can be photographically enlarged and used for artwork templates.

Transparencies of the safe title area can be made in any reasonable size by projection printing on a high-contrast film such as Kodalith ortho film, type 3, for use by artists and photographers.

Legibility Requirements

To be legible, lines, letters, and symbols should contrast adequately with the background, there must be distinct separation of tones, and the colors selected should be strong and attractive. Tonal contrast is particularly important when preparing artwork for television, since the television receiver may display the colored artwork in a black-and-white mode.

Letters and symbols should be bold and simple, with no small openings that will tend to fill in when projected. All elements such as lines, letters, symbols, and figures require a size big enough to be seen easily by everyone in the audience. Therefore, these elements have to be at least a certain minimum size on the screen, the size depending on the height of the artwork area in relation to its distance from the farthest viewer.

In typical viewing situations—screen-to-viewer distances ranging from short (in small conference rooms or in homes), through medium (in class and meeting rooms), to long (in large auditoriums and theaters)—the maximum viewing distance should be about eight times the height of the projected image. To put it another way, if the projected material is legible for the farthest viewer, who is seated eight times the projected image height from the screen, it will be legible for all other members of the audience. This maximum viewing distance (expressed as 8H) can be used in determining the minimum size of significant detail in the material to be projected.

Television images are frequently viewed at distances greater than 8H. For example, an image only 315 mm (12½ inches) high on a 533 mm (21-inch) picture tube may often be viewed from 7–9 m (20–30 feet) in the home or in a classroom. Therefore, when material is being prepared for such use, legibility requirements for comparatively great viewing distances must be considered.

In addition, some area of the original transparency will be lost in the television chain and in the receiver. The amount lost is not always the same; it will vary with such things as receiver adjustment and line voltage. To help provide minimum loss, any essential information must be confined to a central "safe title area." Even so, the usable portion of the art should extend to a minimum area of 175 × 250 mm (7″ × 10″). Minimum letter height (lowercase character less ascender or descender) can be 6–9 mm (¼–⅜ inch). These letter heights allow 16H–24H viewing and provide legibility at distances of 5.5–7.3 m (18–24 feet), 6.4–8.2 m (21–27 feet), and 7–9.1 m (23–30 feet) respectively from a 432, 533, or 635 mm (17-, 21-, or 25-inch) picture tube.

Where possible, it is recommended that the finished artwork be reviewed both in color and black-and-white on the telecine chain before being broadcast. This procedure will indicate any changes in the artwork (contrast, separation of tones, letter height, and color) needed to make it acceptable for broadcasting. If it is not practical, the artwork must be created to take these elements (of the artwork) into account. One color that reflects or transmits the same amount of light as another color will cause the two colors to appear as the same neutral tone on a black-and-white television receiver.

If the artwork is to be used for both TV transmission and regular projection, the lettering and title area should be designed to meet the TV requirements. When the material is being photographed for a projection slide, an extreme close-up can be made so that unnecessary background will be eliminated.

 **Temperature Control**

Accurate, consistent control of photographic processing conditions is necessary for predictable, repeatable results. Particularly critical is the control of processing solution temperature in color and photomechanical work, which may have to be controlled within 0.3 C (½ F).

Small-Scale Control

When you have only small quantities of photographic materials to be processed, you can get along with manual adjustment of temperature. For example, you can fit the drain of the darkroom sink with a standpipe, and allow water from an ordinary mixing faucet to surround processing tanks to the level of the standpipe. With such an arrangement, you must watch a thermometer placed in the water flow to make sure that varying loads on the water-supply lines do not change the temperature of the mixture.

Solutions in metal (stainless steel) containers will adjust temperature more rapidly than those in plastic or glass. Be sure to stir the solution in a container thoroughly before checking its temperature so that the thermometer will not encounter a warm or cool pocket and give a false reading.

Solutions in open trays can also be brought to temperature by placing in them a bottle or other closed container filled with hot or cold water, or ice, as required. Laying a bottle on its side brings more area in contact with the tray solution, and rolling it back and forth helps speed the control. Ice in a plastic bag can also be used. Do not add ice directly to a solution because that will change its strength.

Larger-Scale Control

With certain processes, or with appreciable quantities of sensitized material, the manual control of temperature in processing is often cumbersome. Therefore, you will need an automatic temperature-control system that is both accurate and dependable. The following are some methods for maintaining uniform solution temperature.

Immersion Heaters. Small immersion-heater units control the temperature of the water bath in which the processing vessel stands. These units maintain the water temperature in the bath within

±0.3 C (½ F) and are capable of tempering several cubic feet of water. Most of these units have an electrical heater element, an agitator or circulator pump that keeps the water flowing over the heater, and a temperature-sensing device.

Individual immersion heating elements are also available in a variety of sizes and shapes to fit tanks or trays, or to be used in stirring solutions.

Mixing Valve. If you require a supply of tempered water greater than that provided by an immersion heater, try a thermostatically controlled, manually operated mixing valve as an inexpensive alternative. These valves operate by mixing the hot and cold water to obtain the desired temperature. The one chosen should deliver at least 11 litres (3 gallons) of tempered water per minute, control the temperature of the mixed water within ±0.3 C (½ F), and recover quickly from variations of pressure and temperature in the water lines.

Water Chillers. In some parts of the country, the temperature of the incoming cold water may be higher than required for the photographic processing. In these conditions you must have an auxiliary water chiller. As an alternative, you can install an entire sink unit with the chiller as well as all other processing requirements already fitted.

A chiller can be constructed by running a coil of copper or plastic tubing through a large tank or container that can be filled with water and cracked ice when required. The degree of chilling that takes place depends upon the temperature of the incoming water, the total length of the coil, and the rate of flow. The tank must have a provision for draining away the water and melted ice.

Recirculation Units. Tempered-water recirculating units can provide valuable savings in water usage. These units include both heating and chilling capacity and can be connected either to a water jacket that surrounds a tank or to a sink.

Vacuum Breaker. If the tempered-water-line outlet is installed below the surface of the water in a water bath or washing tank, you must also install a vacuum breaker on the supply pipe from the temperature-control unit. This fitting prevents contaminated water from the tank from being siphoned into the water lines if the main supply fails or is shut off. Both drinking water and processing solutions can be contaminated in this way. Proper installation is best accomplished by a professional installer or plumber; it is required by law to do so in most localities.

• *See also:* Darkroom, Professional; Temperature Scales; Thermometers.

Temperature Scales

Two scales for the measurement of temperature are in common use in the United States. The common metric scale is the Celsius scale (C, previously called Centigrade), which places the freezing point of water at 0 C and the boiling point at 100 C. On the U.S. customary scale, the Fahrenheit (F) scale, the freezing point of water is at 32 F, the boiling point at 212 F (0 F was originally determined as the temperature of a mixture of equal parts of salt and ice).

On both scales the unit of measurement is the degree. Although the degree symbol (°) is often dropped because of typographic expediency, its use is preferred for clarity. Because the two scales divide the same range (freezing–boiling points of water) into a different number of intervals, the degrees are not of equal size; there are 9 Fahrenheit degrees for every 5 Celsius degrees. The following formulas permit conversion from one scale to the other:

$$F = \frac{9\,C}{5} + 32$$

$$C = \frac{5\,(F-32)}{9}$$

The following table shows a direct comparison between the two scales over a much greater range than will be encountered in photography.

When rounding off to the nearest degree in making comparisons or conversions, or when making temperature measurements, note that a change of 0.5 C is equivalent to a change of 0.9 F, or essentially a full degree. This may be important when temperature control is critical. For example, in some color processes the developer should be held to ± ½ F, which is equivalent to 0.3 C. The need for a thermometer calibrated for great accuracy in the relevant range and for precise methods of measuring and reading the temperature should be obvious.

In the International System of Units (SI), the Kelvin (K) is defined as an absolute unit of thermo-

COMPARISON OF TEMPERATURE SCALES*

C	F	C	F	C	F	C	F
+120	+248	+80	+176	+40	+104	.0	+32
119	246.2	79	174.2	39	102.2	−1	30.2
118	244.4	78	172.4	38	100.4	−2	28.4
117	242.6	77	170.6	37	98.6	−3	26.6
116	240.8	76	168.8	36	96.8	−4	24.8
115	239	75	167	35	95	−5	23
114	237.2	74	165.2	34	93.2	−6	21.2
113	235.4	73	163.4	33	91.4	−7	19.4
112	233.6	72	161.6	32	89.6	−8	17.6
111	231.8	71	159.8	31	87.8	−9	15.8
110	230	70	158	30	86	−10	14
109	228.2	69	156.2	29	84.2	−11	12.2
108	226.4	68	154.4	28	82.4	−12	10.4
107	224.6	67	152.6	27	80.6	−13	8.6
106	222.8	66	150.8	26	78.8	−14	6.8
105	221	65	149	25	77	−15	5
104	219.2	64	147.2	24	75.2	−16	3.2
103	217.4	63	145.4	23	73.4	−17	1.4
102	215.6	62	143.6	22	71.6	−18	−0.4
101	213.8	61	141.8	21	69.8	−19	−2.2
100	212	60	140	20	68	−20	−4
99	210.2	59	138.2	19	66.2	−21	−5.8
98	208.4	58	136.4	18	64.4	−22	−7.6
97	206.6	57	134.6	17	62.6	−23	−9.4
96	204.8	56	132.8	16	60.8	−24	−11.2
95	203	55	131	15	59	−25	−13
94	201.2	54	129.2	14	57.2	−26	−14.8
93	199.4	53	127.4	13	55.4	−27	−16.6
92	197.6	52	125.6	12	53.6	−28	−18.4
91	195.8	51	123.8	11	51.8	−29	−20.2
90	194	50	122	10	50	−30	−22
89	192.2	49	120.2	9	48.2	−31	−23.8
88	190.4	48	118.4	8	46.4	−32	−25.6
87	188.6	47	116.6	7	44.6	−33	−27.4
86	186.8	46	114.8	6	42.8	−34	−29.2
85	185	45	113	5	41	−35	−31
84	183.2	44	111.2	4	39.2	−36	−32.8
83	181.4	43	109.4	3	37.4	−37	−34.6
82	179.6	42	107.6	2	35.6	−38	−36.4
81	177.8	41	105.8	1	33.8	−39	−38.2

*Celsius (C), Fahrenheit (F).

dynamic temperature. The temperature interval one degree Celsius equals one Kelvin exactly. The temperature 0 K is called "absolute zero", or 273.15 K (or C) below the zero point on the Celsius scale. Since the Kelvin is a unit on an absolute scale, the degree symbol should *not* be used with the symbol K, and reference to "degrees Kelvin" is also inap-propriate, although still widely used. In photography, the Kelvin is used with reference to the color temperature of a light source. (*See:* COLOR TEMPERATURE; KELVIN.)

• *See also:* COLOR TEMPERATURE; KELVIN; TEMPERATURE CONTROL; THERMOMETERS; WEIGHTS AND MEASURES.

Tent Lighting

The technique of surrounding a subject with white reflecting surfaces is known as "tenting." Although the reflecting material generally used is white paper stretched over a light frame, an additional dimension can be obtained by constructing the tent from translucent plastic sheeting. By directing spotlights onto the plastic sheeting from the outside of the tent, a very diffuse lighting can be shed upon the subject inside. Accents of color can be added by placing acetate gels over some of the lights. Strips of black paper taped to the inside of the tent will add necessary dark accents to completely reflecting subjects, thereby giving roundness and shape. Colored paper can be used to liven up a colorless subject. For specular light, cut a hole in the tent and shine a spotlight through.

The general purpose of tent lighting is to control specular reflections (mirror-like effects) to avoid causing dark areas in extremely shiny objects, and to provide very soft, nondirectional lighting. Shiny objects, of course, pick up and reflect light sources; they will reflect dark surfaces as well.

To photograph this silverware setting, it was necessary to build a white tent completely around the set to eliminate all reflections of dark objects. Five electronic flash units were placed inside the tent, aimed to bounce off the tent. Photo by Jerry West for B. Altman Company.

Tent Lighting

Styles in the photography of shiny objects have changed over the years, with the very flat, retouched look of the 1950's giving way to a more natural look with a wider range of reflections of light and dark areas. Thus, the task of the modern photographer is to control rather than eliminate the appearance of light and dark areas in shiny photographic subjects.

Reflection

Light behaves in an entirely predictable way when it is reflected; the angles of incidence and reflection are always the same. This can be useful in working with reflective surfaces in tent lighting. Obviously, if the camera is aimed at a shiny object head-on, it will be reflected directly on the specular surface as in a mirror. By changing the angle of either the camera or the reflecting object, reflections can be controlled and the setup for the tent lighting determined.

Materials

Modified tent lighting does not necessarily require a tent. The term is broad enough to include everything from a flat white card to completely surrounding the subject with tenting.

Photographers are individualistic about tenting materials, but the technique is most often applied by using translucent material and shining lights through it, or by bouncing light off white opaque reflecting surfaces. Some tenting involves the use of both techniques.

A cylinder of translucent paper is often a simple and workable tent. Lights are placed to evenly illuminate the outside of the cylinder. Shiny, engraved, or pitted surfaces lend themselves to cylinder lighting. The nature of the subject governs the diameter and height of the cylinder. The use of wide cylinders introduces some directional, or modeling, effect, especially when only one lamp is used. Small cylinders, when completely lighted, provide a very diffuse illumination.

The height of the cylinder is another control factor. The higher the wall, the greater is the specular component (toward the lens) of the reflection of the wall in those surfaces of the subject perpendicular to the lens axis. A dark shiny surface needs this specular reflection in order not to record blank. On the other hand, a silvery surface requires a low cylinder to prevent too much specular reflection from

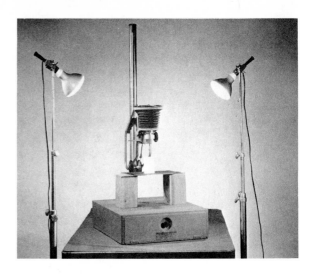

A setup for providing tent illumination for small, shiny objects uses a white, translucent paper cylinder. The lamps are directed so as to evenly illuminate the outside of the cylinder.

washing out the details. Sometimes, especially with silvery or white surfaces, it is advantageous to illuminate the cylinder with a single spotlight. Varying the height of the spot impinging on the paper wall yields differing amounts of specular reflection and modeling. The effects of all these lighting adjustments can be studied visually before the camera is put into position.

• *See also:* COMMERCIAL PHOTOGRAPHY; FLASH PHOTOGRAPHY; LIGHTING; REFLECTORS; SILVERWARE AND JEWELRY, PHOTOGRAPHING; UMBRELLA LIGHTING.

Testifying in Court

If your photographs are submitted as evidence in court, you may be required to testify about the circumstances related to making those photographs. Some courts do not require the photographer to testify unless there is something unusual about the technique used that should be explained to the jury. Other courts may require the photographer to testify before they accept the photographs as evidence.

If you are asked to testify, review the following suggestions, which stem from the experience of legal-evidence photographers and attorneys.

1. Discuss your knowledge of the pictures with the attorney *before* you go into court.
2. Be sure that the attorney understands the extent of your photographic knowledge, experience, and general educational background.
3. Avoid being qualified as a "photographic expert." Generally, it is best to permit yourself to be qualified only in the general practice of photography, that is, making pictures of objects and scenes by conventional techniques.
4. Suggest to the attorney that the investigating officers who were at the scene of a crime or accident testify to the accuracy of the photographs. That is, the officers can state whether the photographs fairly represented what they saw when they arrived at the scene.

As a photographer, you can testify only that the scene or object in the photograph appears as it did to you at the time the picture was taken. The judge will decide whether the photographs are relevant to the issues at hand and whether they will help the jury to a better understanding of the case and the testimony to be given. Usually, it is best not to burden them with testimony on exposures, developing, and other details that are standard practice in producing a photograph. It is possible for the judge, as well as the jury, to be confused on such matters. If you can simply certify that the exposure and processing were carried out in accordance with the manufacturer's recommendations, such a statement will usually suffice.

When you are testifying in a civil case, you are far more likely to be required to testify to the details of photographic technique. Lighting, accuracy of perspective, or point-of-view may be issues.

5. Make sure that you understand clearly each question put to you. If you do not understand the question, say so. If you do not know or cannot remember the answer to a question, say so.
6. Testify accurately. You will normally be allowed to consult notes that you have made while making photographs. If you make a mistake or an apparently contradictory statement, say so, and correct it as soon as possible. Answer questions completely, but do not volunteer additional information; the attorneys and the court will see that the case is properly developed. Remember that you are not deciding the issues; you are only testifying with respect to the making of photographs.

• *See also:* CRIME PHOTOGRAPHY; EVIDENCE PHOTOGRAPHY; FIRE AND ARSON PHOTOGRAPHY.

Testing

Most photographic materials and equipment are thoroughly tested by manufacturers to insure that they will perform at a certain quality level within a normal (typical, or average) range of conditions.

From time to time, individual conditions of use will fall outside the normal range. For example, processing recommendations are based on freshly mixed solutions at controlled temperatures, but many photographers replenish developer and save stop bath and fixer for reuse; thermometers also vary in accuracy. With use, equipment ages and may no longer perform to tested standards. A noticeable difference in negative quality might be caused by major changes in lens apertures, shutter speeds, solutions, or temperature control. Or it might be the cumulative result of small errors in several of these. Many other kinds of deviations from normal can also occur.

A photographer can conduct a number of tests without special equipment or complex procedures to insure that solutions are usable and equipment is performing acceptably. A variety of practical tests are outlined here.

Chemical Tests

Stop Baths and Fixers. An acid stop bath or fixing bath should not be overworked, since an exhausted bath frequently leads to stains and markings in the prints. When produced by a fixing bath, such stains show up only after a period of time.

Since the appearance of a fixing bath (or of an acid stop bath without an indicator) changes very little during its useful life, some means of determining when it is unfit for further use should be employed. The following solutions permit a quick check on the acidity of the stop bath and the silver content of the fixing bath.

Kodak stop bath test solution SBT-1

Water (distilled or demineralized)	
at 26.5 C (80 F)	750.0 ml
Sodium hydroxide	6.0 g
With stirring add:	
Bromocresol purple (*Eastman*	
organic chemical) No. 745	4.0 g
Mix for 15 to 20 minutes, then add:	
Phosphoric acid (86%)	3.0 ml
Water to make	1.0 l

CAUTION: The stop bath test solution contains chemicals that can be hazardous. *Sodium hydroxide* is caustic and is capable of causing severe burns in all tissues. Special care should be taken to prevent contact with skin or eyes. A face shield or goggles should be worn when handling the solid compound. *Phosphoric acid* is a strong, nonvolatile inorganic acid. It is corrosive to tissue and can cause severe skin or eye burns. Impervious gloves and goggles should be worn when handling the concentrated solution. In case of contact with either of these chemicals, immediately flush the involved areas with plenty of water; for eyes, seek out prompt medical attention.

To test a print stop bath, fill a clean, empty 30 ml vial about three-quarters full with the acid stop bath. To this, add 2 drops of the SBT-1 test solution. An acid stop bath that is still useful will remain yellow. When the acid has been neutralized, the bath will turn purple.

Under a light amber safelight, the yellow color is not noticeable but the purple color appears dark.

The stop bath test solution can also be added directly to the tray containing the stop bath. Add the test solution directly to the stop bath, while stirring, as recommended in the accompanying table.

Again, if the liquid darkens under safelight illumination or turns a light purple in room light, the bath is exhausted and should be discarded. Prints should not remain in the stop bath containing the test solution longer than 2 minutes; otherwise, slight yellow stains may result.

Kodak fixer test solution FT-1

Water at 26.5 C (80 F)	750.0 ml
Potassium iodide	190.0 g
Water to make	1.0 litre

To test a print-fixing solution with a single-bath fixer, add 5 drops of the fixing bath to be tested and 5 drops of water to 5 drops of FT-1 fixer test solution. Discard the fixer if a yellow-white precipitate forms instantly. Any slight milkiness should be disregarded. If a two-bath fixer is used, the first bath should be tested as described above for a single-bath fixer. For the second bath, add 5 drops of the fixing bath to be tested and 15 drops of water to 5 drops of the fixer test solution.

If both tests result in a yellow-white precipitate, replace both with fresh fixing baths. If only the first bath forms a precipitate, replace the first bath with the second, and replace the second bath with a fresh one.

Mixed solutions can be stored in brown, stoppered glass bottles for one year.

RATIO OF STOP BATH TO TEST SOLUTION						
Solution	**Metric**			**U.S. Liquid**		
Acid stop bath	1 litre	2 litres	4 litres	1 qt	2 qt	1 gal
SBT-1	1 ml	2 ml	4 ml	20 drops	40 drops	80 drops

To test a used film-fixing solution, compare the time required to clear an emulsion with that of a fresh solution. In darkness, immerse an *unexposed* piece of film in the solution being tested. After the normal (fresh solution) clearing time, check the test film briefly by safelight at 1-minute intervals to see when it has become completely clear and transparent. If the time required is twice as long (or longer) than the normal clearing time, discard the solution. If the time is less than that limit, the solution is still usable and the proper total fixing time is twice as long as it took the test film to clear.

The normal clearing time can be established at any time by immersing an unexposed piece of film in a small quantity of freshly mixed fixer and checking the progress, as with the test. Record the results for future reference.

Tests for Silver. An overworked fixing bath contains complex silver thiosulfate compounds that are retained by films or prints and cannot be removed completely by washing. If they are left in the images, they will cause an overall yellow stain in time. The following tests applied to film and prints will reveal the presence of silver, which can then be removed as described.

Kodak residual silver test solution ST-1

Water . . . .   125.0 ml
Sodium sulfide (anhydrous) . . . .   2.0 g

Store in a small stoppered bottle for not more than 3 months.

Dilute 1 part stock solution with 9 parts water. The diluted solution keeps for a limited time and should be replaced weekly.

To determine whether films and prints retain any silver complexes, place a drop of ST-1 test solution on the margin of a squeegeed film or print (or on an unexposed piece of photographic paper of the same type as the prints being processed and treated in the same chemicals). Remove the solution with a clean white blotter after 2 or 3 minutes.

Any yellowing of the test spot other than a barely visible cream tint indicates the presence of silver.

NOTE: If the test is positive, residual silver can be removed by refixing the print or negative in fresh hypo and rewashing for the recommended time.

Prints toned in a sulfide toner or a selenium toner will not yield to this treatment, however, because the residual silver has been toned together with the image. The yellow stain so formed is permanent.

Testing with Kodak Rapid Selenium Toner. If you wish to use a more stable reagent than ST-1 test solution, a dilute solution of Kodak rapid selenium toner can be used to test whether prints are thoroughly fixed.

To use, dilute 1 part Kodak rapid selenium toner with 9 parts water. These proportions are not critical. Using this solution, follow the directions given for the use of ST-1 solution.

NOTE: The test fails where a very large excess of hypo is present, as in stabilized prints.

Tests for Retained Fixer. The residual hypo content of films and prints after washing can be accurately determined only by actually testing the processed photographic material. This is particularly true in the case of prints, because the paper support retains hypo in its fiber structure.

Kodak hypo test solution HT-2

Water	750.0 ml
28% acetic acid*	125.0 ml
Silver nitrate, crystals	7.5 g
Water to make	1.0 litre

Store in a screw-cap or glass-stoppered brown bottle away from strong light. Do not allow the test solution to come into contact with hands, clothing, negatives, prints, or undeveloped photographic material; it will stain them black.

Testing Prints. To determine whether prints are thoroughly washed, wipe the excess water from the face (emulsion side) of an unexposed piece of the same paper being used in the batch of prints being processed, or from the extra margin area of one of the prints. Place 1 drop of the test solution on the face of the processed paper sample. Allow the solution to stand on the sample for 2 minutes, rinse to remove the excess reagent, and compare the stain with the tints shown in the Kodak hypo estimator, available from photo dealers.

---

*To make approximately 28% acetic acid from glacial acetic acid, dilute 3 parts glacial acetic acid with 8 parts water.

For long-term keeping qualities, use hypo eliminator and hypo clearing agent during the washing process.

If you want prints to have good long-term keeping properties, use washing aids such as Kodak hypo clearing agent and Kodak hypo eliminator HE-1. If the above spot test is used after washing aids other than Kodak hypo clearing agent, it may give misleading results. The face may show less stain than a print washed only in water, and yet the hypo content of the two prints may be equal.

Testing the Degree of Washing of Films. After washing, cut off a small strip from the clear margin of the film and immerse a portion of it in a small volume of the test solution for about 3 minutes. Well-washed films, including those for record purposes, should show very little or no discoloration.

The spot technique should not be used on wet films because of the danger of spreading the reagent. It is very useful in testing dry films.

Camera Tests

The most common problems with cameras are light leaks, inaccurate shutter speeds, framing differences between the viewfinder and the film gate, and mechanical vibrations.

Light Leaks. With a bellows camera, lock the bellows at maximum extension and either cap the lens or put a blank lens board in its place. Remove the ground glass and observe the interior of the camera in a darkened room, using a focusing cloth to exclude stray light. Move a bright light bulb around the outside of the camera; flashes of light will reveal pinholes and cracks as the bulb moves past them. It may be possible to repair some leaks with opaque black tape; photographic black masking tape has an adhesive that is less prone to softening and oozing than electrician's plastic tape and similar products. If the camera is large enough, place the light bulb inside the bellows (in the dark) as an alternative method.

Light leaks in rigid-body cameras are less easy to locate. They most commonly occur around the edges of the panel that opens for loading film, or at the edges of interchangeable viewfinders. To check for the presence of leaks, cap the lens or remove it and secure a body cap in place with opaque tape all around its edges. Put tape over the eyepiece of the viewfinder as well to exclude light that would normally be blocked by your eye. Load the camera with a short piece of film, or with a piece of fast enlarging paper cut in a strip that will reach across the film plane from the supply chamber to the take-up chamber. The paper is convenient because it can be loaded under a safelight and can be processed in much less time than film.

Slowly move a strong light such as a No. 2 photolamp around the camera. With a single-lens reflex camera, make separate tests with the mirror down, with the mirror up and shutter open (on the "B" or "T" setting), and—in cameras with a separate mirror lock-up control—with the mirror up and the shutter closed. Any leaks will appear as black spots or streaks on the processed test emulsion. From the position of the test piece in the camera, it may be possible to trace back to the leak. Examine the camera interior carefully for bare surfaces that might have reflected the light from a leak onto a new path.

To test sheet-film holders for light leaks, load them with fast enlarging paper cut to size. Mark each side of the holders for identification and mark the test sheet correspondingly. Move a strong light source slowly around each side for at least a full minute; moving the film holder around in direct sunlight provides a realistic test. The dark slide entrance slot and the hinged flap are the two most common locations of leaks. Process and examine the sheets of enlarging paper for evidence of leaks as shown by dark marks on the paper.

Roll-film holders can be similarly tested by loading them with a strip of paper, as described for camera body tests.

Shutter Speeds. There are two kinds of shutter speed problems: speeds that vary in relation to one another, and speeds that are significantly different from their marked values. Camera repair services and some camera stores have instruments to check shutter speeds quickly and accurately. Many offer this as a free customer service or make only a nominal charge. Less accurate tests can be performed as follows.

Relative Speeds. The progression of shutter speeds should double or halve the exposure at each step; if the lens aperture is changed to counterbalance the speed change, exposure should remain constant. Photograph a neutral surface such as an 18 percent reflectance gray card. Light the surface evenly, rate the film at the manufacturer's ASA speed, and base exposure on a reflected-light reading from the card, or an incident-light reading taken from the card position. Make a separate exposure at each shutter speed, and adjust the lens aperture each time to keep the exposure constant. (That is, as you change to the next higher speed, open up one stop.) Process the film normally.

The results should be visually identical, but significant differences in printing density may not be apparent. For a closer evaluation, place each exposure over a light-meter cell aimed at an evenly illuminated bright surface such as a light box. If the film area is too small, mask down the size of the cell with a tube or cone of black paper. The actual reading obtained does not matter, only the comparisons between readings are significant. The readings should all be the same, within one-third of a stop. A higher reading indicates a speed that is faster than it should be—the film received comparatively less exposure and its reduced density lets more light reach the meter. A lower reading indicates a speed that is slow, which produces more exposure and greater corresponding density.

A more accurate measurement of results can be made with a densitometer. Take readings from the center of each exposure. Each density difference of 0.10 is the equivalent of about one-third stop exposure difference on color transparency films, and the equivalent of about one-half stop on black-and-white film developed to a normal contrast (CI of 0.56).

If you prefer, you can make the exposure series to a gray scale, or to a full-range subject. Base exposure on a gray card or on an incident-light meter reading. If color reversal film—which has little latitude and will receive standard processing in a lab—is used, exposure variations of one-half stop will be readily visible in most cases. If negative film is used, the processed results can be compared on the basis of densitometer readings from corresponding areas of each exposure, or on the basis of comparison prints. To make prints, use exactly the same enlarger settings and exposure for every print, use paper from the same package, and process them all together if possible. There should be no visible differences among them. A print that is lighter than the rest indicates a fast speed; one that is darker indicates a slow speed. However, no image-comparison method will indicate differences in terms of *f*-stops.

Actual Speeds. A motor with a known number of revolutions per minute (rpm) can be used to make a simple device for measuring actual shutter speeds with a fair degree of accuracy. A speed of between 100 and 1000 rpm is best; a 78 rpm record turntable is too slow for accuracy above 1/60 sec. Measurement is based on the principle that when the rate of travel is known and the distance traveled can be measured, the time of travel can be computed.

Take a dark-colored disk about 30 cm (12 inches) in diameter and attach it securely to the motor shaft, centering it accurately. Place a white mark at the exact center and another at the outer edge; pieces of white tape or self-adhesive label material are suitable. Align the camera so that it looks straight at the center of the disk. Turn the motor on and make a separate exposure at each shutter speed.

The processed results will show a center dot and an arc traced by the movement of the outer dot. Since the outer dot was traveling a 360-degree circle several times a minute, the number of degrees traveled in 1 second is: $(360 \times \text{rpm}) \div 60$. For example, with a motor running at 120 rpm, the dot on the circumference moves $(360 \times 120) \div 60 = 720$ degrees per second.

With a protractor, measure the angle between lines that join the ends of the arc with the center dot. It may be possible to do this directly on large-format film, but it will probably be easier to make a quick enlargement of each exposure and draw the connecting lines on it. The protractor should be centered on the middle dot.

The actual shutter speed is the ratio of the angle covered to the degrees traveled per second. That is, Speed = Angle $\div$ Degrees per second. For example, with the 120 rpm motor, a measured test exposure angle of 12 degrees indicates a speed of $12 \div 720 = 0.0166$, or 1/60 sec.

Manufacturing standards allow some variance from marked shutter speeds. For blade shutters, the standards are $\pm$ 25 percent for speeds longer than 1/125 sec. and $\pm$ 30 percent for speeds of 1/125 sec. and shorter. Standards for focal-plane shutters are $\pm$ 25 percent for speeds longer than 1/250 sec. and $\pm$ 33 percent at 1/250 sec. and shorter. Care must be taken with focal-plane shutters to make each exposure when the outer dot is traveling *across* the direction of the shutter slit movement. If it moves in the same direction as, or in the opposite direction to, the shutter, its trace will be elongated or compressed

on the film and an inaccurate measurement will result.

With blade shutters, exposure time is an averaged figure that is less than the total time as measured angularly. This is because the shutter takes part of the time to open and part of the time to close. At high speeds, such as 1/500 sec., all the time is spent opening and closing. Therefore, actual exposure time will be less than the time measured by the angular method just described.

Framing. Most small-format cameras include a slightly larger area on the film than is shown in the viewfinder. One explanation for this is that it allows for the overlap of some slide mounts into the picture area. It also compensates for inaccuracies in the finder-camera alignment and insures that everything seen in the finder will be on the film.

The test for comparing the area covered by the finder and the camera is a pragmatic one. Set up the camera on a tripod and aim it at a scene with clearly defined details at each border of the picture for reference; the distance should be at least 3 m (10 feet). A simple but precise test target can be made by placing four measuring tapes or rulers with bold markings on a wall so that they cross each of the picture borders at right angles. Note how much of each tape or stick is visible at each edge of the viewfinder. Take a picture, process and print it, and compare the results. Any difference between the two will not necessarily be the same at all four borders.

Rulers placed across the borders of the viewfinder field (colored line) will permit accurate comparison with the field actually covered by the film (black lines). The film field may be smaller or larger, as shown, and may not be centered in the viewing field.

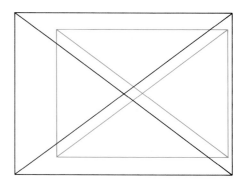

A white mark on the rim of a revolving disk traces an arc during exposure. The shutter speed is equal to the angle of the arc (A) divided by the rate of travel in degrees per second. Text explains how to compute travel rate.

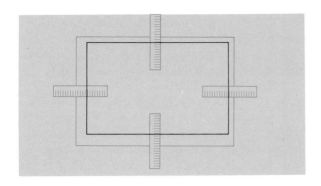

Alignment template. When viewing and camera fields have been determined, draw them at a large scale on acetate in different colors to create a mask for aligning flat copy. Use the diagonal of the viewing field (color) to center the mask in the viewfinder and tape one edge in place on the copyboard. Use the diagonal of the field (black lines) to center the copy; then hinge the mask out of the way. By extending the diagonals, the mask can be used at any practical camera distance.

If the viewfinder shows more area than the film, it is usually possible to mark the viewing screen of medium- and large-format cameras with a china marker, or to lay a framing mask drawn on acetate in position. If the viewfinder shows less area than the film, the problem is not serious except at close distances when framing is critical, as in copying. For flat subjects, it is useful to draw outlines of the two areas on acetate (see the accompanying diagram) and use that to locate the copy after the mask has been oriented so that the viewing field is centered in the viewfinder when the camera is in position.

If a single-lens reflex camera or view camera is being used for copying or other close work, the marks showing the camera coverage will apply at all distances. However, if the finder is separate, as in a twin-lens reflex camera or a camera with a separate viewfinder, the coverage changes as the distance changes. In these cases, it is necessary to make a series of marks showing the top of the camera coverage when the finder is exactly above the camera lens, or two marks—one showing the top, and one the left edge of the camera coverage—for each distance used. Depending on the conditions, it might be useful to mark the edges for a series of distances every 100 mm (6 inches) over the camera distance range required.

Steadiness. To determine whether significant camera movement occurs as the shutter fires, mount the camera on a tripod, attach a small mirror to the front of the lens, and aim a beam of light—for example, from a slide projector—into the mirror so that it reflects onto a wall or other plain surface about 3 m (10 feet) away. Fire the shutter repeatedly and observe the movement of the reflected spot of light —there should be none. If there is movement, the tripod is not an adequately firm support.

To make a more revealing test, aim the camera at a detailed target and make an exposure at each shutter speed. Process and print the results and carefully examine the sharpness of the details. It will soon become apparent what the slowest speed is practical to use with each lens and what degree of enlargement begins to reveal slight movement.

It is also instructive to make this mirror test while hand-holding the camera. Most photographers are surprised to discover how much movement occurs at what they thought were "safe" speeds and stances. The problem increases in proportion to increasing focal length: thus, a 1.6 mm ($\frac{1}{16}$ inch) movement will record six times as large when imaged with a 300 mm lens as it will when imaged with a 50 mm lens.

Lenses. Three aspects of lenses can be checked by practical methods: (1) the relative accuracy of f-stop settings, (2) the sharpness of a recorded image, and (3) in the case of projector and enlarging lenses, the sharpness of a projected image.

f-Stops. The aperture settings of most modern lenses are marked with a high degree of accuracy. When a difference in performance is noticed, it can often be traced to causes other than f-stop inaccuracy. Common causes of exposure errors include forgetting to remove a filter, or accidentally setting the wrong film speed on a meter. And, errors in shutter speed ratings or changes in shutter performance are far more common than lens aperture problems. However, the balance between apertures— whether exposure is doubled or halved at each step —can be checked as follows:

Use a black-and-white film with a long, straight-line characteristic curve. Kodak Plus-X pan 35 mm or roll film and Kodak Super-XX sheet film are examples. Illuminate a medium- or light-gray surface evenly so as to have an exposure of 1/60 or 1/125 sec. at an aperture two stops larger than the smallest opening. That would be *f*/16 for an *f*/32 lens, *f*/11 for an *f*/22 lens, or *f*/8 for an *f*/16 lens. The idea is to not underexpose more than two stops during the test so as to not place any results on the toe of the characteristic curve of the film's response. Exposure should be measured with an incident-light meter or by means of a reflected-light reading from an 18 percent reflectance gray card.

Make one exposure at each *f*-stop setting—including half stops if there are click stops for them—using the *same* shutter speed each time. Process the film normally. Each exposure should be visibly different from the others, but visual evaluation is not possible because densities with equal printing differences do not necessarily have equal visual differences. Use a densitometer, or mask down the area of a light-meter cell with a tube or cone of black paper to read within the center of each exposure.

When one of the black-and-white films suggested earlier is being used for the aperture test, it should be given the recommended development, which will result in a contrast index of 0.56. At this contrast level, the density differences between whole-stop exposures should be about 0.15, and this should read as approximately half-stop differences if an exposure meter is used to measure the negatives. Half-stop exposure differences should measure just one half of the whole-stop differences.

Any significant variation indicates an inaccurate aperture setting. Too little change means that the aperture is not opening sufficiently; too much change means that it is opening too far.

Sharpness of Recorded Image. Although lens-testing (resolving power) charts are available from various sources, it is seldom possible to use them with the precision required to obtain accurate resolution data. It is usually more useful to select or improvise a target with fine detail and make a visual examination of the results.

A distant, sunlit brick wall makes an excellent target; dark red bricks with light mortar between will provide sufficient contrast in the processed image for easy evaluation. Indoors, a target can be made by mounting pages of newspaper classified ads or pages of a telephone directory on a wall about 3 m (10 feet) from the camera. It is not necessary to cover the entire field; a sheet in the center and one at each of the four corners will suffice. The camera back must be absolutely parallel to the test surface, which must be evenly lighted. Sunlight presents few problems of unevenness if there are no shadows on the wall. Inside, take meter readings at the corners and the center of the field; they must be within one-third stop of one another.

For an evaluation of lens performance alone—for example, to determine the *f*-stops that produce

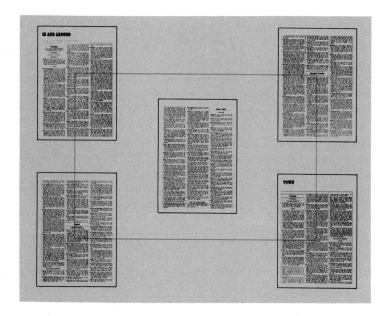

Lens-sharpness test. A resolving-power target can be improvised by mounting sheets of fine print, such as classified ads, on a flat surface so that they fall at the center and corners of the field covered. Even lighting and parallel alignment of film plane with test target are essential for this test.

optimum sharpness—use a high-contrast film. For a more meaningful evaluation of overall performance, use the film that you most commonly use for actual photographic work. Base the exposure on an incident-light reading, or a reflected-light reading from an 18 percent reflectance gray card. Make an exposure at each *f*-stop, changing shutter speeds as required so as to vary no more than one stop over or under the meter-indicated exposure.

Process the results normally and examine the film with a low-power (10 to 20×) microscope. Compare the center definition to edge definition within each exposure and overall definition among exposures. Because of residual aberrations, the greatest sharpness will not be at the maximum aperture, and because of diffraction, the greatest sharpness will not be at the minimum aperture. If you wish to evaluate the total system performance, make enlargements for comparison. But first be sure that the enlarger is aligned and that you use the optimum aperture of the enlarging lens, as described in the following sections.

Projected Image Sharpness. The procedure for checking projected sharpness is simple: Project the test image and examine it with a magnifier. Although test negatives and slides can be purchased, it is perfectly satisfactory to improvise one by scratching X's through the blackened emulsion of a scrap piece of film. Use a needle or other fine point to scratch marks in the center and at the corners of a small-format film. Add intermediate marks with larger formats.

Place the film in the enlarger or slide projector; use the same kind of negative carrier or slide mount that you would normally use. Focus the image visually and examine it carefully.

Use a hand magnifier to examine an enlarger image; many grain-focusing magnifiers cannot be used at the very corners of the projected field because of the extreme angle of reflection. Check carefully how corner sharpness improves in relation to center sharpness as the lens is stopped down. A mid-range setting will probably produce the optimum sharpness throughout the field.

This test can also be used to determine how long it takes a film to expand and "pop" out of focus when a glassless negative carrier or slide mount is used. Focus the center of the image carefully, and turn off the light to let the film cool. Then turn the

light on again and begin timing as you observe the center of the image with a magnifier. A dense black-and-white negative is best to use for this check because the large amount of dense silver will absorb more heat than a thinner negative or a color negative. Thus, the "pop" time you arrive at is a minimum safe time; exposures shorter than that should be free of this problem in the course of normal work.

Checks of overall image sharpness will be accurate only if the film plane of the slide projector is parallel to the screen, or if the enlarger is properly aligned.

Enlarger Alignment

The negative stage, lens board, and baseboard or easel of an enlarger must all be exactly parallel. If they are not, one side or end of the projected image will not be as sharp as the others. Misalignment can be observed by placing a test negative between sheets of glass at the negative stage and comparing sharpness from end to end and side to side in the image. It may be possible to adjust the enlarger, using this negative as a guide, but it is far easier to use an alignment level, which is available from some photo dealers.

The level consists of a metal bar whose top and bottom surfaces are parallel. A small bubble level is mounted on top, near one end, so that when the bar is inserted across the negative stage or held across the lens board, the level will be clearly visible at one side. The level is mounted to a pivot at one end and has a screw adjustment so that it can be raised or lowered at the other end.

To use this level, place the bar on the baseboard or easel so that it runs left-to-right across the image area. Adjust the level screw until the bubble is centered. Move the bar up to the negative stage in the

Enlarger alignment tool. A bubble level with an adjusting screw is mounted on a metal bar which can be laid across the baseboard, lensboard, or negative stage of an enlarger. Alignment must be checked in two directions at right angles to each other to insure parallel alignment.

same orientation. If the bubble is not centered, loosen the negative-stage positioning screws and raise or lower one end of the stage until it is level. *Do not change the adjusting screw on the level.*

Next, move the bar to the lens board and adjust the lens stage until it is level. Repeat these three steps with the bar placed to run at right angles to its previous orientation—front to back—on the baseboard or easel as a starting point. Then recheck with the bar in the first positions; it may be necessary to readjust more than once in each direction to achieve final alignment. This procedure insures parallelism of the enlarger planes; it does not matter whether the enlarger itself is completely level with the floor. If required, this alignment must be completed before checking the sharpness of the projected image, as previously described.

Illumination

The evenness of illumination from a continuous source can be checked by taking readings with a sensitive light meter at various positions throughout the subject field. If an incident-light meter is not used, take reflected-light readings from a card held at various locations. It is not necessary to use a standard gray card unless specific exposure information is needed; a card of any tone will reveal lighting variations. Readings should be made at the principal plane of the subject in most cases; then readings at other distances will reveal how much light must be added or removed to achieve a desired balance.

The evenness or coverage pattern of a flash source is best measured by making exposures on a high-contrast film, which will exaggerate falloff at the edges of the field so it can be seen more easily. Aim the flash unit at a flat, even-toned surface such as a white wall, and align it directly along the lens axis. Use a wide-angle lens to show the whole coverage area of the flash, but note how much of the test area would be included by a normal lens; it may be useful to place reference marks such as yardsticks within the test area for this purpose. Then it will be easy to determine whether light falloff begins outside the normal lens field. If the flash unit has adapters to change its coverage, make exposures with these as well, both with a wide-angle lens and with the lens for which they are intended. In each case the results should be easily interpretable visually either from the negative or transparency, or from a print.

Safelight illumination in a darkroom should be tested to make sure it will not fog emulsions in the course of normal handling. Testing procedures are given in the article SAFELIGHTS.

• *See also:* BRACKETING EXPOSURES; RING-AROUND; SAFELIGHTS; SHARPNESS.

Further Reading: Consumer Guide Magazine Editors. *Consumer Guide: Photographic Equipment Test Reports.* New York, NY: New American Library, 1974; ———. *The Best of Photographic Equipment.* New York, NY: Simon and Schuster, 1975; Mason, L.F. *Photographic Processing Chemistry.* New York, NY: Halsted Press, 1975; Tydings, Kenneth S. *Instant Lens Testing Chart and Book.* Garden City, NY: Amphoto, 1967.

Test Strips

Test strips are small sample prints with a sequence of exposures usually made to aid in determining the proper exposure for a print. They may also be made to determine filtration with color or variable-contrast black-and-white papers. The same techniques can be used with films when an enlarger or contact printer is used to make film transparencies or to duplicate negatives.

General Procedures

In photographic printing, the overall subject in the picture determines the basic exposure; if necessary, certain elements are held back (dodged) or burned-in to bring them into tonal balance.

If the major subject covers a large enough area, the test exposures can be made on a single strip of paper—usually a piece that just covers the main subject is sufficient. Landscapes, full-face portraits, and similar subjects commonly provide enough area for five or six different exposure areas at least 19 mm (¾ inch) wide. Anything narrower than this is usually ineffective because the results are difficult to interpret accurately.

The paper is placed on the easel and exposed in parallel strips by either covering or uncovering it with an opaque card at various exposure intervals. The card *must* be opaque; one or two thicknesses of photographic paper will not do, because enough light may be transmitted to add exposure to areas that are supposedly protected.

The ideal card is white on top (as used) and black on the bottom, so that it is easy to see the projected image no matter how much of the printing paper is covered. This aids in judging how far to move the card for each successive exposure. If the card is black on the bottom, it will not reflect light back onto the paper and affect the exposure of the uncovered portions.

If the main subject is small, or if exposure information is needed about more than one area, it is better to use several strips that are sequentially placed to take in the same part of the image each time. This insures that no test exposure misses the important area, and makes it possible to get more information than would be available from one strip. For example, if a figure is standing in a landscape with a dark foreground and a light sky, it is likely that one strip will indicate the basic exposure for the figure; another one, the total exposure required to print-in the sky; and a third, the reduced (dodged) exposure required for the foreground.

To make a series of strips, cut a piece of paper into pieces about 50 mm (2 inches) wide. (Cut lengthwise or across the width of the paper, depending on the image area to be included.) With the strips in a protected place, turn the enlarger on and place the finger and thumb of one hand to mark spots that are to be included. Turn off the enlarger, place one strip in position, using your hand as a guide, and expose it. Turn off the enlarger, position the next strip in place of the first, pull out the first, and make the second exposure. Repeat this action for the remaining strips.

It is a good idea to mark the exposure times given each strip on the back before going on to the next. It is easy enough to remember the exposures and to sort out their order visually immediately after

they have been processed, but if you wish to refer to them later in the printing session, you may forget the times or apertures that were used for earlier test strips.

There is no point in keeping test strips after a session. The exposure data may be recorded on the back of an extra print so that you have a visual as well as a written record of what was required. Although some factors may vary later, this information will give a starting point when you wish to reprint.

Timing the Exposures

The most useful information will be gained from a series of exposures that doubles at each step. In black-and-white printing it is preferable to set the enlarger lens to the aperture that gives the best overall sharpness, and to vary the exposure times. With color materials it is better to use the time suggested by the manufacturer and to change the f-stop setting; this will avoid color shifts caused by reciprocity effect.

As the accompanying table shows, a convenient series of exposure times for the cover/uncover method is 4, 4, 8, 16, and 32 seconds: This will provide five strips of doubled exposures from 4 to 64 seconds. When a series of individual strips is made, each must receive a different exposure of appropriately doubled length.

When using dial-type timing switches, many photographers prefer to set the dial for the shortest exposure and push the "on" switch repeatedly to build up a longer exposure. For example, with the timer set at 4 seconds, four successive exposures will total 16 seconds. This procedure avoids the delay

EXPOSURE SERIES FOR A SINGLE-SHEET TEST STRIP
(Time in Seconds)

	Start here for a series that uncovers the paper ▼				Start here for a series that covers the paper ▼
Exposure Time of Each Step	32	16	8	4	4
	16	8	4	4	
	8	4	4		
Cumulative Exposure in Each Strip	4	4			
	4				
Total Exposure of Each Strip	64	32	16	8	4

and inaccuracy of having to make a different dial setting each time. It also makes it much easier to time burning-in and dodging procedures when making the actual print. Dodging for three out of five "bursts" and burning-in another area for an additional four bursts is easier to remember and more accurate than trying to keep one eye on the timer and the other on the printing manipulations.

Test strips may also be made at a single f-stop and time (or a compensated time) setting, with filtration changed for each strip. This provides contrast data in black-and-white, and color balance data in color printing.

Single-Exposure Tests

Several manufacturers offer a color-printing matrix by which filtration and exposure can be determined from a single exposure. The matrix covers a sheet of printing paper and allows exposing light to pass through a series of windows; each window has a different balance of color compensating filters or different neutral density filtration. Light projected from the negative is thoroughly mixed by a diffuser placed under the enlarger lens so that the light passing through every portion of the matrix represents all the colors in the negative. The processed results are interpreted by comparison with neutral gray patches or other standards, as indicated in the manufacturer's instructions.

The Kodak projection print scale can be used to determine exposure time with a single test. The scale consists of a circle divided into a series of neutral density wedges. The scale is centered over the most important area of the image in contact with the test paper, and a 60-second exposure is made through it. When processed, the best-looking segment is selected by examination; the number of seconds required to produce a print of that tonality will be found printed alongside the segment's outer edge.

Evaluating Test Strips

It should be obvious that for test strips to be accurate they must be made on paper from the same package and processed in the same way as the final print. Some color materials must be dried before they can be evaluated; others can be examined while wet. Black-and-white papers can be examined under white light after they have been in the fixer long enough for any cream or yellow tinge in the image

to disappear; this is a minimum of 1 minute in most cases. If the strips are to be referred to throughout a printing session, they should be returned to the fixer after examination for the normal total time and then kept in a water bath. If underfixed, they may change tonality. It is often useful to expose a sample of paper to white light and process it along with an unexposed sample at the beginning of a printing session in order to have maximum black and paper-white standards for comparison.

In color printing, exposure controls density. If a print from a negative is too light overall, it needs more exposure; if too dark, it needs less exposure (in printing on reversal materials, the opposite is true). This will be apparent across the range of test strips. The color balance is determined by the filtration used, but this is difficult to evaluate until the exposure is close to being right. Changes in filtration will usually call for minor exposure adjustments.

In a black-and-white test series, look at the dark tones to judge whether the contrast grade is proper; look at the key subject tone or the light areas to evaluate the exposure time. Wet prints will "dry down"; that is, they will look darker when dry than they do when wet. The amount of change is different for various papers and for the various surfaces of a single paper. The intensity of the white inspection light in the darkroom will also affect your evaluation of the results. Only experience under your own working conditions will develop your ability to anticipate what a dry print will look like on the basis of wet test strips.

• *See also:* BLACK-AND-WHITE PRINTING; COLOR PRINTING FROM NEGATIVES; COLOR PRINTING FROM TRANSPARENCIES; CONTACT PRINTING; ENLARGERS AND ENLARGING.

Texture Lighting

It is common to think that "texture" means roughness. When referring to a newly plowed field, for instance, it does, but a frozen pond can have a texture that is as smooth as glass. Texture is the *relative* roughness or smoothness of a surface as revealed by small, overall details. Texture is immediately perceptible to the touch; visually it depends on the clarity with which surface details are perceived, and that is primarily determined by the quality and direction of the light falling on the surface.

Texture and Light

In a photograph, rough texture is revealed by the degree of contrast between the light and dark sides of details, the difference between the highlighted peaks and the shadowed valleys. Smooth texture is revealed by the way light glances off a surface with a minimum of scattering, often with a single, major highlight area.

In both cases, the effect is created by direct, specular, or semispecular light coming from a definite source. It must come from one side of the surface rather than head-on, so that discernible shadows are formed or so that the reflective path is not back toward the source, in which case it would be much less visible.

Overall diffuse, "soft" light de-emphasizes details—hence, texture is minimized. Especially when head-on to a surface, it illuminates evenly so that irregularities cannot be seen; the surface becomes uniformly bright and thus appears to be uniformly smooth.

From these principles it is easy to derive the techniques of lighting to control texture.

Lighting for Texture Emphasis

To emphasize texture, use a specific, intense light source such as a spotlight, a narrow-angle flash unit, or a bare bulb in a polished reflector. The narrower the beam, the more specular the light will be, which in turn will create darker shadows and more intense specular reflections. Use direct sunlight outdoors.

Aim the light at an angle *across* the major direction of the texture details. A light shining parallel along the ridges and valleys of a piece of corduroy, for example, will not reveal the texture nearly as well as one shining at right angles across the ribs of the fabric. Often it is easier to turn the subject than to move the light source.

Keep the angle of light low relative to the surface. As with late afternoon sun, the lower the angle, the longer the shadows that are cast. However, if the angle is too low, texture will be obscured because shadows will fall on what should be the highlight side of adjacent details. It is easy enough to find the optimum angle by watching along the lens axis as the light is moved up and down, or as the subject is moved in relation to the position of the sun.

If only a raking, low-angle texture light is used, the shadows will photograph as black with no detail, even if they do not appear that way to the eye. You can lighten the shadows by filling in with light from the opposite direction. A reflector is often better for this than another light source; it simplifies equipment requirements and avoids the possibility of double shadows.

In a studio, the main texture light adds little to the overall illumination. When other qualities of the subject are at least as important as the texture, establish lighting for them first; then add a raking texture light. This technique is valuable for recording both the full color and the impasto (surface variations) of an oil painting, for example.

Smooth Textures

To emphasize the smoothness of a surface, use a single light source at a somewhat higher angle than a raking texture light. The light should be directed toward the camera, with the source in a position that might be used for angled backlighting. The idea is to create surface reflections without directing the main specular reflection straight into the lens. Reflections directed off to one side, or away from the camera, cannot be seen. Of course, the angle of the light must not be so low that the source is seen directly by the lens; a deep lens shade is a great help.

Suppressing Texture

To de-emphasize texture, light the surface from the front with broad, diffused sources. Open shade, bright overcast sky, diffused floodlights, umbrella reflectors, and bounce flash all provide light that tends to suppress surface detail. If specific, rather than general, light sources must be used, aim matched sources at the surface from equal but opposite frontal angles. This arrangement is used in copying—the shadows cast by the light from one side are completely washed out by light of equal intensity from the other side.

Uses of Texture Lighting

Often it is texture that makes a major point about the subject. For example, in product photography it may be desirable to emphasize the texture of "home-style" whole-wheat bread or the "nooks

Texture lighting is best achieved by brushing the surface with light placed at a 90-degree angle. This allows as high a contrast ratio as possible between light and dark values. Note the considerable contrast between the top surface and the shadowed edges of this wood siding. Photo by Michael Waine.

Cross lighting from a single source placed perpendicular to the subject brings out the wood grain and the delicate features of the cameo. Fill light, if used at all, should be handled with considerable care, as too much can reduce the lighting ratio, with resultant loss of texture detail. Photo by Michael Waine.

Texture Lighting

and crannies" of a breakfast muffin, and to de-emphasize the texture of "soft, delicious" white bread spread with "creamy smooth" peanut butter. The different approaches required to bring out texture are implicit in such materials as tweeds, flannels, silks, and satin, or skid-resistant stair coverings and "never-needs-waxing" kitchen floor surfaces.

In portraiture, the skin textures of a young child and an adult outdoorsman will demand very different lighting, as will that of someone beginning to show age lines.

Scenic pictures may concentrate on the colorful masses of foliage or flowered fields, or may show the dense, spiny forestation of a mountainside. The "texture position" of the sun is important in both cases. It should be above and behind the camera, shining along the lens axis, for the color effect, but lower and to one side to catch the trunks as well as the tops of the needlelike trees.

In works of art, a created texture may be a major expressive element. The marks of the woodcarver's gouge, the contrast between polished marble and the surrounding rough original material, and the dappling left by the silversmith's hammer are only three examples. Strong side texture lighting is exactly what is required to bring out incised relief carving, while smooth texture lighting is essential for an object of polished obsidian.

Natural texture lighting on a large scale is required to make many kinds of aerial photographs interpretable; on a controlled small scale it may be the key to understanding the content of a scientific close-up.

Thus, whatever the situation, the texture characteristics of the subject and how they are to be revealed or concealed is something that ·must be considered in every photograph.

• *See also:* ELECTRONIC FLASH; FLASH PHOTOGRAPHY; LIGHTING; PORTRAITURE; PRODUCT PHOTOGRAPHY.

Texture Screens

Texture screens are used to add the appearance of texture to photographic print images. Prints made on smooth papers have either textureless smooth images or grainy images resulting from grainy nega-

tives that are given considerable magnification in enlargement. On the other hand, prints made on textured-surface paper exhibit either more or less texture depending on how the actual, three-dimensional texture is illuminated when the print is viewed. For example, grazing, hard illumination emphasizes the texture. Prints made on both smooth paper and textured paper can be modified by using texture screens. Texture screens change the densities in the print image, so that the texture is apparent rather than being real.

Materials such as textured paper or cloth require a plastic screening; or, sheets of textured glass or plastic can be used as texture screens.

Commercially Made Texture Screens

Commercially produced texture screens are in the form of processed film images of a variety of textures. Many textures imitate the appearance of different art forms, such as oil paintings, etchings, and mezzo tint. Others are unique to photography, such as screens that produce the appearance of photographic grain when there is none.

Commercial texture screens come in two types: small screens that are laid over a negative and enlarged with it, and large screens that are printed in contact with paper.

Small Screens. Small screens give good results and are less expensive than large screens. They are easier to use because they are easy to clean and because they can be kept in complete contact with the negative by using a glass negative carrier. To use the small screens, place the emulsion of the texture screen next to the emulsion of the negative in a glass negative carrier and print them as one negative.

Large Screens. Large texture screens are used in contact with the emulsion of the enlarging paper on the easel. It may be necessary to place a sheet of clear glass over the texture screen to hold it in contact with the paper. If a heavy piece of glass is not used, a blurred texture effect may result where the screen is not in good contact with the paper. The screen can be kept in position during all or part of the exposure, depending on the degree of effect that is desired. If the screen is to be in place for only part of the exposure, divide the total exposure time in parts so that the screen can be removed when the enlarger is off. Be sure the paper is not moved between exposures.

2416

◄ *This color print was made with a canvas texture screen placed in direct contact with the emulsion of the enlarging paper during printing. A sheet of clear glass should be placed over the texture screen to keep it in complete contact with the paper. Photo by Donald J. Maggio.*

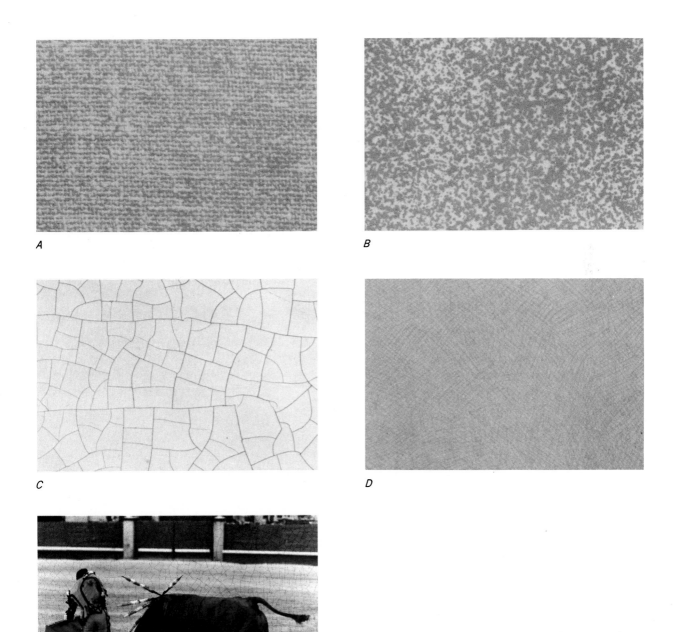

A

B

C

D

Numerous commercially produced texture screens are available. Shown above are four prints made from texture screens alone: (A) canvas texture screen; (B) grain texture screen; (C) Mona Lisa texture screen; (D) etch texture screen. The print at left was made with a Mona Lisa texture screen in contact with the paper. Photo by Donald J. Maggio.

Texture Screens

2418

A texture screen (below) was made for the photograph at left by contact-printing a piece of lens-cleaning tissue on a sheet of high-contrast film. A sandwich of the texture screen and a color negative was then enlarged to produce the color print. Photo by Barbara Jean.

Dodging and Burning-In

It is possible to dodge and burn-in with any kind of texture screen, just as when printing a negative without a screen. Since a texture screen may cause slight loss of print contrast, it may be advisable to use a paper of a higher contrast grade than would be used if the negative were printed normally.

Making Texture Screens

A simple texture screen can be made by tightly stretching a sheer cloth over a frame that can be placed over the enlarger easel. The cloth should be in contact with the paper. Flocked nylon cloth with designs woven into it will add an overall texture and also reproduce the design in white on the print. If the design is to be printed black, contact-print the flocked nylon onto a piece of Kodalith ortho film 6556, type 3. After printing the original negative,

remove it and print the Kodalith film texture screen onto the same sheet of paper.

Photographic Textures. Other varieties of texture screens can easily be made by photographing textured surfaces. For example, use strong sidelighting to bring out the texture of the following or other surfaces:

> Canvas or burlap
> Gravel, pebbles, or sand
> Rugs
> Wall covering
> Window screens
> Wicker
> Bark
> Leaves or grass
> String mops or brooms (the working end)
> Tire treads

By taking a close-up picture of the surface, a negative can be produced that can be used as a texture screen. Put the texture screen in the negative carrier together with the negatives that are going to be enlarged, and print them both at the same time.

Textured Plastic Screens. A sheet of clear plastic with a textured surface can make a good texture screen. A plastic-supply company will have a variety of textures to choose from, and they will cut the plastic to the proper size to fit the easel. Simply place the plastic over the enlarging paper, with the textured side toward the lens and the flat side on the paper, and then print through it.

Dot Textures. Contact halftone screens can be used to convert a continuous-tone image to a dot image. Use a screen such as the Kodak PMT gray contact screen, which is specially designed for making halftones on paper. It should be a relatively coarse screen—for example, one with 65 lines per inch. Place a sheet of film such as Kodalith on the easel, with the screen on top of the film, emulsion to emulsion, and hold together in contact by vacuum or by a sheet of glass. Enlarge a negative or slide

(Above) A color slide of a wooden sidewalk was sandwiched with a slide of pink daisies to make this interesting texture effect. An internegative was then made. Printing is greatly facilitated by this process, as there is only one piece of film to handle. Photo by Barbara Jean. (Left) This texture screen is built right into the negative, which in this case is on Kodalith Autoscreen ortho film 2563 (Estar base). Photo by John Fish.

Texture Screens

onto the Kodalith film and process it in a lith-type developer.

If a negative is used, the halftone will be a positive. This can be enlarged to make a halftone negative print. If a positive print is desired, contact-print the halftone positive on Kodalith film to get a halftone negative.

If the image on the screened negative is kept small, the dots will be of a visible size when the negative is enlarged. For example, if initial enlarging of the negative is 1:1 with a 65-line screen, and the negative is enlarged $20\times$ to make a print, the result will be three dots to the inch in the print.

• *See also:* COMBINATION PRINTING; MULTIPLE PRINTING; SPECIAL EFFECTS.

Theatrical Photography

Depending upon the area, there are three levels of theater photography that may be encountered. The first is the photography of professional theater. Here, all entertainers are paid for their time. The second level is the semiprofessional company with a professional star or stars working with amateurs. Summer stock companies are a good example of this level. The third level is the all-amateur group. These range from the community theater organizations that present a season of surprisingly professional performances to groups that stage a single annual community production.

Each of these groups may require photographs from time to time. However, if a photographer has not been given an assignment, permission should be obtained before photographing begins.

Getting Permission

Whether or not permission will be granted to photograph in a theater will depend upon the particular company or entertainer that is to be recorded. Many actors in Broadway shows have contracts that require them to be paid for photography sessions. This arrangement requires the management to refuse the right to photograph the shows to anyone except the professional hired to handle publicity pictures. Each program handed out to members of the audience warns that taking pictures during the performance is forbidden.

The same restrictions exist with many other professional theater groups. However, this should not be a discouraging factor. The photographer should speak with the theater manager or the public-relations person for the company and explain his or her interest in photographing and the fact that flash will not be permitted. The photographer should ask if there is a way to make photographs during a performance or even a dress rehearsal. Permission may be granted; however, a major company may not want an amateur photographer roaming the stage area or audience during a dress rehearsal. This is especially true if the rehearsal is being recorded by a professional photographer for publicity.

In many cases, the management will allow photographs to be made and will ask to see the finished pictures. If the photographs are good, the theater management may want to use them for publicity. Cast members may want prints as well.

Equipment

For theater photography, an adjustable camera that is capable of using high-speed film is necessary. Extra lighting, including the use of flash, usually will not be permitted in most theaters unless the photographer is working for the production group.

Equipment Noise. The sound level of the equipment that is used will be a consideration if photographing during a production. Many older single-lens reflex (SLR) cameras have mirrors that make a relatively loud noise during exposure. The sound could travel throughout the theater and shatter the mood woven by the performers.

Many of the new 35 mm SLR's have special mechanisms that make them exceptionally quiet. Twin-lens reflex cameras and rangefinder cameras are also quiet, since they do not have a moving mirror to make extra noise.

If the equipment is noisy, photography will have to be limited to periods when this will not be a problem. Dress rehearsals, for example, have all the excitement of a regular performance and everyone is in full costume. But the theater will be empty except for cast and crew, so the sound of a camera will not disrupt the activities on stage.

Lighting and Exposure

Theatrical performances seldom have even illumination, which would allow an average reading

with a normal light meter. The use of spot- and floodlights means that certain areas will be brilliantly illuminated while other sections of the stage go to black. A normal light meter, either built into the camera or held separately, takes in a wide enough angle of view that it is "fooled" by the areas of darkness.

Spot Meters. There are several approaches to the metering problem. The first is to use a 1-degree spot meter. Such a meter records a very narrow angle of view (even narrower than what would be viewed if a 1000 mm lens were used on a 35 mm camera). The light falling on the face of individual performers can then be recorded using this type of meter even if the photographer is in the last row of the balcony.

Spot Attachments. Spot attachments for light meters are somewhat of a compromise. These at-

tachments narrow the normal viewing angle from 5 to 10 degrees in most cases, although various 1-degree attachments are available. If the photographer is close to the performer, a spot attachment can be reasonably accurate when covering 5 to 10 degrees. However, a careful reading must be taken of a single, spotlighted entertainer on an otherwise darkened stage. The 5- to 10-degree attachment would probably read enough dark area to cause overexposure.

Built-in Meters. A behind-the-lens light meter in a camera can be of great assistance even when not of the spot or weighted-center variety. Many photographers use a very long lens to take a light reading that is narrower than would be possible with a normal lens. Then the camera is set according to the original reading, the telephoto lens is removed, and shorter-focal-length lenses are used for the actual photography. Each time the light changes on stage, the long lens can be used to take a new reading.

Incident Reading. The best approach with a hand-held meter is to use it as an incident-light meter from the stage itself. If permission has been granted, the photographer can stand on the stage before the audience is allowed inside and have the lighting crew illuminate the stage as though the production were in progress. Then readings can be taken for use when the show is actually being performed. This is still only a guide, because the use of local spotlighting can increase the light intensity on certain areas of the stage.

Suggested Exposures

There are some guidelines to follow to get a basic exposure, to bracket this exposure, and to adjust according to the film being used. The following suggestions are based on films rated at ASA 400. Black-and-white and color films rated at this speed will provide adequately fine grain to allow for reasonable enlargement and plenty of shadow detail. They will enable the use of a reasonably fast shutter speed for hand-held work.

Stage Show. A typical stage show is fairly bright. Generally, a speed of from 1/60 to 1/125 sec., bracketing from $f/2.8$ to $f/4$, will provide usable images. A small stage or set with a low ceiling tends to be brighter than a larger one with a high ceiling.

When the basic exposure setting is used, pictures will become lighter or darker as the stage lighting changes, reflecting the mood of the different scenes. When spotlights emphasize one stage area with the rest of the stage dark, the pictures will capture the same effect. When all of the stage is dimly lighted, open the lens one stop from the basic exposure. If the lighting is *very* dim, open the lens two stops from the basic exposure.

School Auditorium. The stage and auditorium illumination found in schools is usually quite low compared with that found in professional theaters. Usually, a shutter speed of 1/30 sec. and an aperture of $f/2$ to $f/2.8$ will be necessary.

Ice Shows. Floodlighted and spotlighted performances, especially with ice shows, offer high illumination levels. Basic exposure will be 1/125 sec. between $f/2.8$ and $f/4$ for floodlighted performances and one stop smaller for the brighter, spotlighted performances. (*See:* AVAILABLE-LIGHT PHOTOGRAPHY.)

The type of film used is a matter of personal preference. A floodlighted stage, the most common

Stage lighting changes constantly, depending upon the mood of the different scenes. While a basic exposure setting may be used as a general guide, bracketing is advisable. If the lighting is dim, the lens should be opened one or even two stops from the basic exposure. Photos by Ken Stevens.

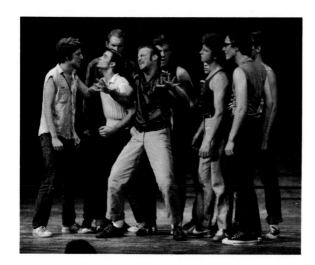

Choice of film is a matter of personal preference, although different types of lights require different films. (Left) Outdoor performances require daylight-balanced film (top) while flood-lighted stages (bottom) require film balanced for tungsten light. (Right) Spotlighted stages using carbon-arc lighting require daylight film to be accurate. Photos at top left and at right by Ken Stevens; photo at bottom left by Joseph Abeles Studio.

with theater photography, requires film balanced for tungsten light to record colors accurately. Spotlighted stages using carbon-arc lighting require daylight-balanced film to be accurate.

Camera Supports

Most theaters will not allow the use of a tripod during a performance because it could become a fire hazard. A tripod in the aisle may trip people hurrying toward an exit. Its presence may even be a violation of city ordinances.

Unipod. Unipods may be allowed by the theater management. If some weight is put on the unipod, it becomes almost as steady as a tripod. More important, it can be braced against a wall, on a chair, or on almost any other surface.

Shoulder Pod. A shoulder pod helps to improve camera steadiness. If a sharp picture can be obtained by hand-holding a camera and lens combination at 1/60 sec., the same combination can be used with a shoulder pod at between 1/15 and 1/30 sec. A unipod will usually allow work at 1/8 sec., and the tripod can keep the camera steady for considerably longer exposure times.

The Performance

Generally, an opportunity arises to make photographs from one of three places: (1) from the audience level where, during a performance, heads may be visible in the picture, (2) from above, usually from the balcony, or (3) from the side of the stage. The side area provides an excellent view of single entertainers, rock groups, and the like. It is not good for plays.

Special Cases. Certain productions require the use of special photographic techniques. Dance companies are a prime example of the need to plan carefully how the images will be recorded. Dancers are usually in motion—spinning, leaping, and moving at paces that will most likely be too fast for photographing at the relatively slow shutter speeds the light allows. A dancer's movement might be stopped with a shutter speed of 1/500 sec., or faster if the light is controlled. Working with available light

forces the photographer to find ways of stopping the motion.

The simplest approach is to pan with the dancer. The photographer moves as the dancer moves, with the camera traveling at a pace exactly matching the dancer's leaps. This keeps the dancer sharp and blurs the background as well as the other dancers.

Peak of Action. A better solution is to watch for moments of peak action. When leaping into the air, a dancer reaches zero vertical velocity for an instant at the peak of the leap. At this moment of peak action, even a shutter speed as slow as 1/15 sec. will render a sharp photograph.

There are countless moments of peak action in other productions as well as in dance. However, in

At moments of peak action, a leaping dancer reaches zero vertical velocity for an instant; at this moment, a sharp photo can be obtained with a shutter speed as slow as 1/15 sec. To anticipate such a moment, the photographer must have prior knowledge of the movements, either by reading the script or, preferably, by attending a rehearsal or a previous performance. Photo by Ken Stevens.

order to catch peak action, it must be anticipated. The photographer can read the script of the play or watch any of the dance rehearsals prior to taking the picture. This prior knowledge will enable the photographer to know what movements are coming and when a brief pause can be expected in the action.

To anticipate this moment, the photographer must start to release the shutter *before* the peak action is reached. There is a delay of a fraction of a second between the time the photographer begins to release the shutter and the moment it actually opens. By starting this process before peak action is achieved, the photographer can be sure that the shutter will be open at the precise moment when the actors, dancers, and other performers are still. This technique takes practice and luck.

The Cast

In addition to photographing theatrical productions, the photographer may want to photograph the actors and actresses themselves. Performers need photographs of themselves in different poses to help them sell their talents to producers, directors, and others. They use the pictures much as a model uses her portfolio.

Actors and Actresses. When an actor or an actress is photographed for a portfolio, the photographer should allow the person to show as much versatility as possible. Different changes of clothing, makeup, and expression should be suggested. The photographer should show the many ways the individual can appear. If a beautiful young woman can realistically portray a middle-aged, harried housewife and an aged, ugly old crone, this is ideal. She might look sexy, or mousy, or just like the "girl next door." She may dress in rags and furs, a period costume, or the latest bikini. Whatever roles an actor or an actress can assume should be shown.

Photographs of actors and actresses should be taken under controlled conditions. Work in the home, studio, or at the theater when it is closed to the public. Use drapes or set up a roll of seamless background paper. Inexpensive floodlights will serve this purpose, but by all means use umbrellas and electronic flash if you have them. At the theater, work with the person in a stage setting, using the curtain for a background. (*See:* PORTRAITURE; GLAMOUR PHOTOGRAPHY.)

Semi-Pros. When pictures are taken for summer stock companies and other semiprofessional groups, the photographer will undoubtedly be asked to take more than just publicity photographs. For an amateur actor or actress, the high point of the performer's career may be working with a "name" star. Everyone will want individual portraits taken with the star, and this can be profitable for the photographer. In addition, photos of the performance and group pictures of the cast may be taken.

Amateurs. With totally amateur groups, pictures are usually taken of the performance and the cast. This might include one picture of everyone in costume lined up on stage as though taking their bows. Each person may wish to buy one of these as a souvenir. Occasionally, individual pictures may be taken as well, either as souvenirs or for those who want to start a portfolio for use when they go after professional parts.

Other Considerations

Once the techniques of photographing a play or other theatrical performance have been practiced, consider the ultimate use of the pictures. Will they be printed 8" × 10" or larger and displayed on the walls of the box office or theater lobby? Will they be used by cast members as souvenirs and for portfolios carried when applying for future work? Or will they be sent to newspapers and magazines, either as advertisements or in the hope of free publicity?

If the photographs are going to be reproduced in newspapers or magazines, several factors must be taken into account. First there is the matter of space. Large photographs are seldom used except for dramatic news pictures or strong human-interest images. Picture format may be square, or a horizontal or vertical rectangle.

When photographing specifically for newspaper or magazine publicity use, place the actors close together. Concentrate on no more than three performers, no matter how many are in the show. Just two people interacting would be even better. Fill the frame, limiting the background shown. Do not try to include the whole stage because this will reduce the relative size of the actors. Such a photo is unlikely to be printed.

By including a horizontal and a vertical photograph for consideration, chances are increased for a picture's use.

Actors need photographs of themselves as part of their port-folios, to show their experience and the type of roles they have played. In addition to formal studio poses, some photographs taken in performance (either real or simulated) are highly desirable. Photo above from the Van Damn Collection; photos at right by Alfredo Valente.

Getting Started

There are several ways to make contact with the theatrical groups and entertainers. Check the Yellow Pages of the telephone book and the entertainment pages of area newspapers. Call the entertainment editor or the theater critic at the local newspaper. Schools and social organizations also stage amateur productions.

Once the photographer decides which groups to contact, he or she should call and ask to speak with the theater owner or manager, the play's producer, or the person handling public relations for the group or show. When dealing with singers and similar per-formers rather than actors, it may be necessary to contact a theatrical agent.

The photographer should explain his or her interest in taking photographs and ask for an appointment to see the individual in charge. It is very easy to have a request to photograph turned down over the phone. When a person is seen face to face, a favorable response is more likely to be obtained.

The photographer should take a portfolio of 10 to 20 photographs to the theater to represent his or

When photographing specifically for newspaper or magazine publicity use, show a maximum of three, or preferably two performers, and place them close together. Fill the frame and eliminate as much background as possible. Black-and-white is preferable to color for these purposes. Photos by Ken Stevens.

her best work. This will serve as proof that the photographer is competent even if the photographs are not being made for pay. Few theatrical groups will give a complete beginner special picture privileges. However, a competent amateur may be welcome and the photographs speak for the photographer's ability.

• *See also:* AVAILABLE-LIGHT PHOTOGRAPHY; COLOR PHOTOGRAPHY; DANCE PHOTOGRAPHY; GLAMOUR PHOTOGRAPHY; LIGHTING; PORTRAITURE.

Thermal Photography

All bodies above absolute zero (-273 C [-460 F]) emit radiant energy. The wavelength of the energy varies with the temperature of the body. When the radiated wavelengths are between about 700 and 1200 nanometres (nm), in the near infrared region of the spectrum, they can be recorded by their direct action on infrared-sensitive photographic emulsions. This technique is called thermal infrared photography, or simply *thermal photography*. The object being photographed must be shielded from light and outside sources of infrared radiation so that the exposure is created only by radiated, not reflected, energy.

The infrared region extends beyond 1200 nm—the practical limit to which emulsions can be sensitized—to about 1,000,000 nm. Photographic records in this range can be made by means of *thermography*.

Thermography

Thermography is the name given to a family of infrared imaging systems that employ some intermediate means of converting variations in infrared radiation into a visual display. These displays can then be photographed by conventional methods and film materials.

Modern thermographic methods rely primarily on electronic means. A widely applied technique employs infrared detectors to scan the scene. The resulting electronic signal is easily amplified and displayed on a television monitor. This method permits infrared imagery of the human body and of scenes as cold as arctic snowfields.

Another rather simple method of recording heat patterns involves the use of temperature-sensitive, liquid crystalline materials. In practice, a liquid-crystal mixture is selected that has a color response range that encompasses the temperature range of interest. The mixture is applied to the surface area under investigation and responds to temperature differences by changing color. The color patterns produced can then be recorded on ordinary color films. In similar fashion, liquid-crystal mixtures can be used for nondestructive testing of materials, such as flaw detection.

Temperature and Radiation Wavelength

At all temperatures above absolute zero, every object emits energy from its surface in the form of a spectrum of differing wavelengths and intensities. The particular spectrum that the surface emits depends upon its absolute temperature and its emissivity.* As the temperature increases, the amount of energy emitted at each wavelength increases. In addition, the wavelength at which *peak* radiation occurs becomes shorter. This peak moves from the long wavelength end of the infrared spectrum (about 1,000,000 nm at 3 C [5 F] above absolute zero) toward the short wavelength end as the temperature increases. When the temperature approximates 4000 K, the emission peak reaches the visible region of the spectrum.

Thus, radiation is very much temperature dependent. An object below 250 C (482 F) radiates wavelengths that lie roughly between 1400 and 100,000 nm. For example, an object whose temperature is roughly that of the earth's surface (−50 C to +50 C [−16 F to 122 F]) will emit radiation at peak wavelengths ranging from 9000 to 13,000 nm. The human body radiates infrared energy at wavelengths between 4000 and 20,000 nm with a peak wavelength of approximately 9500 nm.

If the object becomes hotter, it radiates more energy at every wavelength because its molecular activity increases. At the same time, the energy distribution is shifted to shorter wavelengths until ultimately some wavelengths in the visible region begin to appear. However, below about 500 C (932 F), the radiation is mostly infrared energy, and at these subincandescent temperatures the intensity of visible radiation is extremely small.

*The emissivity of an object is the ratio of the amount of radiant energy it emits to that emitted by a perfect radiator at the same temperature. A perfect radiator, known as a "black body," has an emissivity of 1.0.

Photographic Sensitivity

In spite of the fact that the infrared spectrum extends from 700 nm out to approximately 1,000,000 nm, very little of it can be recorded photographically. Silver halide films with sensitivity beyond about 1300 nm are fundamentally impossible. At longer wavelengths, the energy of a photon is insufficient to create a latent image. Furthermore, films that might respond to longer radiations would present serious problems as thermal sensitivity increased. Even warmth approximating body temperature in the camera and surroundings would fog the film.

Most infrared films have little sensitivity beyond 900 nm, although certain specialized materials for astronomy reach out to about 1250 nm.

Thermal Infrared Photography

When an object reaches incandescent temperatures above 500 C (932 F), it begins to glow. It emits actinic radiation, and it can be photographed without any other source of illumination. Its visible emanations can be recorded on panchromatic or color film, and its infrared radiation can be recorded on infrared-sensitive film.

An object at a temperature below 500 C (932 F) is nonincandescent, and it cannot be photographed with panchromatic or color film unless illuminated by an external source. However, if its temperature falls between 250 C (482 F) and 500 C (932 F), it emits enough energy in the actinic region to produce an image on infrared film if the exposure time is sufficiently long. Its radiation can be photographed directly as emitted or as it is reflected from colder bodies around it. Only infrared film can be used because no visible emanation is present. Such photography, of course, must take place in a darkened room where there is no source of shorter-wavelength radiation. This, then, provides a means of determining the temperature profile of objects that are just below red heat.

Measuring temperatures photographically is based on the premise that, for a given surface, radiation increases with temperature, and the higher the temperature, the more density will be produced in the film to record it. Furthermore, areas that produce equal densities in the negative are at the same temperature, provided that their emissivities are equal.

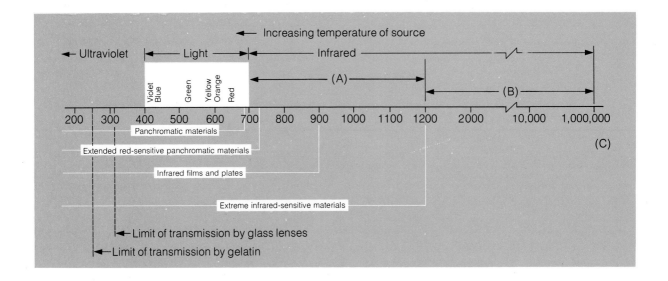

Photographic records of the temperature variations in objects are made by infrared thermal photography or by various methods of thermography. The technique employed is largely determined by the wavelength of the energy radiated by a heat-emitting body. The following are represented here: infrared thermal photography (A), electronic, liquid crystal thermography (B), and wavelength in nanometres (C).

The technique of using such photographic films to record the temperature profiles of bodies at temperatures above 250 C (482 F) differs little from pictorial photography in the type of equipment used and in the manner of its use. A large-aperture lens, preferably *f*/2, with the equivalent of a Kodak Wratten filter No. 87, a sturdy tripod, and a means of calibrating exposures will suffice for most studies. The actual exposures will have to be determined by experiment, however, since they can be extremely long—in some cases, amounting to hours. Furthermore, in order to be able to interpret the infrared exposures of hot bodies quantitatively, a calibration of some sort is necessary. One way of calibrating is to include a series of exposures of a standard hot object held successively at a variety of known temperatures within an applicable range. These exposures should be made on the same roll of film used to record the object under investigation. A calibration curve can then be derived by plotting density versus temperature.

The temperature range that can be covered by any one exposure is in the order of 60 to 120 C (108 to 216 F); the actual position of this range on the temperature scale determines the exposure required. If the temperature variations over the surface of the body are greater than 120 C (248 F), the density range on the film will not easily translate into accurate temperature measurements. If such is the case, two exposures are a better choice: a long exposure to record the cooler parts and a shorter exposure for the hotter areas. When the record is confined to a range of 60 C (108 F) or less, temperature differences of 15 C (27 F) are easily distinguishable.

Objects at temperatures below 250 C (482 F) cannot be photographed directly using self-emitted energy as the source of exposure. Although such bodies emit infrared radiation, the wavelength of this radiation lies in a region of the spectrum to which photographic emulsions do not respond. To be photographed, these objects must be irradiated by an external source, or they must be photographed indirectly with the help of an electronic thermographic process.

• *See also:* INFRARED PHOTOGRAPHY.

Thermometers

The importance of the thermometer in the photo laboratory cannot be minimized. Indeed, the thermometer may be considered the most important measuring instrument used by the photographer, more important even than the exposure meter.

Approximately correct exposures can be secured by estimation based on experience, by following the printed guides packed with film, or—particularly in the case of color—by bracketing. Moreover, moderate deficiencies in exposure can be compensated for by modifying the standard time-temperature relationship. But, there is no way of estimating water temperature with any reasonable degree of accuracy and, in color processing, there is no way of arriving at acceptable results without a consistent, accurate thermometer.

Thus, one of the priorities in equipping a photo lab is to secure an accurate thermometer reliable in the range of normal working temperatures of from 18.5 to 24 C (65 to 75 F) for black-and-white, and from 29.5 to 43.5 C (85 to 110 F) for color, depending upon the processes used. This may mean buying a fairly expensive thermometer—one of the "process" types, for instance.

A practical approach is to use a very good thermometer as the standard, and calibrate working thermometers against that standard. The working thermometers need not be as accurate, but they should provide consistent repeatability. Trying to work with a very cheap thermometer of unknown variability is not just a hardship, it is false economy.

Types of Thermometers

There are three types of thermometers generally used in photography. The first is the liquid-filled thermometer—a sealed glass tube filled either with mercury or with colored alcohol, either red or blue. The second type is the dial thermometer, in which two metals having different coefficients of expansion are bonded together. They expand or contract at differing rates in response to temperature changes, which cause them to curl. This curl is translated into the movement of the dial to display the temperature. A third type, now coming into common use, is the electronic thermometer in which a probe is used to sense temperature. The data are displayed either on a dial or in digital form with light-emitting diodes.

Liquid-Filled Thermometers. The oldest type of thermometer in continuous use, the liquid-filled thermometer, was invented in 1714 by Gabriel Daniel Fahrenheit. This German instrument-maker who lived in Holland gave his name to the temperature scale he developed for use with his thermometer.

The liquid-filled thermometer remains the most important type of thermometer today. It is supplied in a wide range of types and models. They vary in price and accuracy from low-priced, less accurate thermometers to extremely precise, highly accurate mercury-filled models.

It is necessary to differentiate between the terms *accuracy* and *precision*. Accuracy refers to the ability of the instrument to measure temperature correctly and to respond uniformly to changes in temperature. Mercury is the most accurate of materials commonly used in high-quality thermometers. An alcohol thermometer is somewhat less accurate.

Precision refers to the degree of fineness in reading the thermometer and depends upon the diameter of the tube (which controls the length of travel of the liquid) and the fineness of markings. For example, a thermometer may be extremely accurate, but if it is marked in 2-degree increments, the user will have a problem in reading the working temperature with a precision of ½ degree.

Thermometers to be Avoided. The photographer should avoid the lower-priced alcohol thermometers, particularly those consisting of a glass tube anchored to a calibrated metal backing. In time, the tube may slip from its fastening and the improper placement of the glass on the scale will cause gross inaccuracy. A longer thermometer is usually more useful and probably more precise than a shorter model, because the longer scale will permit easier reading of the temperature markings.

Avoid the combination stirring rod and thermometer. Thermometers are rather delicate instruments and should not be subjected to any more vibration or shaking than is absolutely necessary.

Another type of thermometer of dubious value is the model designed to fit into the hollow shaft of a film developing tank. Presumably, this type of thermometer would provide a convenient method of monitoring the developer temperature during the complete process. However, such a thermometer is usually neither accurate nor precise enough for this monitoring. Also, inversion agitation makes the use of tanks with hollow spindles impractical.

Mercury Thermometers. For the photographer interested in doing serious work, the mercury thermometers are preferred. The more expensive "process" thermometer is extremely accurate and is generally used to calibrate other thermometers. An alternative standard thermometer is a clinical model, which is most accurate in the range of body temperatures 37 $\pm$4 C (98.6 $\pm$7 F). Therefore, it must be used only in this range as a check. This type of thermometer provides a maximum reading; it must be shaken down to give the correct response.

Color Thermometers. Good thermometers made for color work (generally identified as "color" thermometers) have working ranges from about 10 to 60 C (40 to 140 F). The prime accuracy must be within the middle range, however. If several thermometers are used, they should agree to within a degree. In use, thermometers have a way of losing accuracy so that the role of a standard calibration thermometer remains extremely important.

Dial Thermometers. Dial-type thermometers are the easiest to use and to read, but instruments of this sort are inherently less accurate than the best mercury thermometers. One reason is that the bimetallic strip may change over the yeàrs so that the degree of response to temperature changes may not be the same as when the thermometer was initially purchased.

For the most accurate readings, the dial must be viewed straight on rather than from an angle. Some of the newer dial thermometers use a reflective band around the scale so that two needles are seen if the dial is viewed at an angle, while only one needle is visible if the dial is viewed correctly.

Dial thermometers should normally be immersed in at least 2 inches of solution to provide an accurate reading. Follow the manufacturer's instructions if they vary from this recommendation.

In general, dial thermometers are more expensive than liquid-filled types, but they offer considerable convenience. Dial thermometers are much sturdier, resisting dropping and shock. Dropping a dial thermometer can, however, affect the accuracy of the reading. It is a good idea to calibrate dial thermometers periodically to make sure that they continue to record accurately.

In reading both liquid and dial thermometers, allow sufficient time for the instrument to register properly. Thermometers normally come close to a final reading in 15 seconds, but it may take as long as 2 minutes with the thermometer sufficiently immersed in solution to reach a final, stable reading.

Electronic Thermometers. The electronic thermometer is the newest (and most expensive) type available for photography. It has a very sensitive probe to record extremely fine variations in temperature. Essentially, the temperature variation is used to monitor a current, similar to the operation of a CdS exposure meter. Thus, a variation of as little as 0.05 C ($\frac{1}{10}$ F) is recorded and the exact temperature can be easily read on a dial or digital readout. These thermometers may also span a much wider range of temperatures than the conventional liquid or dial types.

Recording Thermometers. A variation of precision thermometers is the recording thermometer, in which a recorder is coupled to the thermometer to provide a record of processing temperatures. This type of installation is commonly used in photofinishing operations involving large volume, constant replenishment, and periodic quality-control checks.

Accuracy

The increasing use of color processes and the growth of small-batch color processing by amateurs and professionals has increased the importance of accurate, precise thermometers. In color, an accuracy of $\pm$0.3 C ($\frac{1}{2}$ F) at the working range is a prime requirement. For black-and-white, an accuracy of $\pm$0.6 C (1 F) is quite acceptable. Few thermometers meet this standard over a long period of time so that the photographer should get the best thermometers available, take care not to drop them or to attempt to read temperatures too hot or too cold for their scales, and calibrate working models periodically.

• *See also:* TEMPERATURE CONTROL; TEMPERATURE SCALES.

2-Thiobarbituric Acid

Used as a blue-black image-forming agent in fogging developers for reversal processing of black-and-white films; also has been used in higher concentrations as a silver complexing agent in monobaths.
Formula: $C_4H_4N_2O_2S$
Molecular Weight: 144.15
White powder, slightly soluble in water.

Thiourea

Thiocarbamide, sulfocarbamide, sulfourea

Used as a toning medium to convert silver bromide to a silver sulfide image. It is also used in gold toning baths, mordants for dye toning, stabilizers, and as a fogging agent in some reversal procedures.
Formula: CH_4N_2S
Molecular Weight: 76.12
White, prismatic crystals, soluble in water, ammonium thiocyanate solution, ether, and alcohol.

Time Exposures

A time exposure is one in which the camera shutter remains open about 1 sec. or longer. In making time exposures, certain camera adjustments are necessary. Some cameras have built-in slow-speed settings for time exposures up to 8 or 15 sec. Or an auxiliary timer, which connects to the shutter cable-release socket, may be used. However, usually the photographer must open the shutter, monitor the time, and close the shutter after the proper interval.

Shutter-Speed Settings

Time exposures are made at either of two shutter settings: "T," time (in older European shutters, "Z" for zeit), or "B," bulb, or brief. At the T setting, the shutter opens when the release is pushed once, and closes when it is pushed again. At the B setting, the shutter remains open as long as the release is held depressed; when pressure is removed, the shut-

ter closes. Some shutters have a locking device to hold the release button depressed for long time exposures at the B setting; with others it is necessary to attach a locking cable release. Few modern shutters built into cameras have both T and B settings; most between-the-lens shutters for view cameras have both T and B settings.

Preventing Movement

For sharp pictures with time exposures, the camera must be mounted firmly on a secure support to prevent movement during the exposure. More than one photographer has developed blurred negatives because the weight of a large-format camera pushed a tripod leg into the soft earth during a long exposure.

Subject movement during a time exposure will leave a trace of the path traveled, known as a ghost image. This is the cause of light streaks through pictures of night traffic scenes. Time exposures of star trails in the sky at night are caused by the earth's rotation while the shutter is open.

In daylight scenes, traffic and passersby can often be eliminated by deliberately creating the need for a time exposure. A slow-speed film and a very small aperture may be enough, or neutral density filtration may have to be added. The total required time is divided into an equivalent number of short exposures, each less than 1 sec., which are given at intervals so that no unwanted moving element is in the same position in two or more exposures.

The length of the individual exposures should be short enough that an average subject in the scene would be underexposed by at least the equivalent of four stops. The camera and the major subject must not change position at any time during the exposure series. The frequency of the exposures will be well below the rate at which exposure is affected by the intermittency effect. Many photographers use a dark slide as a shutter, holding it in front of the lens. Thus, they avoid having to touch the camera for shutter cocking, and avoid the hazard of moving the camera.

Reciprocity Effect

The major exposure consideration in planning a time exposure is compensation for reciprocity effect. During a time exposure, the light reaching the film is not strong enough to build up the same effect as

Time exposures are frequently used for taking photographs of fireworks displays. Several bursts may be recorded on a single frame of film while the shutter is held open on "Time."

a shorter exposure with more light, even though the two exposures may be mathematically equal. If compensation is not given, black-and-white negatives will lack density and contrast, and color pictures will exhibit color shifts.

Compensation for color reciprocity effect requires additional exposure and, in some cases, corrective filtration. Data are given in most film instruction sheets.

Compensation for black-and-white films may require additional exposure, additional development, or both. For methods of determining the required compensation, see the article RECIPROCITY EFFECT.

Time-Lapse Photography

Time-lapse photography is a means of recording and revealing events that happen too slowly for human perception. One can capture in a single set of photographs the growth of a sheaf of wheat, the life cycle of an insect, or the precipitation of a solution and its ultimate crystallization. As the term time-lapse suggests, successive images of phenomena are made, and time is allowed to pass between exposures. The technique records actions and events at rates with intervals from 1 second to many hours between exposures. Scientists, engineers, and technicians know how important time is in their work. Many of the phenomena or processes studied are evaluated on the basis of time. Motion pictures have long been an aid in this area. The motion picture records the data or action in relation to a time base—the rate at which the successive frames are exposed.

A motion picture consists of a series of still pictures, called frames, that are taken at regular intervals. Thus, at a frame rate of 18 frames per second, if an event occurs in frame number 72, it occurred 4 seconds after the beginning of filming. For time to appear normal, this succession of pictures must be viewed at the same rate at which they were exposed. However, some actions, motions, or processes occur over such long periods of time that significant changes cannot be detected by the human eye when the changes are viewed in normal time.

Time-lapse photography records actions at very slow rates, with intervals from 1 second up to many hours in between frames. When these frames are viewed at a faster frame rate of 6 to 18 frames per second, we effectively compress time; actions that occurred over a long period of time, such as days or weeks, can be speeded up so that the observer can appreciate their intricacies.

Equipment

The equipment needed for time-lapse photography consists of a motion-picture camera that is capable of exposing a single frame of film at a time, a device to actuate the single-frame release on the camera, and a timing device to control the time interval between the successive frames. Generally, 16 mm and 35 mm equipment have been the favorites for this photographic technique. There are, however, a number of super 8 cameras that are readily equipped for time-lapse photography.

Mounting the Camera

Because a time-lapse camera exposes a frame every few seconds, minutes, or hours, it is extremely important that the camera be secured to a rigid mounting, one that will not allow the camera to move between exposures. For temporary installations, a tripod is essential. Once you have mounted the camera on the tripod and positioned it to cover the subject, tighten everything down. Above all, do not try to pan or tilt the camera during the filming of a time-lapse sequence. Any slight movement of the camera, or any change in the setting of a zoom lens during shooting, will have a jarring effect, with the entire scene jerking about when the action is viewed on the screen.

Although the camera is mounted rigidly, unwanted subject motion can present problems—such as in photographing plant development outdoors. Here, even a slight breeze can make flowers jump wildly around on the screen when the movie is projected. You may want to build a windscreen around the subject to keep any draft from moving it.

Make the screen from clear plastic sheeting stapled to wooden dowels. Push the dowels into the ground, outside of the field of coverage of the lens,

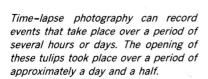

Time-lapse photography can record events that take place over a period of several hours or days. The opening of these tulips took place over a period of approximately a day and a half.

Time-Lapse Photography

to support the screen. The clear plastic will not cast shadows; and if it is out of focus, it will not show in the picture.

In situations where a tripod will not work, some manufacturers supply camera-mounting clamps. Sometimes these devices offer the only means of attaching a camera to a fence post, a machine bench, or the dashboard of a vehicle.

Positioning the Camera

Correct placement and aiming of the camera can play an important part in the success of a time-lapse film. Study the subject carefully. Are there likely to be obstacles between the camera and the subject during the shooting session? Such things as vehicle traffic, people walking past, and shadows moving across the subject as the sun changes position during the day can distract the observer from the subject's action.

With the camera mounted on a tripod or mounting clamp, sight through the viewfinder to determine the *field of coverage*. It may be necessary to move the camera to get the coverage you need.

The lenses on many cameras must be focused for the camera-to-subject distance so that the subject will appear in sharp focus in the picture. However, an area in front of the subject and an area behind the subject will also be in acceptably sharp focus. This range of sharpness *(depth of field)* depends on the lens opening or aperture (which is automatically controlled by the lighting conditions on cameras with automatic exposure controls); for cameras with zoom lenses, it also depends on the position of the zoom lens between the wide-angle and telephoto positions. For example, a bright-light condition (small lens opening) or a zoom-lens setting at the *wide-angle* position provides the greatest depth of field.

Subjects closer to the lens than the lowest value of the depth of field will appear fuzzy or out of focus. This will also be true of those elements of the scene that are farther from the lens than the larger value of the depth of field. The camera manufacturer can provide depth-of-field data for the specific camera lens.

Lighting

There must be adequate lighting to provide sufficient exposure. If the subject is outdoors or in a room with a large window area, the level of lighting will change during the course of a day. An automatic exposure control on the camera will, within limits, adjust the exposure according to the changing conditions. If the area to be covered is rather large, evenness of the illumination is also important. If a portion of the area is lighted with subdued illumination, this portion should be "filled in" with supplementary lights if significant action may occur in it.

In cases where poor lighting exists and supplementary lighting is not possible, a poor photographic record may still be better than no record at all. Sometimes your film processor can make adjustments in processing to help overcome this problem.

Determining Frame Interval

There are a number of different ways to determine what frame interval to use for a particular situation, depending upon your needs.

1. Do you want to cut up the action into small pieces by using a fast frame rate?
2. Do you want to cover a particular time period with just one roll or cartridge of film?
3. Do you want to have a certain amount of projection time filled with time-lapse footage?
4. How many rolls or cartridges of film will be required to cover a particular time period at a certain frame rate?

Consider one or all of these questions before you start shooting. Probably the easiest way to begin is to take a critical look at the subject. What does it do, and how long does it take to do it? Use a stopwatch and see how much time is required for various sections of the action. This will give an approximation of what kind of action will be captured on film.

For instance, if cloud cover is recorded for a period of time, watch the clouds through the camera's viewfinder and time how long it takes for a cloud to pass through the field of view. As an example, say that it takes 5 seconds. If a frame interval of one frame every 5 seconds is used, you would get only one picture of the cloud, and the action would be fairly fast. It would be better to get two pictures of the cloud, and this can be done by simply reducing the frame interval by half—or one frame every 2.5 seconds.

Computations

Here are some formulas that will be useful in determining your needs.

Determination of Frame Interval. If the length of time the total event will last is known and a certain projection time is desired, then

$$\frac{\text{Event time (sec)}}{\left(\begin{array}{c}\text{Projection time (sec)}\\ \times\\ \text{Projected frames per sec}\end{array}\right)} = \begin{array}{c}\text{Frame}\\ \text{interval (sec)}\end{array}$$

If the event time is known, and the event must be photographed in a certain number of frames (such as one 50-foot super 8 cartridge = 3600 frames), then

$$\frac{\text{Event time (sec)}}{\text{Number of frames}} = \begin{array}{c}\text{Frame}\\ \text{interval (sec)}\end{array}$$

Determination of Total Number of Frames Needed to Cover an Event. Since the event time and the frame interval are known, then

$$\frac{\text{Event time (sec)}}{\text{Frame interval (sec)}} = \begin{array}{c}\text{Total number}\\ \text{of frames}\end{array}$$

Determination of the Number of Cartridges or Rolls Needed to Cover an Event.

$$\frac{\text{Total number of frames}}{\begin{array}{c}\text{Number of frames}\\ \text{per cartridge or roll*}\end{array}} = \begin{array}{c}\text{Number of}\\ \text{cartridges or rolls}\end{array}$$

Determination of Projection Time.

$$\frac{\text{Total number of frames}}{\text{Projected frames per sec}} = \begin{array}{c}\text{Projection}\\ \text{time (sec)}\end{array}$$

$$\frac{\text{Event time (sec)}}{\left(\begin{array}{c}\text{Frame interval (sec)}\\ \times\\ \text{Projected frames per sec}\end{array}\right)} = \begin{array}{c}\text{Projection}\\ \text{time (sec)}\end{array}$$

---

*3600 frames per 50-foot super 8 cartridge or
7200 frames per 100-foot super 8 cartridge or
4000 frames per 100-foot 16 mm roll or
8000 frames per 200-foot 16 mm roll

An Example

Assume a subject is to be recorded over a 24-hour period, and a frame interval of 15 seconds seems to be adequate for the action to be photographed.

1. How many frames of film will be exposed?

$$\frac{\text{Event time (sec)}}{\text{Frame interval (sec)}} = \begin{array}{c}\text{Number}\\ \text{of frames}\end{array}$$

$$24 \text{ hours} = 86,400 \text{ sec}$$

$$\frac{86,400}{15} = \begin{array}{c}5\,760 \text{ frames will}\\ \text{be exposed}\end{array}$$

2. How many 50-foot cartridges of super 8 film will be required?

One 50-foot cartridge of super 8 film = 3600 frames

$$\frac{\begin{array}{c}\text{Total number}\\ \text{of frames}\end{array}}{3600} = \begin{array}{c}\text{Number}\\ \text{of cartridges}\end{array}$$

$$\frac{5760}{3600} = 1.6 \text{ cartridges}$$

3. What will be the projection time at 18 fps (the normal projection speed for super 8 film)?

$$\frac{\text{Total number of frames}}{18 \text{ fps}} = \begin{array}{c}\text{Projection}\\ \text{time (sec)}\end{array}$$

$$\frac{5760}{18} = 320 \text{ sec} = 5.3 \text{ min}$$

What will be the projection time of 6 fps?
$$\frac{5760}{6} = 960 \text{ sec} = 16 \text{ min}$$

Time-lapse photography is but one of many applications of photo-instrumentation imaging or, more simply, applications of photography as a tool.
• *See also:* MOTION STUDY; SCIENTIFIC PHOTOGRAPHY; STROBOSCOPIC PHOTOGRAPHY.

Timers

Control of the proper timing for film developing, print exposures, and processing—whether color or black-and-white—cannot be accomplished without using an accurate timer.

Film Development

During film development, it is extremely important to have precise control of the exact time for each step: development, rinse, fixing, wash, and drying. Too short or too long a time with any step can mean poorly processed negatives that may be difficult or impossible to print. Most photographers (both amateur and professional) and a great many processing labs rely on time and temperature for satisfactory negatives and slides. No photographer or technician would think of processing without the use of a thermometer. A reliable timer is equally important.

Printing

At the enlarger, a timer is indispensable for consistent results. A high-quality timer, which provides consistent accuracy with the least amount of attention and effort, can save time and paper.

Safelights. Most timers used with enlargers provide an outlet for both the enlarger light and the safelights. Such timers control both. A "focus" switch on the timer turns on the enlarger light for focusing and at the same time turns off the safelights. Focusing is much easier. Some timers provide an outlet for an optional foot switch so that both hands can be free for paper handling.

Color Printing. Precise timing is particularly important in color printing. With color printing paper, a change in exposure not only affects the lightness or darkness of the print, but also alters the color balance.

Types of Timers

The type of timer to use is a matter of personal preference, although some types are more suitable for particular tasks than others.

Mechanical. The standard mechanical, large-face timer is most useful for film processing because the size of the dial makes it easy to read in total darkness. Since this type of timer must be reset for each timing cycle, it is not convenient for making prints.

Timers generally used for enlarging reset themselves after each successive exposure to the time originally set. Once exposure time has been determined by test strip or densitometer, the timer is set. It may be left at that particular time for any number of prints from the same negative.

Some timers may be left on the principal exposure setting and also be utilized for burning-in and dodging. If, for example, the time for the overall exposure is 10 seconds, it may be possible to move the hand on the timer dial to 5 seconds while still keeping the original 10-second time set. Other timers may need to be reset for print manipulation and main exposure. These are features to look for when purchasing the timer that will be most suitable to your printing needs and working habits.

Electronic. Electronic dial or digital darkroom timers offer advantages and disadvantages when compared with standard mechanical timers. Electronic timers have solid-state construction, which means quiet operation and fewer moving parts. Digital timers usually use LED's (light emitting diodes) to display the interval information. The light emitted is paper-safe red so that it can be used while printing, but the read out should be switched off when color enlarging papers are used. The timer will still control exposures without displaying the exposure time.

Mini-Computer. Other timers are designed to operate with enlarger color heads to compensate for color pack changes as well as changes in exposure. These are really mini-computers and are suitable for professional applications where standard results are necessary for a large number of prints per day.

Kitchen Timers. A simple kitchen timer may be useful for timing longer, less precise processing steps such as washing and drying. These timers are best if they sound a bell or buzzer at the end of their cycle so that they can be heard through a closed darkroom door.

Use and Care

It is important to protect timers from chemicals and chemical vapors by placing them in the dry area of the darkroom. The timer must be visible and accessible. When prints are being made, the best location for the timer is next to the easel, where timer controls can be easily reached without moving through the beam of the enlarger light source or disturbing the arrangement of the printing paper.

Time, "T"

Camera shutter-speed dials often have a setting marked "T" (for time) or, in German equipment, "Z" (for zeit). At this setting, the shutter opens at the first pressure on the release and remains open until the release is pressed a second time to close it. Thus it differs from the "B" (bulb) or "D" (Dauer) setting, at which the shutter opens when the release is pressed and closes when it is released.

The "T" setting is used mainly for long exposures, where continued pressure on the camera release or even on a cable might cause vibration and a blurred picture. Many modern cameras do not have a time setting because it would interfere with the interlock used for double-exposure prevention. On such cameras, long exposures can be made by using a locking cable release. Pressure on this type of cable release opens the shutter, and it is then held open by a setscrew or latch, which is released to end the exposure.

To avoid blurring due to camera vibration, many experienced photographers use the following procedure. They hold a piece of black material, such as a black card or the slide of the film holder, in front of but not touching the lens, while they open the shutter with finger release or cable. They allow a few seconds for vibration to die down and then take the card away from the lens to start the exposure. At the end of the required time, the lens is again covered with the black card, and the shutter is then closed.
• *See also:* BULB, "B"; SHUTTERS; TIME EXPOSURES.

Tintype

Sometimes called "ferrotype," this process for making direct positive photographs originally utilized black-enameled iron plates coated with a wet collodion emulsion. Later, the plates were commercially supplied with a dry gelatin-bromide emulsion instead. In either case, the plates were exposed in a simple camera with a developing tank underneath and a lighttight black cloth sleeve at the rear. Through the sleeve, the photographer could reach in, take the plate from the camera, and drop it into the tank, which contained a kind of primitive monobath developer-fixer solution. After development, the plate was rinsed in water and mounted in a cardboard folder for the customer. The entire process, which took only a minute or so, was widely practiced by itinerant street photographers up to World War II. Because of the slow emulsion and the developer used, the image was very thin and composed of fine-grained silver. Since it was rather whitish in appearance, the image, viewed against the black-enameled background, appeared to the eye as a positive.

One might expect that images produced in this simple way, with minimal washing, would be very impermanent. However, for reasons that are not entirely clear, they actually last a long time. With age, the emulsion does darken to some extent, but it does not seem to fade. Old tintypes are easy enough to copy, and if a fairly high-contrast film is used for the copy negative, good copies can be obtained. See the article COPYING for more details.
• *See also:* COPYING; FERROTYPE; WET COLLODION PROCESS.

Titling

In the creation of motion pictures, effective titles can contribute impressively to the impact of the entire film. They can summarize, symbolize, foreshadow, establish suspense, and present basic information through visual (and aural) elements that also introduce mood, characters, setting, and story. Many of the techniques covered here concerning titles for motion pictures can also be used in slides and filmstrips; for more information see the article SLIDES AND FILMSTRIPS.

Titled messages should be characterized by clarity, brevity, and novelty. In conventional story production, titles should be used sparingly within the body of the film; they are used to best advantage in situations where they can state the message most economically. The title, *In the Year 1866*, or simply *1866*, superimposed over a long shot of, say, a period town, village, or castle, can pinpoint a time in history. Titles of this kind often improve and lend polish to sequences in motion-picture work.

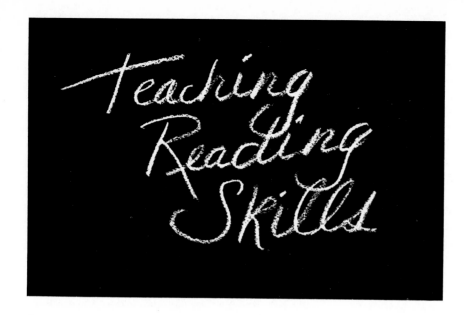

The content of a title and its very technique should relate to the film with which it is used. Lead and end titles, especially, should be appropriate to the film's theme, mood, and tempo, and be pitched to the intended audience. A film about auto racing should have a title with a sense of movement and excitement; the title of a religious film should suggest reverence. A lead title should stir the imagination and make the audience want to see the picture.

A credit title acknowledges the contribution of individuals to the total film production. It is in a sense like the signature of an artist on a painting. Such a title is generally a simple list of the names of the people who acted in the film or assisted technically. If this list is lengthy, it can be presented on a scroll or on several separate title cards with the names grouped according to the larger divisions of work in the film (for example, the casting might appear on one card; writing, art direction, music, and so forth, on another; and filming, editing, and sound recording on still another). It is customary to give stars, producer, and director separate title cards in elaborate productions.

Title Lettering

A number of title-lettering sources are available to the film producer. The most suitable source is frequently determined by factors such as production time, budget limitations, and availability of talented personnel. However, regardless of whether a title is hand-lettered, hot-pressed, stenciled, or scrawled with a crayon, remember that the primary consideration is *legibility*.

Hand-Lettered Titles. This method is excellent when it is well done. It can be quite costly, especially when performed by a professional. When hand lettering is used, the artist must know which sizes of letters will be suitable for various formats, and must be aware of the ways that color combinations will reproduce if the title is to be filmed in color.

Printed Titles. Most print shops stock a number of typefaces in a variety of sizes. There are several basic typesetting methods, and each has its particular advantages and disadvantages. Elaborate and ornamental styles are to be avoided, if possible; they are apt to be difficult to compose and hard to read. A consultation with the typographer will help determine which style is best for specific title needs.

Lettering Devices. In addition to supplies for hand lettering and printing of titles, artists' supply stores stock a number of lettering devices that yield uniform, professional-looking letters for use in commercial art and art for reproduction. Some of these employ stencils as a guide to letter formation. Stencils for a variety of lettering types can be had in several sizes.

Three-Dimensional Title Letters. These white, ceramic, block letters can be obtained in many styles and sizes; they are relatively inexpensive and can be used almost indefinitely. Such letters have been used extensively in amateur filming and have served well in numerous nontheatrical film productions.

Hot-Press Title Lettering. This is available from most motion-picture service organizations and title shops. This lettering, supplied in many commercial typefaces and colors, offers the advantage of being easily applied to most cards and background materials, especially cellulose acetate. Also, such lettering is opaque and is therefore not subject to "show through" when superimposed over a desired background.

Hot-press lettering is produced by stamping heated printer's type on colored foil laid over a thin sheet of clear acetate. The hot type transfers the colored pigment from the foil onto the acetate in much the same way that ink is transferred onto paper in the conventional printing process. The sheet of acetate containing the title can then be laid over a background and photographed as a title.

Once the type has been set up initially to print a cel, it is often relatively economical to print two cels in different colors of ink—such as one cel printed in white letters and a duplicate printed in black. Then, by placing the white cel over the black and "slipping" the position of the black type a trifle, a shadow effect can be obtained. The white letters will seem to be casting a three-dimensional black shadow over the background viewed through the pair of "sandwiched" cels.

Other Lettering Systems. There are other lettering systems that can save time and money. Included are some typewriters that can be used to make neat lettering, and dry-transfer letters (transferred by a burnishing technique). These letters, which adhere easily to most surfaces, are marketed under various trade names and are supplied in many styles, sizes, and colors. Transfer letters are adaptable to the labeling of graphs, diagrams, flowcharts, and organization charts.

Title Layout

The successful arrangement of type with pictures or other decorative elements depends largely upon the artistic taste of whoever does the work. It has been common practice in title layout to use formal or symmetrical balance; however, much can be said in favor of informal balance because it helps to solve the problem of precise centering when aligning the title. Whichever arrangement is chosen, the layout, composition, subject matter, and related elements should be created with regard to simplicity and clarity of thought.

Title-Card and Artwork Size. Motion picture title cards can be made almost any size. A good argument can be made in nontheatrical filming for having the cards fairly large; this minimizes prob-

Transfer letters can be put on clear plastic sheeting. The plastic is then laid over a photograph, and a title slide is made with a camera. This is a particularly good technique for when the same title is to be used with different backgrounds.

lems of parallax, and sharp images can be recorded even with fixed-focus lenses. However, the cards should not be so large that they become unwieldy. Large cards can present storage problems, so consider title cards that will be small enough to store easily. Also, it is essential that a size be chosen that will be convenient to work on (for both lettering and pictorial material). The size should be compatible with other photographic materials to be used for backgrounds or other illustrative purposes. A title-card size of about 254 × 305 mm (10″ × 12″) should prove satisfactory with a working-area ratio of 3:4.

Perhaps even more important than the overall size of the title cards used is the size of the lettering relative to the projected image height. For good screen legibility, the smallest letters in the title should be at least $\frac{1}{25}$ of the projected image height. To achieve this relationship, the lettering on an artwork working area of 152 mm (6 inches) would need to be no less than 6 mm (¼ inch) high. (Ascenders and descenders of lowercase letters should not be included when letter height is measured.)

Sufficient margin area should be left around the edges of a title layout to allow for the screen dimensions of the medium for which the title is designed. Information helpful in determining the legibility requirements of projected visuals is contained in the article SLIDES AND FILMSTRIPS.

Superimposed Titles

Superimposed white titles can be made in the camera or during the printing operation at a professional processing laboratory. Titles made in the camera are accomplished through double exposure of the same length of film. There are several satisfactory methods from which to choose.

White Letters on Black Velvet. One method is to set up three-dimensional white letters against a black velvet background, photograph them, rewind the film in the camera (this cannot be done with some cameras), and then shoot the desired background scene. Since the order of shooting is of no consequence, the lettering can be filmed first and pictorial material second, or vice versa. Slightly overexposing the titles will help to prevent the background from "bleeding" through the letters.

Also, it is possible to make superimposed white titles by double-exposing an original film and a high-contrast negative title in a motion-picture printer, using the technique of A and B roll printing. Consult a professional laboratory for further information.

Light-Box Method. Another method utilizes a small light box. Black lettering is first painted or set up on a white background and photographed on a sheet of lith film. Then, the resulting negative (with white-on-black lettering) is mounted on the light box. Any space around the negative is masked with black paper and tape, the light is turned on, and the title is filmed in the same manner used for the velvet and white lettering.

Animation. Superimposed titles can be made to appear one letter, or a portion of a letter, at a time from either side of the frame or from the center outward by animation of the scene when the title lettering is being filmed. Several techniques are available:

1. Place a high-contrast title negative on a light box and cover it with a piece of black paper. Then, remove the paper one title letter at a time, exposing about six frames for each move of the black paper.
2. To reveal portions of each letter, use the procedure just described, but move the black paper a fraction of an inch at a time, exposing one or two frames with each move.
3. To make the title appear from the middle of the frame outward, use two pieces of black paper, placing them so that their edges overlap slightly at the middle. Then, move the papers outward, one exposed frame at a time, until the entire title is revealed. Marking the top and bottom edges of the light box with uniformly spaced lines will assist in equalizing the amount of movement for each half of the title as it unfolds.

Title lettering that seems to rotate into or out of position or flop up from the bottom of the frame into proper reading position is made easy with the light box. Simply adjust the axis of rotation of the box to the desired position. For titles that turn from a horizontal to a vertical position, the axis should be set at the center of the lettering. For lettering that seems to swing up from the bottom, or down from the top, the axis should be set below or above, as needed. The exact location should be determined by checking visually through the camera viewfinder.

Plate-Glass Technique. A fourth method of superimposing titles is called the "plate-glass technique." A sheet of plate glass (large enough to cover the background completely) is supported a few inches above the background (this distance depends upon how out of focus the background should be), and block letters are placed on the glass so that they can be photographed along with the background. Both levels should be illuminated carefully to control reflections and shadows.

• *See also:* ANIMATION; COPYING; COPY STAND; HOME MOVIES; SLIDES AND FILMSTRIPS.

 # Tone-Line Process

The tone-line process is a method of converting a continuous-tone image to a line drawing by means of photographic operations. This line conversion will produce an effect similar to that of a pen-and-ink drawing. This process also makes possible the photomechanical reproduction of illustrations without the use of a halftone screen.

Tone-line conversion involves combining a negative with a positive of nearly equal contrast, the positive being used as a mask. This method should not be confused with solarization methods of producing outlines or with the pseudorelief effect obtained by using a negative and a positive slightly out of register with each other.

A positive and a negative that exactly match each other in contrast are taped together, back to back, in exact register. Except at the boundaries of images, the positive and negative neutralize each other's tone values. A little light leaks around the boundaries of images, and if a print is made from the combined images onto a high-contrast lith film, a line positive is produced.

If desired, a line negative can be made from this line positive by contact-printing. If artwork or lettering is to be combined with the line positive, the line positive can be produced directly on high-contrast paper.

A tone-line reproduction can be made from either an original negative or a photographic print. In the latter case, it is necessary to make a copy negative. The original can be black-and-white or color, as can the final image. By using filters for the printing light, a color image can be produced from a black-and-white original. Not every subject will give a pleasing result by this method, and experience is necessary for judging whether the method will be useful in a given case.

The Continuous-Tone (Original) Negative

Any good film negative with sharp detail can be used for the tone-line process. If the negative is specially made for this process, however, the following factors should be considered.

A large-size film should be used, and the negative should be given full exposure. The lighting should be such as to accentuate the outlines of the subject without producing sharp-edged shadows. The use of large light sources will produce the necessary softening of the edges of the shadows. The utmost care should be taken to make the negative as sharp as possible.

For pictorial purposes, it is desirable to have more and thicker outlines in the shadows than in the highlights. This can be achieved by using continuous-tone negatives in which the shadows have more contrast than the highlights—that is, negatives that would normally be considered overexposed. The contrast in the highlights should not be so low, however, as to cause too much loss of highlight detail.

The greater the density range of the transparencies, the easier it will be to make a satisfactory outline print, provided that the positive mask and the negative are matched over the whole range. The density range over which they can be matched is limited, however, by the length of the straight-line portion of the sensitometric curve of the mask emulsion. A range of about 1.5 is usually satisfactory.

Creating a Black-and-White Tone-Line Image

Start with a black-and-white negative and make a contact positive on any black-and-white film. A blue-sensitive film is easy to use for this step because it can be processed under a safelight. The contrast and density of the positive should be as close as possible to that of the negative. Register the images

A line conversion from a continuous-tone image will produce an effect similar to that of a pen-and-ink drawing. Any good film negative with sharp detail can be used for the tone-line process.

of the negative and positive with the base sides together, and tape them together along the edge.

Place the film sandwich into a printing frame with a sheet of high-contrast film. Put the printing frame on a turntable and rotate it during the exposure, or move the light source in a circle over the printing frame. Expose the film to the light from a 100-watt frosted bulb placed 1 m (about 3 feet) above the printing frame at an angle of about 45 degrees, as illustrated in the accompanying diagram. It is necessary to experiment in order to determine the exposure; small pieces of film can be used until the desired exposure is achieved. The processed lith film will be a true outline picture of the original. This

(Left) A single image was printed at three different magnifications to create the illusion of a flight of gulls. To get a color print with a green background, expose color negative-positive paper through a magenta filter. (Right) This tone line was made from a film sandwich where the negative and positive films had different densities. Because the densities did not match, some detail throughout the subject, as well as the tone-line outline, was exposed. Photo by Stanley W. Cowan.

Tone-Line Process

can be contact-printed to another lith film to make a negative for subsequent printing. Artwork can be done at each stage by opaqueing.

High-Contrast Masks

Another way of producing tone-line images is by using high-contrast masks. Color can also be added by printing one or more combinations of line images through color filters onto color paper. The following steps are used in the high-contrast film masks method.

1. Use an enlarger, or a process or view camera, for changing reproduction size. Focus carefully for the sharpest reproduction of detail. With a camera, strip the negative into a window cut in a sheet of processed, blackened film, so that the flare will not degrade the image.
2. From the negative, make four separate line exposures onto four sheets of high-contrast film. One exposure should record highlight detail only. A second exposure should record only extreme shadow detail. The other two exposures should record two different levels of middletone detail. Process the films.
3. Make contact negatives of each of the four line positives produced in Step 2.

The tone-line on the left looks like the negative used to print the tone-line print on the right. To produce a print that looks like a tone-line negative, it is necessary to contact-print that negative onto another sheet of high-contrast film, and then use the resulting positive film to make the print. Photos by Richard M. Warner.

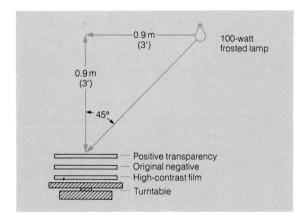

This setup is used to expose a high-contrast tone-line positive. The films used must be in contact in a printing frame, or under a heavy sheet of glass that is taped in position so it will not slide during rotation. The turntable should rotate at about 60 rpm during the exposure. (A simple ball-bearing "lazy Susan" can be turned by hand or an ordinary record-player turntable can be used.) Control exposure by time, not by moving the light source, in order to standardize procedures.

4. Register each negative and corresponding positive, *emulsion to emulsion,* on a light table. Study the visual line effect of each combination. Now switch the combinations around—combine a highlight negative with a middletone positive, for example—and study the differences in visual effect.

5. Choose the negative-positive combination that is the most satisfying.

6. Reregister the chosen negative and positive *base to base*. Use register pins or tape to hold the films firmly together.

7. Place the chosen negative-positive combination (sandwich) in a spring-loaded contact-printing frame or easel; the image should be *wrong-reading* when viewed through the glass cover of the frame.

8. Over the film sandwich, place a sheet of high-contrast ortho film with its emulsion side facing the sandwich. Close the cover.

9. Use one of the following two methods of exposure. The first method is preferred, but with either method, you will have to experiment to find the correct exposure.

   a. Place the easel below a diffuse or point-source contacting lamp, and cover the easel with a sheet of opalized plastic or several thicknesses of diffusion sheeting. Make an exposure onto the high-contrast orthochromatic film.

   b. Use a turntable as a base for the frame or easel. (A phonograph turntable or a "lazy Susan" will work, but make sure the easel is

Tone-line images may be produced by using high-contrast masks. Color can be added by printing one or more combinations of line images through color filters onto color paper. Shown at left is the original color photograph from which the two-color tone-line conversions were made. Photos by Neil Montanus and Ken Starr.

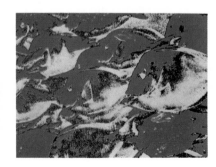

Tone-Line Process

Sometimes a rather busy photograph can be improved by a tone-line conversion. In this photo, the tone-line helps isolate the subject. The diagonal composition adds to the feeling of action. Photo by Mark Packo.

secured to the turntable with clamps or through-bolts.) Position the turntable beneath a point-source contacting lamp at an angle of approximately 45 degrees to the lamp. Make the exposure onto the high-contrast orthochromatic film while rotating the easel rapidly on the turntable—about 60 revolutions per minute.

10. Process the resulting line positive.

Selecting a Negative-Positive Combination. This procedure may help you choose the best negative-positive combination of line images to print. Although it is a somewhat tedious exercise, take each combination—there are ten in all—and print them in register, base to base, onto a sheet of high-contrast photographic paper, using one of the expo-

sure techniques described in Step 9 above. When the photographic paper has been processed, the result will be a permanent visual record of the line effects possible with a representative sampling of masks.

Unequal Outlines. The exposure methods described above will produce an outline *around* each intricate element of detail. For example, a tree branch will have a thin line of equal width above and below the branch. To produce an *unequal* outline—one line heavier than the other—deliberately misregister the two films in the film sandwich; or, if the turntable approach is used, tilt the easel on the turntable and spin in the recommended fashion.

Positive Originals. The procedure for making tone-line reproductions from *positive* transparencies is exactly the same as that for original negatives—you simply have to reverse the language of "negative" and "positive." However, the nature of the original positive dictates the exposure and development requirements for making the subsequent masks. Generally, black-and-white reflection copy has a longer density range than a black-and-white negative; color reflection copy has a longer density range than a color negative; color transparencies have longer ranges than any of the other forms of original copy. As a rule of thumb, the longer the density range of the original copy, the higher-contrast film will have to be used to make the first-generation negatives from the original positives.

When working from color originals, positive or negative, the first line exposures will have to be on high-contrast panchromatic film.

• *See also:* BAS-RELIEF; HIGH CONTRAST; POSTERIZATION; SABATTIER EFFECT; SPECIAL EFFECTS.

  Tone Reproduction

Human vision sees by distinguishing between various visual aspects of surrounding objects. The three characteristics that are distinguished are brightness, hue, and saturation. Form, line, shape, texture, gradation, and depth are all seen by variations in the three basic characteristics.

Images in photographs are seen by the same variations. In color photographs, variations in brightness, hue, and saturation are all evident. In black-and-white photographs, only the characteristic of brightness is involved.

Photography is a process by which the visual aspects of subjects are reproduced. In black-and-white photography, films record the subject brightnesses as latent images that are converted to negative black-and-white tones in development. Negatives are printed on photographic paper which, on development, yield positive images of the original subject brightnesses. Color photography yields images that have variations of color as well as brightness. In photographic practice, the variations in brightness are called *tones.*

In the early days of photography, just getting the images was sufficient. It soon became apparent that to get the best possible reproduction of tones, some method of measuring the tones of subjects, camera images, and photographic negatives and positives was required. About 50 years after the invention of photography, two Englishmen, Hurter and Driffield, developed the first steps of the science of sensitometry—the study of the effects of measurable amounts of exposure on films, and the amount of darkness (density) in the films after development. In the 1920's, Dr. L. A. Jones of the Kodak Research Laboratory developed an objective method of interrelating the various factors in the photographic process to show how the brightnesses of subjects are converted into the tones of the final photograph. In this article the method is called the *quadrant method.* This procedure is now carried even further and can include the viewing of the photographs and the effects of the viewing conditions.

This article discusses the reproduction of tones at each step of the typical photographic processes, how and where the tones are expanded and compressed, methods by which tone reproduction is measured, and ways in which tone reproduction is displayed so that it is possible to visualize what is happening in the tone reproduction process.

Units of Measurement

Brightness is a visual attribute; it is the lightness or darkness of a subject tone as seen by the eye. Any study of tone reproduction requires measurable units, and the measured correlate of brightness is called *luminance.* Luminance is the amount of light coming toward the eye on the camera from each elemental area of the subject. The intensity of light falling on a subject is *illuminance.* Illuminance can be measured in footcandles, while luminance can be measured in candles per square foot, or in other units. (*See:* LIGHT: UNITS OF MEASUREMENT.)

The illuminance on a subject in bright sunlight on a clear day is typically about 7200 footcandles. The luminance of a vertical, white, diffuse surface is about 2000 candles/ft^2. An 18 percent neutral test card with the same illuminance has a luminance of about 400 candles/ft^2, while a very black object in the sun has a luminance of about 16 candles/ft^2.

Light that has been imaged by a lens and is falling on the film during exposure is the illuminance on the film. It is typically measured in metre candles. Exposure is the illuminance multiplied by the time of exposure in seconds, and is given in metre-candle-seconds. Log luminance and illuminance values are used in plotting tone reproduction curves.

The tone values in negatives and transparencies are measured in transmission density units, while the tone values in prints are measured in reflection density units. (*See:* DENSITY.)

Tone Compression and Expansion

The overall luminance ratio of a typical outdoor subject is about 160:1. This is measured from a diffuse white to a dark tone that is to be reproduced just lighter than black. The 160:1 ratio is a logarithmic range of 2.2, and is just slightly over a seven-stop range. A typical negative density range, depending on the method of printing, is from about 0.80 to 1.25. A print density range is typically from about 1.5 to 2.0, depending on the paper. The tonal range is therefore compressed considerably from the subject to the negative, and then expanded again when printed.

The density range of a transparency is about 3.0, so that the original luminance range is expanded when it is recorded as a transparency. The density range of color negatives is similar to that of black-and-white negatives, so overall tone compression takes place in the negative, and overall expansion occurs when making a print from the negative.

Because the original subject has a 160:1 luminance ratio (log range of 2.2) and paper prints typically have a 60:1 reflectance ratio (log range of 1.8), there is overall compression in the tonal range from subject to paper print.

However, the tones are not all compressed equally for various photographic reasons. The highlight tones and shadow tones are compressed the most while the middletones are actually expanded slightly in the typical reproduction.

Subject Luminances

The different brightness levels of a subject are readily seen. Light sources and direct reflections of light sources are the brightest part of a scene, and are called specular or semispecular reflections. White objects are seen as the next brightest tones, and these are called diffuse highlights. The highlight region consists of light tones and diffuse and specular highlights.

The middletones cover a fairly broad range from the highlight region to the shadow, or dark-tone, region of the brightness scale. There are no accepted breakpoints between the three regions, but it is useful to think of the brightness range as being divided in this way.

Dark tones are usually shadowed tones. The eye sees into the shadows and distinguishes very dark tones that are generally reproduced as black in photographs. Usually subjects that are light and medium-toned when seen in sunlight appear as dark tones when shadowed. Subject tones that are dark in sunlight become "black" when shadowed from the sun. Very dark objects in direct light also appear as dark tones.

There are a number of units used in luminance measurement, but the photographer may find it easier to think in terms of exposure, in shutter speeds and f-stops. The typical subject that has a luminance ratio of 160:1 has a log luminance range of 2.2 (2.2 is the logarithm of 160), and has a 7⅓-stop range. (A 1-stop difference is an exposure factor of 2; the logarithm of 2 is 0.3; 2.2 ÷ 0.3 is 7⅓.) In the article CONTRAST, the normal subject is considered to have a 7-stop range, while the range of subjects from the lowest to highest luminance ranges usually photographed is from 5 to 9 stops.

Subject luminance range can be measured with a reflection spot meter, from the luminance of the diffuse highlight to a shadowed tone that is to be reproduced just lighter than black. If the exposure is calculated for the typical diffuse highlight and the exposure is calculated for the typical dark tone to be reproduced just lighter than black, it will be found

that there are just about seven stops difference between the two tones.

Camera Flare

The camera lens forms an optical image of the scene on the film. If the imaging of tones were perfect, the 7-stop range subject (2.1 log range) would expose the film with the same range as the subject. However, camera lenses, and to some extent the camera itself, lower the range by flare. Flare is light that is scattered evenly over the film by the lens surfaces, edges of the lens mount, and by light reflected off the surface of the film and back to the film by the camera interior. The largest source of flare can be the lens surfaces if the lens has many elements. Before lens coating was used, flare levels were very high, but single- and multi-layer coatings have reduced the flare level in normal lenses to very low levels, and in zoom lenses to moderate levels.

Flare light compresses the dark tones. It is such a small percentage of the highlights in the optical image that they are relatively unaffected, but it can exceed the intensity of the darkest tones. The graphs show how flare is plotted, and the effect flare has on the tones with lenses of various flare levels. The flare levels shown are those used in the CI method of finding developing times as given in CONTRAST.

Two methods of showing tone reproduction are given in illustrations later in this article: a quadrant type of display commonly called tone reproduction diagrams, and a graphic display that shows linearly the expansion and compression of tones at each step of the reproduction process. In both methods, camera flare compresses the illuminance range of the optical image by compressing the shadow tones.

In both types of tone reproduction display, the solid lines represent full-stop (2×) differences. The heavy solid lines in the graphic displays represent the diffuse highlight and dark tone limits. The dotted line represents reproduction of the 18 percent neutral test card. The quadrant diagrams show the tone reproduction from diffuse highlights through a dark tone that reproduces just lighter than black— the dark limit tone. The graphic displays show also a specular highlight and black tone reproduction.

Negative Images

The characteristic curves of films show how the intensities of light in the optical image transfer into negative densities or transparency densities.

In typical negative films, both black-and-white and color, all the tones are compressed, with the dark tones being compressed more than the others. Films that have long straight-line curves with relatively short toes reproduce the mid- and upper tones evenly, while films with long-toe curves have a continually changing rate of tone compression.

In the accompanying quadrant display of negative film reproduction, the film characteristic curve is rotated 90 degrees counterclockwise, so that the illuminance values of the optical image act as exposure values to the film. For correct exposure, the film curve is positioned so that the dark tone to be reproduced just lighter than black lines up with the speed point of the film, which is where the density of the image is 0.10 density units greater than the gross fog level. To show the tone reproduction with underex-

posure, the film curve is moved upward; for overexposure downward.

In the accompanying graphic tone reproduction display, the compression of tones is shown by the closeness of the stop lines in the negative drawing. The dotted line representing the 18 percent neutral test card tone shows what happens to the average tone in reproduction.

The characteristic curves of black-and-white films change with development. The illustration on page 2452 shows how the density range can be kept constant as the optical image range varies, by varying the contrast index of the film development.

Printing on Photographic Paper

In exposing film, the toe end of the characteristic curve is nearly always used. In exposing paper, almost the entire tonal range of the paper is used to get the maximum print tonal range.

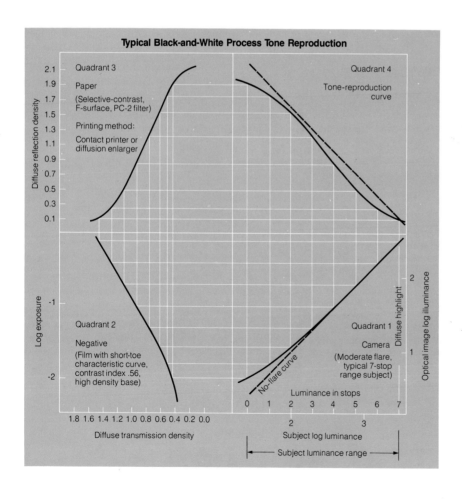

Quadrant 1 shows how the log illuminance range of the camera image is shortened by flare in the camera. The flare curve is the solid line while the dashed line shows that the image would have the same range as the subject if there were no flare. The construction lines are one stop apart in the subject, but change their separation as a result of the flare, showing the tone compression that results. The negative curve (quadrant 2) is the characteristic curve of the film. The construction lines show how the curved toe further compresses the tones in the dark-tone region. Correct exposure places the limit dark tone on the curve at a 0.10 density level. The diffuse density range of the negative is 1.05, and in a contact printer this becomes the log exposure range of the paper, whose characteristic curve is shown in quadrant 3. The paper expands the midtones and compresses the highlight tones. Quadrant 4 shows the tone reproduction of the typical black-and-white photographic process. This is discussed in the text.

Graphical Representation of Typical Photographic Tone Reproduction

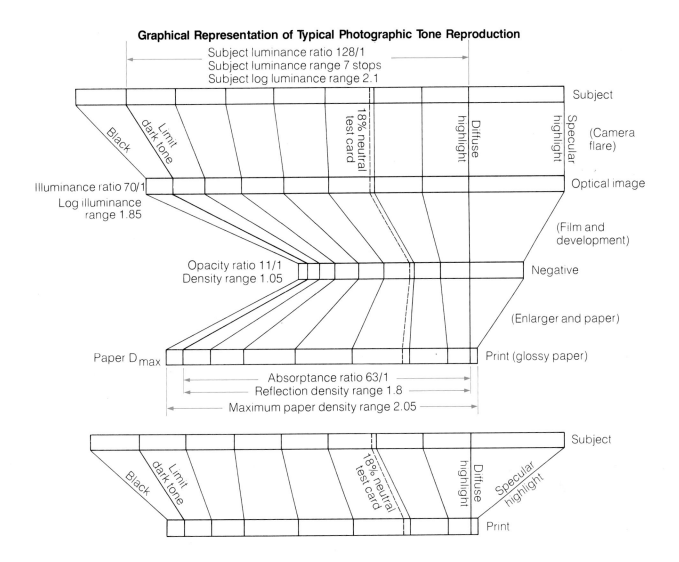

This is a graphic display of the same tone reproduction shown in the first-quadrant display illustration. The distance between each step in the subject diagram is one stop. The relative distances between the lines show how the tones are expanded or compressed in the reproduction process. The lower part of the diagram shows a direct comparison of the subject with the print. This lower part is a graphic equivalent of the tone-reproduction curve.

The midsection of a normal paper curve expands the negative tones, while tones are compressed in both the highlight and dark-tone regions. The highlight region has the greater compression. This means that the overall tone reproduction has about the same amount of compression at both ends of the tonal scale. The dark tones are compressed by camera flare and by being on the toe of the film characteristic curve. Tones in the highlight region are compressed by flare and by the film. The greater compression of highlights by the paper about equalizes the compression of shadows by flare and film.

Paper characteristic curves are not currently published by Kodak. Anyone with a transmission and reflection densitometer can make curves. A step scale is made on the film commonly used, and calibrated on the transmission densitometer. This step scale is used to make paper prints using the enlarger

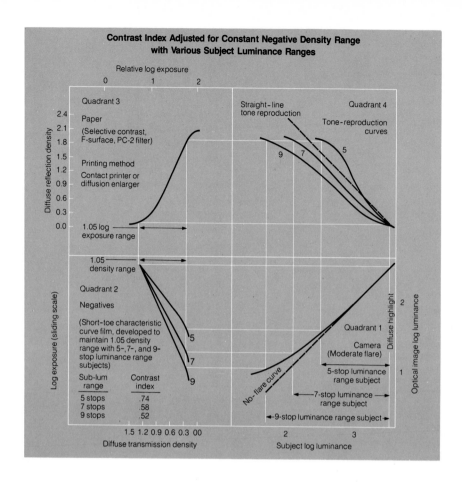

Contrast Index Adjusted for Constant Negative Density Range with Various Subject Luminance Ranges

Relative log exposure

Quadrant 3

Paper
(Selective contrast, F-surface, PC-2 filter)

Printing method
Contact printer or diffusion enlarger

1.05 log exposure range

1.05 density range

Quadrant 2

Negatives

(Short-toe characteristic curve film, developed to maintain 1.05 density range with 5-, 7-, and 9-stop luminance range subjects)

Sub-lum range	Contrast index
5 stops	.74
7 stops	.58
9 stops	.52

Diffuse transmission density

Straight-line tone reproduction

Quadrant 4

Tone-reproduction curves

No-flare curve

Quadrant 1

Camera
(Moderate flare)

Diffuse highlight

5-stop luminance range subject

7-stop luminance range subject

9-stop luminance range subject

Subject log luminance

Diffuse reflection density

Log exposure (sliding scale)

Optical image log luminance

Given in the article Contrast is a method of adjusting developing time to give a consistent negative density range. The control in this procedure is the contrast index to which the negative is developed. This quadrant display shows the tone reproduction that results when 5-, 7-, and 9-stop luminance-range subjects are reproduced by this procedure.

or contact printer to be used in the tone reproduction test. The reflection densities of each step in the print are plotted against the density of the film step. This creates a paper characteristic curve as printed.

A print made by contact and exposed by diffuse light will fairly represent the curve of the paper itself. If this curve is used in the quadrant-type tone reproduction diagram, an extra step has to be included for the enlarger characteristics. Condenser enlargers print with greater contrast than do diffusion enlargers. The exact change differs with the degree of specularity of the enlarger illumination. This is due to the Callier effect. This difference applies only to black-and-white materials, not to color.

The density range of the negative is matched to the log exposure range of the negative. The paper curve shown in the diagram on p. 2450 is positioned so that the diffuse highlight line intersects the paper curve at a density of 0.04 above the paper base den-

sity. If the negative density range matches the paper curve (as printed), the dark-tone limit line will fall on the paper curve where the density is equivalent to $0.9 \times D_{max}$ of the paper. These two values are the determining points for the log exposure range of the paper.

Specular highlights expose as though they have a luminance about two stops higher than that of diffuse highlights. This two-stop separation is maintained in the optical image, and compressed only in a straight-line relationship on the negative.

On the print, however, the difference between specular highlights and diffuse highlights is drastically compressed; there is only an average reflection density difference of about 0.04 units between the print tonal values of the specular and diffuse highlights.

In the graphic tone reproduction display, the print diffuse highlights value is shown directly under

2452

Tone Reproduction

the subject diffuse highlight value. This is because the diffuse reflective density of diffuse highlights in the subject and on the print are essentially the same, although the luminance values may differ greatly. In viewing, the brightness adaption of the eye almost compensates for the luminance difference. (*See:* VISION.)

Overall Tone Reproduction

In the quadrant tone reproduction display, the overall tone reproduction is shown in the upper right quadrant. The stop-tone lines as reproduced are joined to equal spaced tone lines of the subject. The resultant curve is the tone-reproduction curve and is compared to a straight-line reproduction drawn at 45 degrees to the axes, and through the diffuse highlight point.

In this way, the tones of the print can be compared to the original tones. Highlight compression is indicated by the very low slope of the tone reproduction curve as it passes through the 45-degree straight line. Its upward sweep shows that the amount of compression lessens as the tonal darkness decreases. If the tone reproduction curve parallels the straight line in the midtone region, the tone reproduction is one-to-one. If the angle is less than 45 degrees, the midtones are slightly compressed. If the angle is slightly greater than 45 degrees, as it usually is in good reproduction, the midtones are slightly expanded by the reproduction.

As the curve gets into the dark tones, it falls from the 45-degree straight line, showing dark-tone compression. The distance of the $0.9D_{max}$ dark tone below the straight line indicates the amount of overall tone compression by the reproduction process.

In the graphic method of display, the overall black-and-white tone reproduction (the lower dia-

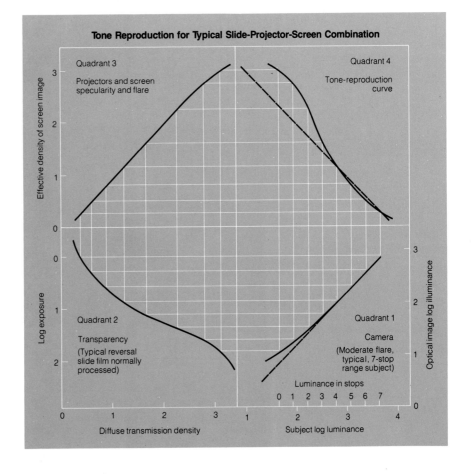

This shows typical tone reproduction of a color slide film, including the effects of the slide projector and the screen. Ambient light would lower the higher densities in the third quadrant and bring the tone-reproduction curve closer to the dashed straight-line reproduction curve. However, this would be viewed as a less-satisfactory reproduction. The preferred slide reproduction is shown in a later illustration.

Tone Reproduction

Graphical Representation of Typical Slide-Projector-Screen Tone Reproduction

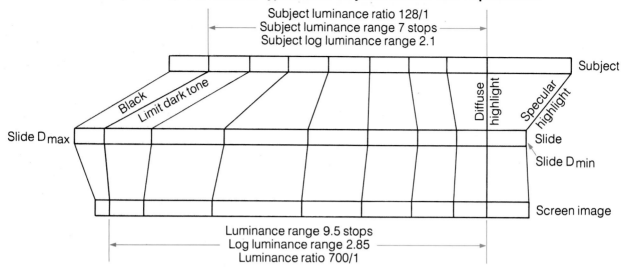

Subject luminance ratio 128/1
Subject luminance range 7 stops
Subject log luminance range 2.1

Subject

Black

Limit dark tone

Diffuse highlight

Specular highlight

Slide D_{max}

Slide

Slide D_{min}

Screen image

Luminance range 9.5 stops
Log luminance range 2.85
Luminance ratio 700/1

The expansion of tones by the slide reproduction and the viewing process can be easily seen in this diagram.

If a negative has a low density range, it can be printed on a high-contrast grade of paper or on a selective-contrast paper with a No. 4 Polycontrast filter. This increases the contrast and takes advantage of the entire density range of the paper. This illustration shows typical tone reproductions that result from these procedures as compared with the normal tone reproduction as shown in a previous illustration. The grade 4 paper has a slightly better tone reproduction than the selective-contrast paper used with the PC4 filter, but the graded paper has a lower D_{max}.

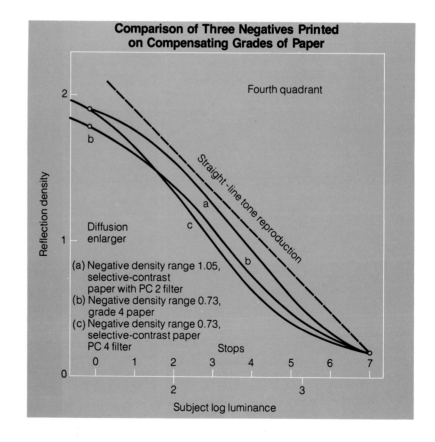

Comparison of Three Negatives Printed on Compensating Grades of Paper

Fourth quadrant

Straight-line tone reproduction

Reflection density

Diffusion enlarger

(a) Negative density range 1.05, selective-contrast paper with PC 2 filter
(b) Negative density range 0.73, grade 4 paper
(c) Negative density range 0.73, selective-contrast paper PC 4 filter

Stops

Subject log luminance

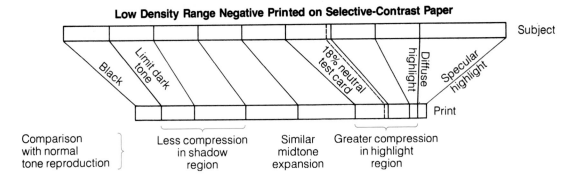

Low Density Range Negative Printed on Selective-Contrast Paper

Subject

Black · Limit dark tone · 18% neutral test card · Diffuse highlight · Specular highlight

Print

Comparison with normal tone reproduction | Less compression in shadow region | Similar midtone expansion | Greater compression in highlight region

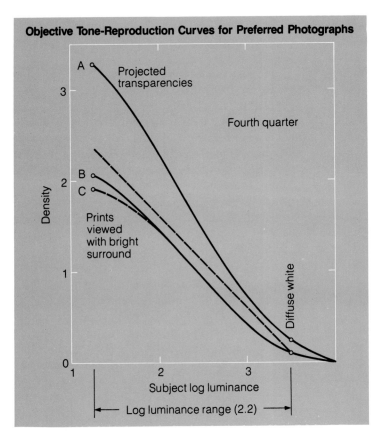

Objective Tone-Reproduction Curves for Preferred Photographs

A — Projected transparencies

Fourth quarter

B
C

Prints viewed with bright surround

Diffuse white

Density

Subject log luminance

Log luminance range (2.2)

(Above) This is the diagram display of the tone reproduction of the selective-contrast paper with the PC4 filter shown in the fourth-quadrant illustration. (Left) A shows the preferred tone reproduction of projected transparencies and transparencies on an illuminator with a dark surround. B shows the preferred tone reproduction of a black-and-white paper print when viewed with a bright surround. It is based on print densities as measured on a densitometer. Not all photographic papers provide a maximum density as high as that shown by curve B. With some papers, the best reproduction that can be achieved is more like that indicated by curve C.

gram of the subject and the final print) shows how the midtones typically have a slight increase in the tone separation, while the highlight and dark-tone regions are both compressed. Further, it shows how the midtones are lightened in tone (decreased in reflection density) by about 0.3 log units, or about one stop in luminance.

Transparency films compress tones mostly in the highlight region, while they expand the tones in the midtone and dark-tone regions. The density range of transparencies is greater than the log luminance range of the original subject.

In the quadrant display of slide transparency reproduction, the effect of projection, screen type,

Tone Reproduction

and ambient illumination on the overall tone reproduction are shown.

Uses of Tone Reproduction

Tone reproduction methodology is important to photographic manufacturers. Their decisions regarding the production of the materials and the publishing of technical data are often based on the study of best photographic reproduction. Such studies can be used by workers in the field to provide aim points for copying and duplicating systems; for improving the quality of black-and-white enlarging procedures; and for comparing the quality of results of various alternative methods, such as projection systems with various screens.

While densitometers and special illuminance meters make the measurements easier, a clever handyman can convert exposure meters to perform nearly all of the density and luminance readings required for most applications. (*See:* LIGHT: UNITS OF MEASUREMENT.) The *KODAK Reflection Density Guide* (pub. No. Q-16) is a visual comparator for finding approximate reflection densities of prints. Kodak calibrated film scales can be used to calibrate densitometers that are made with exposure meters. The article LIGHT: UNITS OF MEASUREMENT gives a method of using a Kodak neutral test card (No. R-27) and an exposure meter for finding illuminance values and luminance values.

Preferred Tone Reproduction

Studies have been made in which many observers selected prints and viewed transparencies for "best reproduction." The graph on page 2455 shows the tone reproductions that were selected as the best. These curves can be useful as aim points in determining the relative quality of comparative methods of tone reproduction.

• *See also:* BLACK-AND-WHITE FILMS; BLACK-AND-WHITE PRINTING; BRIGHTNESS; BRIGHTNESS RANGE; CALLIER EFFECT; CHARACTERISTIC CURVE; CONTRAST; CONTRAST INDEX; DENSITOMETRY; DRIFFIELD, VERO CHARLES; ENLARGERS AND ENLARGING; EXPOSURE; EXPOSURE TECHNIQUES; GRADATION; GRAY CARD; GRAY SCALES; HURTER, FERDINAND; LIGHT; LIGHT: UNITS OF MEASUREMENT; LOGARITHM; PAPERS, PHOTOGRAPHIC; REFLECTION DENSITY; SENSITOMETRY; VISION; ZONE SYSTEM.

  Toning

Many black-and-white prints can be made more interesting and attractive by toning, or changing the color of the existing image. Toning is a means of creating moods and impressions in a picture. In some cases, a slight change in the color of the image gives the desired effect; in other cases, a bold change transforms a drab picture into a spectacular one. The color obtained by toning depends on the formula used, but each toner yields a number of variations on its characteristic hue when it is used with different kinds of paper.

Toning is a technique that may enhance some photographs, but there is no need for this extra treatment unless it will improve the picture. This is a matter that requires careful consideration. Toning is not a way to "save" a picture. A weakly seen, conceived, or executed picture will not become stronger by being brown, blue, red, gold, fuschia, or any other color. On the other hand, a well-done picture may gain in emotional impact and visual beauty from the sensitive addition of overall coloration by toning. So basic expressive strength of the image is an initial requirement.

Basic Considerations

The process of toning converts the black-and-white silver image on the paper to another form having the desired color. As a result, numerous factors enter into the making of a good toned print. First of all, start with a high-quality print that has been developed and fixed with toning in mind.

Although the products of one manufacturer seldom compare exactly with those of another, it is possible to group most enlarging papers into three broad classifications based on image tone: cold tone, neutral tone, and warm tone. The image tone of a print is primarily a matter of the size and condition of the silver grains, so that variations in development that influence the character of the silver particles have a marked effect upon image color. Warm-tone developers will yield a warmer black-and-white image.

The color of the toned image is influenced by the image tone of the black-and-white print. For example, a print on a warm-tone paper yields a warmer

(Above) Blue tones can add mood to photographs of snow, water, and moonlight. Since printing inks do not exactly duplicate toning colors, the appearance of this toned photograph varies slightly from the original. Producing your own blue-toned prints is the best guide to your preferences. (Right) An almost unlimited variety of brown tones are available. The actual color obtained depends on the paper-toner combination and, to a lesser extent, on the processing conditions when the print is made.

Toning

brown tone than a print on a cold-tone paper. By the same token, when a print on a warm-tone paper is blue-toned, the resulting tone will have more blue color in it than would be obtained by blue toning a similar print on a cold-tone paper. Similar effects are observed when the prints are overexposed or grossly overfixed. All of these variations are due to differences in the grain structure of the silver image. Consequently, to avoid variations in the color of toned prints, adhere to the processing recommendations for the paper you are using, except where a different development time is suggested for a particular type of toner.

Processing Prints for Toning

Each kind of photographic paper yields a characteristic image color when toned by a particular toning formula, but this color is modified by variations in developing time, the condition of the developer, and the temperature of the developer. Variations in color can also be caused by erratic fixing time and by the amount of dissolved silver in the fixing bath. Moreover, the presence of hypo in the print after washing may cause a change in color or, in severe cases, staining of the print may occur.

Development. To maintain a uniform tone with a particular paper, always use the developing time recommended for the type of toning to be done. Develop the prints at 20 C (68 F), because variations in temperature alter the rate of development and, consequently, the color of the toned image.

Stop Bath. Always use fresh stop bath of normal strength. An overly strong stop bath may cause mottle in the paper base of a toned print. This mottle is invisible in a black-and-white print, but it immediately becomes visible when the print is toned by one of the sulfide processes or by a selenium toner.

Mottle can also be caused by lack of agitation in the stop bath, particularly during the first few seconds of immersion. Another cause of mottle is overfixation.

Fixing. Improper fixing technique is probably the chief cause of stains in toned prints. Always use a fixing bath in good condition, because incomplete fixation causes an overall yellow stain on prints toned by the selenium or sulfide toners. An exhausted fixing bath contains some relatively insoluble silver compounds that cannot be removed from the prints by washing. As a result, the residual silver

compounds are also toned and form a yellow stain that is most noticeable in the borders and highlights of the prints. Use of the two-bath method of fixing is the best way to avoid the problem. (*See:* FIXERS AND FIXING.)

Agitation of prints in the fixing bath is most important. Stains are often caused by sticking together of the prints or their floating on the surface of the solution. Also, air bells that become trapped beneath or between prints are a frequent cause of circular, purplish stains that appear on prints toned by selenium or one of the sulfide toners.

Avoid Excessive Fixing. Do not fix prints for longer than the recommended time—5 to 10 minutes—because prolonged fixing impregnates the fibers that make up the paper base. Paper in this condition is difficult to free from residual hypo. Also, prolonged fixing tends to bleach the lighter tones in the image and to change the overall color of the toned print. Prints on water-resistant papers should not be fixed longer than 2 minutes.

Washing

Washing is also an important step in processing prints for toning. Traces of hypo remaining in the paper after washing cause stains, a reduction in the density of the image, or in the case of bleach-and-redevelop sepia toning, partial destruction of the image. Gold toning (T-21) and hypo-alum toning are exceptions, however, because the toning solutions contain hypo.

Prints intended for toning by processes other than gold toning or hypo-alum toning should be washed for 1 hour in a tank or tray in which the water changes completely every 5 minutes. To reduce the washing time and to conserve water, use a washing aid; follow the directions on the package. This procedure not only reduces washing time, but it yields a freedom from residual chemicals that is difficult to achieve by washing with water alone. Consequently, toned prints have cleaner, whiter highlights and borders.

It is essential to keep prints moving and separated from one another throughout the washing time. Otherwise, some of the prints may be washed properly and others only partially so. The result can often be seen on toned prints as stains consisting of straight lines and angles where the prints have bunched together or have overlapped in the washer.

Some color toners, such as green, are best purchased as commercial preparations. Here, green toner adds to the lush character of the vegetation in this photograph of a forest cataract.

Toning

(Above) Blue toner enhances the glacial quality of this mountain lake and the expansive sky. Warm-tone papers react best to this toner; there is no noticeable effect on cold-tone papers. (Left) Red toning was used to heighten the fierce appearance of this rooster. The toning effect is achieved by first sepia-toning and then washing the print. The sepia print is then blue-toned, resulting in this spectacular red color. Photo by Jens Karlsson for Hasselblad Corp.

A washing tank, however efficient, cannot perform satisfactorily if too many prints are washed at one time. If necessary, use two or more tanks and wash only a reasonable number of prints in each.

Wash Kodak water-resistant papers for 4 minutes in running water (instead of the longer times given for conventional-base papers) both before and after toning. Water flow should be adjusted so that a volume of water equal to the capacity of the wash tank flows in 4 minutes, and prints should be kept moving and separated during the wash by interleaving. Prolonged washing, soaking, or leaving the prints in the toning solutions for longer than necessary may counteract the advantages of the water-resistant base. Because of the rapid washing of water-resistant papers, the use of a washing aid offers little advantage and is not recommended.

Drying Toned Prints

Most toned prints should be allowed to dry naturally between photographic quality blotters or on drying racks, because hot drying causes a shift to a colder tone. If it is necessary to dry toned prints by heat, as in a continuous-roll process, reduce the temperature of the drying apparatus as far as is consistent with proper drying.

If prints are toned with Kodak Poly-Toner, the change in color can be compensated by toning to a warmer color with a more dilute solution of the toner. For example, if prints toned by the 1:24 dilution of Poly-Toner are too cold after drying, use a more dilute solution, such as 1:40, which yields a warmer tone.

Prints toned in Kodak gold toner T-21 should not be dried by heat unless care is taken to wash residual hypo from the prints and to remove all traces of the sediment deposited on the prints during toning. Otherwise, a patchy yellow stain will result.

Prints toned with Kodak blue toner are not affected by hot drying, but as with all other toned prints, excess water should be sponged from the surfaces before drying.

Brown toner is particularly effective with images of old or weathered wood. The natural appearance of the wood might suggest to the viewer that this was a color print. Photo by Barbara Jean.

For proper procedures with water-resistant and resin-coated papers, see the article DRYING FILMS AND PRINTS.

Brown Tones

Although almost any color can be produced by some type of toning process, brown tones are by far the most popular. Brown tones can be classified into three broad groups: the characteristic reddish to purplish brown tones produced by selenium toners; the cold-toned chocolate browns of the single-solution sulfur-reacting toners; and the warm brown of the bleach-and-redevelopment sulfide toners. Some products produce a series of hues with varying dilutions, and do not quite fit into any of these three categories.

Brown Toning Warm-Tone Papers

Certain warm-tone papers, such as Kodak Ektalure and portrait proof papers, will lose density and contrast when toned in Kodak brown toner or polysulfide toner T-8. This effect is most evident with low-key prints; it is hardly noticeable in high-

key prints. However, most pictures are either medium- or low-key.

A slight bleaching is characteristic of all polysulfide-type brown toners, and the resulting toned image is quite yellowish with normally processed prints. Although a yellow-brown color is preferred by some photographers who wish to oil-color their prints, it is not generally considered a pleasing portrait tone for prints that will not be oil-colored.

It is possible to compensate for density and contrast losses and also produce a more pleasing (less yellow) image tone by changing the technique of developing the black-and-white prints. To make this compensation, first make an exposure to obtain a print of normal quality in the 2-minute development time recommended with Kodak Selectol developer, 1:1, at 20 C (68 F). Use this same exposure time, but extend the development time to 3½ minutes. This increase in development will increase the contrast and density of the print and offset the bleaching effect of the toner. The resulting toned image will be less yellow and more pleasing. Somewhat richer browns can be obtained by using Kodak Dektol developer, 1:3, for 3½ minutes.

Do not increase the print exposure to compensate for bleaching by the above toners; otherwise, you will succeed in compensating for density loss in only the low- and mid-density areas of the print, and when toned, the print will show an appreciable contrast loss and a warmer (yellowish) image tone. Kodak Medalist and Polycontrast papers, however, constitute exceptions to this rule because they have rather cold tones and produce satisfactory sepia colors without an objectionably yellow cast when treated in Kodak brown toner. Prolonging development by only about 25 percent will be sufficient for these papers.

CAUTION: Sulfide-type toners should be used with adequate ventilation. The hydrogen sulfide fumes—the odor of rotten eggs—given off are both disagreeable and poisonous. The need for additional local exhaust ventilation depends on the quantity of work being done. Because hydrogen sulfide causes fogging of unexposed paper and film, make absolutely sure these are not present in the vicinity of the toning operation. It is advisable to use print tongs or wear rubber gloves, since brown toner solutions are quite alkaline.

Do not discard sulfide-type toners with either stop or fixing baths, because the combination of these solutions will liberate additional hydrogen sulfide gas. Flush the drain liberally with water after discarding each solution separately.

Kodak hypo alum sepia toner T-1a

Cold water	2800.0 ml
Sodium thiosulfate (hypo) (pentahydrated)	480.0 g
Dissolve thoroughly, and add the following solution:	
Hot water, about 70 C (160 F)	640.0 ml
Potassium alum, fine granular (dodecahydrated)	120.0 g
Then add the following solution (including precipitate) slowly to the hypo-alum solution while stirring the latter rapidly:	
Cold water	64.0 ml
Silver nitrate, crystals*	4.0 g
Sodium chloride	4.0 g
After combining the above solutions, add water to make	4.0 l litre

For use, pour the toner solution into a tray supported in a water bath and heat it to 49 C (120 F). At this temperature, prints will tone in 12 to 15 minutes, depending on the type of paper. Never use the solution at a temperature above 49 C, or blisters and stains in the prints may result. Do not continue toning longer than 20 minutes at this temperature.

This toner causes losses of density and contrast that can be corrected by increases in exposures (up to 15 percent) and developing time (up to 50 percent). The actual increases depend on the kind of paper.

Thoroughly fix the prints to be toned and wash them for 5 to 15 minutes before placing them in the toning bath. Soak dry prints thoroughly in water. Immerse the prints completely and separate them occasionally, especially during the first few minutes.

---

*NOTE: Dissolve the silver nitrate completely before adding the sodium chloride, and immediately afterward add the solution containing the milky white precipitate to the hypo-alum solution as directed above. The formation of a black precipitate in no way impairs the toning action of the bath if the proper manipulation technique is used.

After prints have been toned, wipe them with a soft sponge and warm water to remove any sediment, and wash them as previously recommended.

Kodak sulfide sepia toner T-7a
Stock bleaching solution A

Water	2.0 litres
Potassium ferricyanide (anhydrous)	75.0 g
Potassium bromide (anhydrous)	75.0 g
Potassium oxalate	195.0 g
28% Acetic acid*	40.0 ml

Stock toning solution B

Sodium sulfide (not sulfite) (anhydrous)	45.0 g
Water	500.0 ml

Prepare bleaching bath as follows:

Stock solution A	500.0 ml
Water	500.0 ml

Prepare toner as follows:

Stock solution B	125.0 ml
Water to make	1.0 litre

First, thoroughly wash the print to be toned. Place it in the bleaching bath (solution A) and allow it to remain until only a faint yellowish-brown image remains. This operation will take about 1 minute.

NOTE: Do *not* use trays with any iron exposed; otherwise, blue spots may be formed on the prints.

Rinse the print *thoroughly* in clean, cold running water (at least 2 minutes).

Treat the print in the toning bath (prepared from solution B) until the original detail returns. This will require about 30 seconds. Give the print an immediate and thorough water rinse; then treat it for 2 to 5 minutes in a hardening bath composed of 1 part Kodak liquid hardener and 13 parts water, or 2 parts Kodak hardener F-5a stock solution and 16 parts water. The color and gradation of the finished print will not be affected by the use of this hardening bath. Remove the print from the hardener bath and wash it for at least 30 minutes in running water at 18 to 21 C (65 to 70 F).

---

*To make approximately 28% acetic acid from glacial acetic acid, add 3 parts of glacial acetic acid to 8 parts of water.

For a packaged toner with similar characteristics, obtain Kodak sepia toner.

Kodak polysulfide toner T-8

Water	750.0 ml
Sulfurated potassium (liver of sulfur)	7.5 g
Sodium carbonate (monohydrated)	2.5 g
Water to make	1.0 litre

This single-solution toning bath produces slightly darker sepia tones than the redevelopment-sulfide toner, Kodak toner T-7a. It has the advantage—compared with hypo-alum toners—of not requiring heating, although raising the temperature to 38 C (100 F) reduces the time of toning from 15 to 3 minutes.

Treat the well-washed black-and-white print for 15 to 20 minutes, with agitation, in the Kodak T-8 toner bath at 20 C (68 F) or for 3 or 4 minutes at 38 C (100 F).

After toning, rinse the print for a few seconds in running water and place it for about 1 minute in a Kodak hypo clearing agent bath, freshly mixed and kept for this purpose only, or in a solution containing 30 grams of sodium bisulfite per litre (1 ounce per quart) of water. Then treat the print for about 2 to 5 minutes in a hardening bath made by adding 1 part of Kodak liquid hardener to 13 parts of water, or 2 parts of Kodak hardener F-5a stock solution to 16 parts of water. (*See:* HARDENING BATHS.) If any sediment appears on the print, wipe the surface with a soft sponge. Wash the print for at least 30 minutes at 18 to 21 C (65 to 70 F) before drying.

For a packaged toner with similar characteristics, obtain Kodak brown toner.

Kodak gold toner T-21
Solution A

Warm water, about 50 C (125 F)	4.0 litres
Sodium thiosulfate (hypo) (pentahydrated)	960.0 g
Potassium persulfate	120.0 g

Dissolve the hypo completely before adding the potassium persulfate. Stir the solution vigorously while adding the potassium persulfate. If the solution does not turn milky, increase the temperature until it does.

Cool the above solution to about 27 C (80 F) and then add the solution below, including the precipitate, slowly and with constant stirring. The *bath must be cool when these solutions are added together.*

Cold water	64.0 ml
Silver nitrate, crystals	5.0 g
Sodium chloride	5.0 g

NOTE: The silver nitrate should be dissolved completely before the sodium chloride is added.

Stock solution B

Water	250.0 ml
Gold chloride	1.0 g

NOTE: Gold chloride is a deliquescent chemical; it will liquefy rapidly in a normal room atmosphere. Store the chemical in a tightly stoppered bottle in a dry atmosphere.

Kodak gold toner T-21 yields a pleasing range of tones from warm black to neutral brown with most warm-tone papers. It has little effect on cold-tone papers. Gold toner is one of the few chemical formulas that tones both highlights and shadows of the print at a uniform rate, thereby allowing the toning action to be stopped when the desired color has been attained.

To prepare a working solution of the toner, add 125 ml (4 ounces) of stock solution B slowly to the entire quantity of solution A while stirring the latter rapidly.

Before using the bath, allow it to stand for about 8 hours. By this time, a yellow precipitate will have formed at the bottom of the container. Pour the clear solution off into another container and discard the precipitate.

For use, pour the toner into a tray supported in a water bath and heat the water to 43 C (110 F). During toning, maintain the water bath at this temperature.

Wash prints to be toned for a few minutes after fixing and before placing them in the toning solution. Soak dry prints thoroughly in water before toning.

Keep an untoned black-and-white print on hand for comparison during toning. Keep prints separated throughout the toning operation.

Some sediment will form in the toning tray, especially if many prints are toned. The sediment is harmless, but it may form a scum on the print surface. If so, wipe the print with a wet sponge or a wad of cotton immediately after toning.

When the desired tone has been obtained (5 to 20 minutes), remove the prints and rinse them in cold water. After all prints have been toned, wash them for 1 hour in running water or use a washing aid as recommended. To prevent the formation of spots, be sure to sponge all the water off the prints before placing them in a dryer or between blotters.

Revive the bath at intervals by adding stock solution B. The quantity to be added will depend upon the number of prints toned and the time of toning. For example, when toning to a warm brown, add 4 ml (1 dram) of stock solution B after each fifty 8" × 10" prints or equivalent have been toned.

Purple Browns and Red Browns

Selenium toners permit either partial or complete toning. Selenium toners produce reddish browns with warm-tone papers and purple browns with neutral-tone papers. They have little or no effect on cold-tone papers.

Prints to be toned in selenium toner must be free from acid and silver salts; otherwise, yellow stains may result. For the shortest washing times, use the following procedures: After fixing in two successive fixing baths, treat single-weight prints at least 2 minutes and double-weight prints at least 3 minutes in Kodak hypo clearing agent solution to which has been added 56 grams of Kodalk balanced alkali for each 3 litres of solution (2 ounces for each 100 fluid-ounces). Then wash single-weight prints for at least 10 minutes and double-weight prints for at least 20 minutes in running water.

When 1 part of the toner is diluted with 3 parts of water, complete toning occurs in 2 to 8 minutes at 20 C (68 F), depending on the type of paper. To produce intermediate tones, dilute the full-strength toner 1:9 or more to reduce the rate of toning. Remove the print from the bath when the desired tone has been obtained, allowing for some continuation of toning in the wash water.

Wash completely toned prints at least 30 minutes and partially toned prints at least 1 hour in

Toning can create moods in a picture. Note how blue toning adds to the nighttime quality of the picture at right. Both prints were made on Kodak Medalist paper, but the print at left was not toned. Photos by Paul D. Yarrows.

running water at 18 to 21 C (65 to 70 F). For shorter washing times, treat completely or partially toned prints in a washing aid; then wash as instructed at 18 to 21 C (65 to 70 F).

CAUTION: Selenium toners leave permanent stains on clothing.

Choosing a Brown Hue. Kodak Poly-Toner offers a seemingly infinite number of tones from one bottle. By varying the dilution and the toning time of this single-solution direct toner, a series of brown hues can be produced at room temperature. A dilution of 1:4 produces a reddish brown, quite similar to that produced by Kodak rapid selenium toner, and a 1:50 dilution gives a very warm brown tone approaching that produced by Kodak brown toner.

Kodak Poly-Toner can perhaps be understood most easily if it is thought of as being two toners in one bottle—the "selenium-type" being the more active at high concentrations and the "brown-type" being the more active at low concentrations.

With this toner, it is not necessary to keep two or three different toners on hand. Neither is it necessary to mix two individual toners to obtain an "intermediate" hue. Kodak Poly-Toner is rapid-acting, its toning time at room temperature ranging from 1 minute for the 1:4 dilution to 7 minutes for the 1:50 dilution. In most cases, the 1:24 dilution, with a toning time of only 3 minutes, will produce the most pleasing tone with Kodak Ektalure paper.

For prints to be toned in the 1:4 dilution of Kodak Poly-Toner, the slight increase in print density can best be compensated for by a slight reduc-

KODAK POLY-TONER—CAPACITY OF DILUTIONS		
	Capacity	
Dilution	Square Metres per 4 Litres	8" × 10" Prints per Gallon
1:4	11	200
1:24	4.2	80
1:50	2.1	40

tion in development time. The amount of reduction depends upon the grade of paper. For prints to be toned in the 1:24 dilution, usually no change in exposure or development time is required. For prints to be toned at the 1:50 dilution, the slight loss in print density can best be compensated for by an increase in print development. Again, the amount of the increase depends upon the kind of paper.

Prints should be fixed as normally recommended, preferably by the two-bath system, and washed thoroughly before toning.

Tones intermediate between those produced by the recommended dilutions can be obtained by altering the dilution. The time recommendations given can be used as guides under these circumstances.

After toning, rinse the prints in running water for about 2 minutes, and then treat them for 3 minutes in Kodak hypo clearing agent solution. Do not use the hypo clearing agent bath subsequently for other purposes.

If hardening is required, as in the case of prints that are to be heat-dried,* treat the prints for 2 to 5 minutes in a bath composed of 1 part of Kodak liquid hardener and 13 parts of water, or 2 parts of Kodak hardener F-5a stock solution and 16 parts of water. (See: HARDENING BATHS.) Hardening may be required for adequate drying properties; it does not affect the color and gradation of the print.

Finally, wash for 30 minutes at 18 to 21 C (65 to 70 F).

Blue Tones

Pleasing blue tones are produced by Kodak blue toner. Warm-tone papers react very well to this toner, whereas neutral-tone papers tone only slightly

---

*Drying toned prints by heat results in a colder than normal tone.

to a rather pleasant blue-black. Cold-tone papers will show no change.

The visual contrast and density of a print treated in this toner appear to increase, but the effect is slight and the maximum compensation should consist of no more than about a 10 percent reduction in normal exposure for most subjects.

Thoroughly wash the prints to be toned; otherwise, uneven toning will result. Soak dry prints in water for at least 10 minutes.

Immerse the wet print in the toning solution and agitate it until the desired degree of toning is obtained. The time may vary from 8 to 45 minutes at 20 C (68 F), or 2 to 15 minutes at 38 to 41 C (100 to 105 F), depending on depth of tone desired.

Toning occurs first in the highlight areas and proceeds slowly until the shadows are toned. For this reason, careful observation is required to avoid partial toning, which results in blue highlights and untoned shadows.

When prints are toned one at a time in Kodak blue toner, the first few prints seem to derive the most benefit, and the last few may not even tone at all. Consistent results can be obtained only by immersing all of the prints in the bath simultaneously. The toning action is so even that only a small amount of normal agitation is necessary to prevent the formation of streaks. This technique will give all prints a uniform blue tone; however, the toner capacity should not be exceeded. Kodak blue toner will tone five to fifteen 8" × 10" prints (or equivalent) per quart of working solution, depending on the degree of toning.

Wash the prints for at least 30 minutes before drying.

Red Tones

If you are inclined to experiment, try for spectacular red tones on photographic papers. Sepia-tone the print and wash it in the normal way; then blue-tone the sepia print. The result is a red to orange color, depending on the type of paper used. Cold-tone papers yield a good red color, whereas warm-tone papers give a more orange hue.

Kodak sepia toner or Kodak brown toner can be used for the first stage, and after the print has been washed thoroughly, toning with Kodak blue toner yields the red color in about 15 to 30 minutes at 32 C (90 F). There is usually a loss of density in

Both these prints were made on the same paper and treated with sepia toner. The print at right was also toned with blue toner for 20 minutes. When making prints for toning, make several exposures and tone them all to provide a selection after the toner has changed the print. Photos by Arthur Underwood.

the shadow areas of the picture with this method of toning; therefore, you should start with a print of higher than usual contrast.

Multiple Toning

Selective, or multiple, toning offers the possibility of making pictures that are strikingly different. In brief, the process consists in toning only certain areas of the print while the rest is covered with rubber cement or frisket. Various colors can be secured by the action of one toner on the image toned by another. For example, an area that has been toned sepia can be changed to red by further toning in blue toner.

Such a procedure can be used to separate the foreground from the background. For example, an extremely effective result is obtained by toning waves a rich blue, while the rocks over which they are breaking remain a natural gray-image color.

The possibilities are practically limitless; a print can contain its original warm image tone as well as sepia, blue, and red tones, yet only two toners need be involved.

Good results will be easier to obtain with scenes that have a clear line of demarcation between subject and background. A clear-cut portrait of a subject with a smooth hairdo or a head covering, a sail

against the sky and water, buildings and mountains against the sky, and still-life setups are the easiest subject types to start with. It is neither necessary nor desirable to run the complete gamut of colors; the addition of just one tone to a particular area, such as the face and hands, will often prove very effective.

About the only materials that are required, in addition to the toners, are a bottle of rubber cement or a frisket material, such as photo Maskoid liquid frisket (obtainable from art-supply dealers), some rubber-cement thinner, a fine brush and a wider one, and an appropriate print.

Maskoid liquid frisket is probably the easiest to use because it is colored a brilliant red, making it easy to see what has and what has not been covered. If rubber cement is used, it must be thinned with some type of solvent, such as regular thinner, benzene, or even cigarette-lighter fluid. Dilute the rubber cement about 1:1 with thinner, and mix well.

Use a reasonably soft but not too large brush that points up well and does not lose its bristles. Another, larger brush will prove a time-saver for filling in broad areas of the print. The rubber cement should be applied in two or three thin coats rather than in one heavy coat. Do not work the rubber cement over to any extent; just flow it on with the brush, perhaps making one or two strokes to smooth it out, and then immediately move on to another area.

For uniform toning, it is generally suggested that prior to immersion in the toning solution a dry print should be soaked in water for about 10 minutes. However, to minimize the risk of having the toner creep under the edges of the mask and ruin the job, it may be better in this case to place the print immediately in the toner. Do not be alarmed if the print buckles and curls due to the uneven wetting as a result of the rubber cement. If the portion of the print that is not to be toned can be held out of the toning solution, there is less chance that the toner will bleed through the protective coating. Make sure, though, that the toner is kept flowing evenly over the uncoated portions.

Wash the print as recommended, and then remove the frisket material. Maskoid frisket is best removed by picking it up with sticky tape, whereas rubber cement can be removed easily by rubbing the fingers across the print while it is still in the wash. Continue washing the print for the full length of time, usually an hour, and then dry it in the usual manner. When two or more toners are used, it is necessary to follow through with the entire procedure each time.

• *See also:* AFTERTREATMENT; DRYING FILMS AND PRINTS; FIXERS AND FIXING; FORMULAS FOR BLACK-AND-WHITE PROCESSING; HARDENING BATHS; SPECIAL EFFECTS; WASHING.

Traffic Accident Photography

Accident investigation is usually the province of a police agency; however, many accidents require no police action in their resolution. Rather, the information from accident investigation frequently provides a source for insurance claimants or parties in civil proceedings. The methods of providing accident reports and photographs to interested parties vary from one legal jurisdiction to another. Many police agencies make accident photographs available to anyone for an established reprinting fee. Such a fee defrays, in part, the costs of photographic coverage of accident scenes.

After an accident, a photographer must work quickly and surely to get pictures before the scene is cleared. There is little time to sort out technical details or to consult a reference manual. In addition to having a good understanding of the capabilities of his or her equipment, the photographer must quickly and accurately determine exposures, camera and flash position, and focus.

In traffic accident photography, following a basic plan formulated beforehand will eliminate many failures due to inadequate equipment, overlooked angles, or misunderstood directions. Following a general procedure to cover basic situations will avoid errors.

A full-time photographer will not usually need to be told to maintain flash equipment, to keep a supply of film on hand, and to check camera operation regularly. For the part-time photographer, the accident investigator, or the on-scene officer, a clear outline of equipment maintenance, film stock, and check-out procedures will be invaluable.

On-the-Scene Responsibility

Some police departments issue simple cameras with built-in flash to each patrol vehicle or investigator. The officer who responds to a reported accident is instructed to assist injured victims, to control traffic, and to make a preliminary investigation including the making of photographs. Even when a serious multiple crash, fatal accident, or accident involving major property loss occurs and a regular photographer makes detailed photographs, the preliminary photographs made by the responding officer are frequently very helpful since there is less chance of that information being disturbed, obscured, or lost.

The photographer should take notes on the photographs that he or she makes; note-taking should not be left to another investigator. Careful identification of the film is necessary. For films exposed by police officers, preprinted labels or envelopes with blanks for the required identification and descriptive information can help the laboratory personnel. Unless processing of the film is done by the photographer, it is usually sent to a central laboratory. A clearly established procedure will eliminate errors and provide a clear chain of evidence where this may be necessary.

Equipment and Film

Any camera is useful for recording the accident scene. Some cameras may be more versatile, but even a simple camera with a flashcube can produce

Responding to an accident call, a patrol officer completed this 12-frame photographic sequence in a single, brief walkthrough with a simple camera. The technical quality of the photographs is excellent, and all relevant views are recorded. (Identifying markings on vehicles and witnesses faces have been deliberately obscured, although they formed an important part of the original photographic record of the accident.)

Traffic Accident Photography

adequate photographs if the photographer uses care. Choice of equipment is perhaps less critical than the proper maintenance of the equipment. Whatever cameras are provided, they must be reliable.

Accident Scene Coverage

What photographs are needed from the accident scene? This will, of course, require some judgment on the part of the on-scene officer, investigator, or photographer. For complete coverage, the following elements should be included in the views made of the accident scene.

Approach. In order to photograph the approach to the scene from the viewpoint of the driver or drivers involved, it may be necessary to make several photographs of the scene at different dis-

These two views of an accident scene made from opposite directions are related by the bridge overpass.

The image of the overpass also establishes the site of the accident.

Traffic Accident Photography

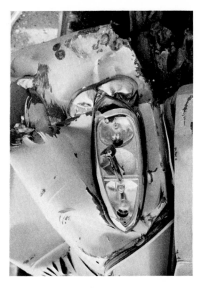

(Left) A piece of tail-light glass was found wedged into the headlight surround of a van suspected of a hit-and-run offense. (Right) The glass matched that of the victim's car. The close-up photographs relate evidence to the two vehicles.

tances. Make these from the driver's eye level as he or she would be seated in the vehicle. Remember that the high cab of a tractor-trailer may place the driver as much as 8 feet from the ground. Climb on a tow truck or station wagon tailgate to get the needed height.

Eyewitness' Viewpoint. To corroborate eyewitness statements, make pictures of the scene from the eyewitness' position and eye level.

Position of the Vehicles. Try to get shots of the final position of the vehicles before they are moved. If they must be moved before they can be photographed, mark their position with chalk or tape.

Position of Victims. Where victims are thrown clear of the vehicles, get photographs of the position of a body, or mark the position of an injured victim who is being removed for treatment.

Point of Impact. If it is possible, determine and photograph the point of impact of the vehicle or vehicles involved in the accident. This may correspond to the final position of the vehicles or it may be some distance from that point. Relate the two in a photograph if possible.

Overall View of Scene. One or several pictures that relate the overall scene elements can be useful to the accident investigator. One viewpoint for such photographs is a high position overlooking the scene; a rooftop, an embankment, a bridge, or even a truck can provide a commanding position. Other overall shots can be made with the camera at eye level in the direction of vehicle travel and then by looking back through the scene from the opposite direction to show the area of approach.

Close-ups of Accident Details. Details of vehicle damage; skid marks; tire marks; worn or damaged tires; registration plates; oil, water, or gasoline spills; and broken parts provide key information to aid the accident investigator. Photograph questionable items within the car such as wine, beer, and liquor bottles; narcotics; or firearms.

Special Situations

All too frequently the accident scene presents problems that challenge the photographer's ability to get useful pictures. Many accidents occur at night or in bad weather.

Existing Light. In night photography there are several methods of getting an image on the film. Light is necessary for photography; therefore, the photographer may use existing light and supplemental light. Existing light simply indicates whatever light is on the scene. At first glance this may seem insufficient for photography. However, with the camera firmly mounted on a sturdy tripod, the photographer can make time exposures that will provide adequate overall photographs of the scene, photographs that could not be made any other way. The skylight of late evening or even moonlight can provide enough light for a time exposure. Many streets and expressways have lighting that provides adequate illumination. Only by experimenting with such lighting and exposures can the photographer expect to get useful photographs in this way. (*See:* NIGHT PHOTOGRAPHY.)

Supplementary Light. There are many ways to supplement the light already existing at the scene. Automobile headlights, spotlights, or emergency vehicle lights can be directed at the scene. By far the most common supplemental light for accident scene photography is the flash lamp—either expendable flashbulb or recycling electronic flash. (*See:* ELECTRONIC FLASH and FLASH PHOTOGRAPHY.)

Painting with Light. A useful technique for photographing large areas indoors and outdoors at night is open shutter, serial flash "painting with light." Its use in accident photography at night is necessary to cover multiple-auto accidents, to show skid marks in relation to the final position of a vehicle, or to relate the vehicle to road conditions, signs, obstructions, and the like. (*See:* PAINTING WITH LIGHT.)

• *See also:* CRIME PHOTOGRAPHY; ELECTRONIC FLASH; EVIDENCE PHOTOGRAPHY; FIRE AND ARSON PHOTOGRAPHY; FLASH PHOTOGRAPHY; NIGHT PHOTOGRAPHY; PAINTING WITH LIGHT.

 # Transparencies from Negatives

Slides and transparencies for projection and display can be made easily from negatives, in either black-and-white or color.

Materials

Black-and-white transparencies are made on fine-grain positive film, or on projector slide plates. (Ordinary panchromatic films give poorer results.) Fine-grain positive film comes in sheet and 35 mm sizes. The 35 mm film can be processed in rolls of 100 feet or more because it is commonly used for motion-picture printing. Plates are commonly available in the standard projector sizes: 50.8 × 50.8 mm (2″ × 2″) and 82.5 × 101.6 mm (3¼″ × 4″).

These materials are usually blue-sensitive, so they can be handled under a red safelight. They can be processed in paper developer, which is often preferred for obtaining neutral image tones, or in other developers for various times to produce different image tones or degrees of contrast. The images can also be toned, just as black-and-white prints are, for special color effects.

There are also print materials available; these are coated on diffusing film bases for making display transparencies from black-and-white or color negatives. The images are not suitable for projection. Kodak Translite film 5561 is one such black-and-white material; Kodak Ektacolor 74 Duratrans print material is a color emulsion on a diffusing base.

Color transparencies can also be made on suitable print films. Kodak Vericolor print film (sheet sizes) and Kodak Vericolor slide film (35 mm and 46 mm sizes) are especially designed for making transparencies from still-film negatives. A number of print films are available for use with negatives made on motion-picture films.

Techniques

There are three basic ways to make transparencies from negatives:

1. Contact printing—for same-size reproduction.
2. Projection printing—for a larger, same-size, or smaller transparency.
3. Copy photography—for a smaller transparency.

The setups and methods suitable for these techniques are explained in the articles DUPLICATE SLIDES AND TRANSPARENCIES and ENLARGERS AND ENLARGING. The only significant difference between the procedures presented is in the nature of the material being exposed. However, note that panchromatic and color materials must be handled in complete darkness. When printing, back the print film with matte black paper to prevent halation from reflected light. To copy a negative onto print film, place the negative on an illuminator, mask off all surrounding areas to prevent flare, and put the print film in the copy camera. Process the materials normally, as recommended by the manufacturer.

• *See also:* BLACK-AND-WHITE SLIDES AND TRANSPARENCIES; COLOR PRINTING FROM NEGATIVES; DUPLICATE BLACK-AND-WHITE NEGATIVES; DUPLICATE COLOR NEGATIVES; DUPLICATE SLIDES AND TRANSPARENCIES; ENLARGERS AND ENLARGING; SLIDES AND FILMSTRIPS.

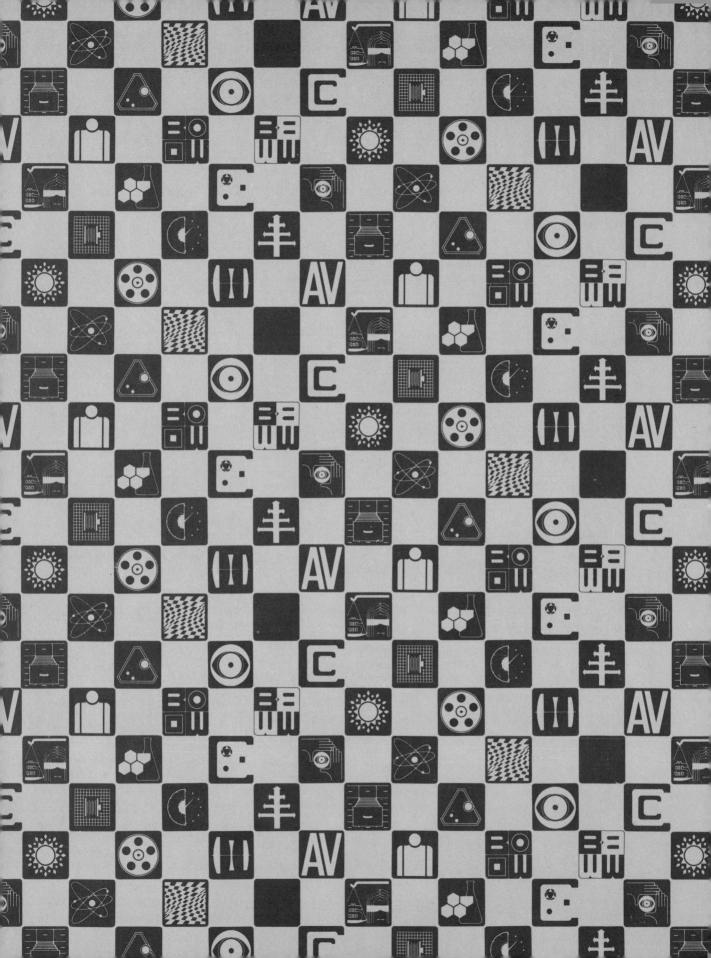